HAIR
OF THE
DOG

TALES FROM ABOARD
A RUSSIAN TRAWLER

HAIR
OF THE
DOG

TALES FROM ABOARD
A RUSSIAN TRAWLER

BARBARA A. OAKLEY

Washington State University Press
Pullman, WA 99164-5910

Washington State University Press, Pullman, Washington, 99164-5910

Library of Congress Cataloging-in-Publication Data
Oakley, Barbara A., 1955-
    Hair of the dog : tales from aboard a Russian trawler / Barbara A. Oakley.
      p. cm.
    ISBN 0-87422-134-X (cloth).—ISBN 0-87422-135-8 (pbk.)
    1. Trawls and trawling—Pacific Coast (U.S.)—Anecdotes. 2. International cooperation—Anecdotes. 3. Women translators—Pacific Coast (U.S.)—Biography. 4. Oakley, Barbara A., 1955- .
I. Title.
SH344.6.T702   1996
639.2'092—dc20
[B]   96-853
                                             CIP

Washington State University Press
Pullman, Washington 99164-5910
Phone: 800-354-7360
Fax: 509-335-8568

To my father, Alfred Grim
who started the adventure

And, as always,
to my beloved Philip,
who keeps the adventure alive

Hair of the dog that bit you. A drink taken to counteract drunkenness; usu. of the same liquor that caused the state the previous night. Frequently shortened to "hair of the dog." The allusion is to an ancient notion that the burnt hair of a dog is an antidote to its bite.

A Dictionary of Slang and Unconventional English

Being in a ship is being in jail,
with the chance of being drowned.

Samuel Johnson

Although I am not a human tape recorder, I have a good memory for dialogue: the events described in this book are pretty much as I remember them and as I recorded them day by day in my journals. Like any writer, I've adapted the rhythms of the real conversations to fit the needs of the written page. But there was no need to resort to fiction: reality was strange enough. I have also changed the names of both ships and people in this narrative, along with a very few biographical details.

Contents

Chapter One
Arrival

"THE CAPTAIN INVITES you to his cabin for tea," said the man in Russian. He stood awkwardly at the cabin door, averting his gaze from our nightgowns.

I glanced at Laura. She tugged at her gown, then scratched her belly. "It's close to midnight, Barb. I don't think people ordinarily have tea at midnight." She grinned. "I know what else they have, though."

I raised my eyebrows.

"Don't be such a fuddy-duddy." She nodded to the crewman and shut the door. "Come on." In seconds she was dressed and out the window.

It was my first evening aboard the *Muis Yegorova*, a Soviet trawler that had put in at Seattle to stock up on supplies, refuel, siphon off wastes, and pick up several observers from the National Marine Fisheries Service, along with another translator: me.

My knowledge of Russian had been instilled during a thirteen-month stint at the U.S. Army's Defense Language Institute five years before, and honed to a dull edge of rustiness with two quarters of third-year Russian at the University of Washington in the months prior to my departure on the *Yegorova*. Somewhere in the back of my mind I'd carried an image of a few romantic months of dreamy work at sea. As Laura, my new cabin mate and fellow translator had put it only hours before: "Welcome aboard, sucker."

I clambered out the window after Laura (it was easier to get to the bridge on the messy walkways outside the window than through the labyrinthine passageways beyond the door), and we picked our way forward, climbing over ripped-up planks, hefty chunks of metal, and bits and pieces of gear. The *Yegorova* was a 270-foot combination trawling and fish-processing vessel of a type referred to as a "Big Mother" by the American fishermen. It was also a rat's nest. Peeling gray and white paint was everywhere, often covered with a bloody patina of rust. I made my way forward with trepidation. Every ship, as the old saying goes, is a reflection of its captain.

I'd met some of the ship's crew earlier, as I boarded. The deck crew had been standing near the railings, huddled in surly little groups and smoking the industrial-strength cigarettes called *papyrosi*. They had eyed me wordlessly as I lugged my baggage up the narrow gangplank, then jumped to assist as the fleet commander, Anatoly Petrovich, appeared.

"I want to meet you," Anatoly said, in heavily accented English.

I think you just have, I thought, and shook his hand. At about five feet, Anatoly Petrovich was short even by Russian standards. He was also dumpy and beetle-browed ugly. I later learned that most of the Russian women in the fleet had a passion for him, which goes to show what power will do for a man.

Having exhausted his store of English, Anatoly switched to Russian: "Welcome aboard the *Muis Yegorova*. I'm sure you will enjoy your stay here."

I mumbled something to the effect that I was glad to be aboard. Mumbling is a potent resource when one isn't sure whether one is saying things properly.

We both stood uncomfortably for a moment, Anatoly unsure of what to say, and I unsure of both what to say and how to say it.

"You should have something to eat. I'm sure you're hungry," Anatoly said.

I protested in vain that I wasn't; then watched helplessly as my baggage was ferried off without me, while I was led off through a Byzantine maze of stairwells and passageways to the officers' mess.

The mess, located in the forward area of the ship, contained a long, empty table, obviously designed to hold most of the officers. I was seated alone at a small stand squeezed into the side. It was covered with leaflets and brochures, all in English, expounding the virtues of communism. I shuffled through them nervously, then glanced about at the walls plastered with banners and pictures of Lenin. At last a waitress darted in with a bowl of cold and greasy fish soup. She smiled.

"Would you like to come down to our cabin when you're through?" she asked shyly.

"Yes, I'd like that." I gulped a bit of my soup, hesitated a few moments out of politeness, and got up.

The woman, Klavdia, was on her third voyage, and as we made our way to her cabin she explained some of the workings of the Soviet pay scales. Each job in the Soviet Union, she explained, had a set salary, but multipliers were used depending upon how far away from Moscow you were. The Ukraine had a multiplier close to one, Soviet central Asia a multiplier around two, and Siberia had a three. The *Yegorova*, she explained, was considered to be even tougher duty than Siberia, and as such merited a multiplier close to four. Therefore, she told me proudly, even though hers was one of the lowest paying jobs on the ship (indeed, the women held all the lowest paying jobs on the ship), she made more money than most college professors in Moscow.

We arrived at her cabin and she opened the door with a flourish.

Inside, perched on inadequate-looking chairs, were three of the stoutest women I'd ever seen. Although none of them could have topped five feet, each was enormously rotund, with fat bursting from tiny frames. They must have weighed around three hundred pounds apiece.

They smiled happily. "Come in! Come in! Have some coffee; have some cookies!"

The women were Klavdia's roommates: the head cook and her two assistants. The obesity, I later learned, was an occupational hazard shared by cooks throughout the fleet. They were often ferried on and off the ship by deck cranes, being unable to climb ladders and unsure of themselves on the narrow gangplanks.

All three were busy eating cookies from a box. "Here, have some," said the head cook, thrusting a handful in my hand. "I'm Alla Nikolayevna, this is Katerina Lvovna, and this is Yelena Sergeyevna. You've already met Klavdia Yurevna."

I nodded, munching nervously on a cookie. The Russian custom of using both first and middle names in ordinary speech tended to leave one bogged down after a while.

"Do you happen to have a Sears catalog?" Alla asked.

"No, sorry."

"Too bad." She pointed to the walls plastered with pictures of fashion models torn from American catalogs. "Beth gave us these last year. They're out of fashion now, no doubt. Ah, well."

Someone thrust a mug of coffee in my hand. It was Soviet instant coffee—even worse than American instant coffee.

"Here, have some sour cream. It's delicious," said Katerina, waving a heaping spoonful in my direction. "Don't be shy, now."

I hesitated. What did one do with a spoonful of sour cream? I took it and stirred it into my coffee.

"No, no, no!" The cabin filled with laughter. "You're not supposed to drink it, silly. You're supposed to eat it!" I looked up. All three cooks had spoons full of sour cream in their hands and were licking them as if they were ice cream. "It's fresh. We just got it here in port, and it's thick and sweet as can be." They poured out my coffee, still laughing, and gave me a refill.

The women chattered happily, and I listened carefully. Although I understood most of what they said, the speed of the conversation was much faster than I was used to; in class the professors had always been careful to speak slowly and clearly. And there was a strange lilt to the speech: a Ukrainian accent. The ships in this fleet, they told me, were based out of Nakhodka, a town near Vladivostok in the far eastern reaches of Siberia. Many of the inhabitants had moved there from the Ukraine during the thirties, for reasons unspecified.

We passed the better part of the evening exchanging bits and pieces of information about each other while the cooks stuffed themselves on cookies and sour cream, and Klavdia drank tremendous amounts of tea. At eleven I excused myself to hunt up my luggage, my cabin, and a little sleep. Or so I'd thought, anyway.

Laura knocked loudly on the captain's door, with a wink toward me. A Harvard graduate with a mass of curly red hair, Laura was working her way through Harvard Business School in her own unorthodox fashion. This was "her" ship—she'd already been on board for a week, and would serve as *Muis Yegorova's* translator throughout the fishing season. I was to be transferred to another vessel, the *Izumrudny* ("Emerald") to serve as translator when we joined back up with the rest of the fleet near the Oregon coast.

The door swung open. "Laura! You have come!" Laura was suddenly enveloped in a gigantic bear hug.

"Barbara! I am pleased to meet you." The captain transferred his embrace to me. "Call me Captain Alex. We will party, okay?" he asked, his bloodshot eyes only inches away.

"Okay!" said Laura enthusiastically. We stepped inside.

The cabin was appointed in a style straight out of the fifties. The furniture was spindly proto-Scandinavian, the walls covered with ersatz wooden paneling. Red velour curtains hung over the portholes. A television set with a small and nearly circular screen stood in an oak cabinet under a porthole; water stains showed white on the wood. A black and white picture of polar bears, probably torn from a magazine, hung framed on the far wall.

"We are ready, then," said the captain in careful, tipsy English. "What will you have?" He spread his arms toward the table.

I glanced over, glanced away, and then looked back again. The table, a large Formica contraption bolted sturdily to the floor, was completely covered with bottles of every conceivable shape and size. Whiskey, brandy, and tequila bottles mingled with large green bottles of "Bear's Blood" wine; Armenian cognac stood before stacked six packs of Buck beer. In the back, marching in a seemingly endless row, stood bottles of vodka, punctuated with splits of Soviet champagne. A number of empty bottles lay in a box on the floor.

"I'll have cognac," said Laura. "And tequila."

"Okay!" said Captain Alex, turning toward me. "Barbara?"

"Guess maybe I'll start with a glass of champagne." I'd sampled Russian vodka, but I'd never even heard of their champagne.

"Good. Soviet champagne much better than French stuff," the captain said. He reached over to brush aside a curtain and open a porthole; then sat down and grabbed a champagne bottle, aiming it, bazooka-like, toward the window. With a pop the plastic cap sailed into oblivion.

"Hope nobody walking by outside," he said, pouring the champagne at a practiced angle. "Here." He handed me a large glass and quickly poured himself a shot of tequila. Laura was already going after the cognac.

"Toast," he proclaimed. "To Soviet and American fishermans. And good season." He downed the shot in a gulp and poured himself another. "Say, Barbara, did you bring Sears catalog?"

I allowed as how I hadn't.

"That's okay. Sears—alright," Captain Alex said, waving his hand in a gesture of ambivalence. "K-Mart—Number One." His thumb shot up in the air. "Too bad no K-Mart catalogs."

"Yes," I said. Laura was working on her second shot. I gulped at my champagne.

"Here you are." Klavdia, the waitress I'd met earlier, came bustling into the room with steaming platters of potatoes and fish balanced on her arms. She set them on some chairs. "Alexei Vasilievich," she said, clapping the captain on his shoulder, "You need to eat something."

"Eat?" Captain Alex said in Russian. "Have I ever told you the one about the pickles?"

"Yes," said Klavdia. "You have." She picked up the box of empty bottles and headed out of the cabin.

"There was this bunch of Muscovites," said the captain, oblivious. "They were sitting at a table with a Frenchman. On the table were ten bottles of vodka and a bowl of pickles."

The captain paused to down his second belt, wiping his mouth with the back of his hand. He poured another shot as he continued.

"The head Muscovite, Ivan, poured a round, and everyone downed his shot without saying a word. Nobody touched the pickles. Ivan poured another round, and everyone drank again, still silent. Still, nobody touched the pickles. Ivan picked up a new bottle and poured another round. Even so, nobody touched the pickles."

Captain Alex stopped to refill my glass.

"Ivan poured once again, and everyone drank. Then another round, and another, until finally the very last bottle of vodka was reached, with still not a pickle being touched." Captain Alex looked down abruptly, as if he had forgotten something important. He located the shot glass in his right hand and upended it into his mouth, then leaned over to fix me with a glazed stare.

"Ivan poured again, and everybody paused for a minute, getting ready to drink, when the Frenchman, Jacques, reached out—and took a pickle."

"'Jacques,' said Ivan, finally breaking the silence. 'Are you here to eat, or to drink?'"

Captain Alex guffawed heartily. "Funny, okay?" he asked, switching back to English.

"Funny, okay," I said, laughing. Actually, everything was beginning to be funny. And my understanding of Russian seemed to be getting better by the minute.

"Barbara, you must also try this cognac. Armenian cognac is best."

"Don't mix drinks," whispered a tiny voice in the back of my mind. "You'll be sorry." I swirled the remaining champagne in the heavy wine glass. It went down in two bubbly swallows. "Okay!" I said.

Captain Alex whipped a shot glass under my nose and extended a palm. "Give me five, baby!"

I slapped his palm and took the glass.

"He's my best student of American idiom," said Laura, her eyes watering with a plastic sheen.

I took a sip of the cognac and wrinkled my nose at its strength.

"No. No good, Barbara. Is bad luck not to finish glass all at once. Like this." Captain Alex poured himself another hefty shot and downed it in one large gulp.

I stared at him, stared at my glass, and took a breath. I wasn't ordinarily a heavy drinker, but there was no graceful way out of this. Not that I could see, anyway. The cognac went down in a burning swallow.

"See—is easy," he said, pouring me another shot.

I nodded, blinking.

"Here," slurred Laura with consideration. "You'd better eat some of these potatoes." She pushed a plate of greasy fries in my direction. "Besides, they've been out of potatoes here for the last month. This is a real delicacy."

I grinned stupidly and grabbed a fry.

"Laura, yo-yo is yes, where?" said Captain Alex.

"Maybe we'd better switch to Russian," she said in Russian.

"*Gdye tvoyo yo-yo*?" Where's your yo-yo?

"I left it in my cabin—why, do you want it?"

"Of course I want your yo-yo," he said. "I love your yo-yo."

"Russians don't have yo-yo's," Laura explained. "I showed him mine today and I think he liked it."

"I love your yo-yo," said the captain again. He began to make yo-yoing motions with his hands, swaying from side to side. "Barbara, would you like to thumb wrestle?"

"Sure," I said. I was beginning to feel very cheerful.

"Shame on you," said the captain, eyeing my glass. "You should tell me when you're all out." He poured me another shot and dribbled the bottle over to his glass, pouring himself one while he was at it.

"*En guard*." He extended a fist, thumb cocked.

"Hey," said Laura, "I've got to get a picture of this."

"No," said the captain. He suddenly looked sober. "Just a minute." He reached over to the bottles and began to turn the labels away from Laura, swinging each bottle around so that its contents could only be guessed at. Easily guessed at, but still guessed at.

"Okay!" he said, all smiles again. "Cheese!" Obviously Laura had been working hard on his English lessons. We mugged for the camera, toasted each other, and mugged for the camera again. Captain Alex poured another round.

And another.

And another.

And another....

"Hey," Laura said, "whamph?"

"Huh?" I replied.

"I said," she spoke slowly now, trying to enunciate, "what time is it?"

The hands of my watch bleared into focus. "It's six o'clock. In the morning."

"Oh," Laura said. She looked at the captain. He was out cold on the floor, his head pillowed in his hands like a sleeping baby. An empty bottle rolled in the slight swell, bumping him every few seconds. "Maybe we'd better go."

I thought for a while. "Yeah. Where?"

Laura thought for quite a while. "I don't feel so good," she said, finally.

"Neither do I."

"Maybe we'd better go get some fresh air."

"Yeah."

We stumbled out of the cabin, carefully shutting the door, and meandered in the mist toward the back deck. It was cold and dank, and the gantry over the stern ramp loomed out of the fog like an archaeological artifact.

"Hey, look," said Laura. "The deck has a hole in it."

Sure enough, a trap door hidden in the planking gaped wide on the deck before us. We tripped down a set of stairs and wandered up to the edge of the hole, gazing with bovine vapidity toward the holds thirty feet below. Ice vapor curled fuzzily out toward the gray husk of morning.

"Look at these hooks." A set of steel hooks were slung onto a gantry that rode like a swing set over the hold. "Wanna play Tarzan?" Laura grabbed a hook and swung herself out over the hole, legs dangling. "Wheee!"

"Stop that! What are you doing?" A tall man appeared from a room tucked away toward the front of the deck.

"Stop what?" said Laura, kicking the edge of the deck to swing wide again. She began to spin. "Look out below!"

"I think you'd better get her," I said to the man. "Otherwise she might fall down." He looked at me strangely. I realized I was speaking English.

The man stationed himself by the edge and nabbed Laura on her next swing, manhandling her away from the edge. "*Mokroye odeyalo*," she said. The man looked confused. She'd called him a wet blanket, and a wet blanket isn't a spoilsport in Russian. It's a soaking bed covering.

"Maybe it's time for you to go to your cabin," said the man. "My name's Volodya, by the way."

"Cabin?" we asked in unison.

"Come on."

We trooped back up a set of stairs. I bumped heavily against the davits of a lifeboat as the deck began to weave. God, I thought, I'm drunk. I watched as the horizon began to bob and tilt. The queasiness I'd been feeling suddenly worsened. Wait a minute, I thought. Is it me or the ship?

Laura grabbed for some handrails. "Everything keeps moving," she complained. "I don't feel so good."

"Just wait," Volodya laughed. "We'll be out of the Strait of Juan de Fuca pretty soon. Then it's open sea. This rocking is nothing compared to that."

Laura and I looked at each other, faces tinged with green.

"There's a big storm out on the coast," Volodya explained. "It's supposed to be the worst one we've had this year."

"I have a bad feeling about this, Laura," I said. My left foot shot out from under me on the slippery deck and my hands splayed ineptly toward a bulkhead. I was definitely having steering problems.

Laura moaned. She had a distant look in her eye, like an animal coping with private pain.

We arrived at last at our cabin.

"Let me get you some *suchari*. It'll help," said Volodya.

"What are *suchari*?" I asked. Volodya was gone.

"It means rusks," Laura murmured. "I looked it up."

"What are rusks?"

"I don't know. I didn't think I'd need an English dictionary out here."

I glanced around our cabin, the former dispensary. The glare of the naked light bulb on the stark white walls was downright nauseating in the swell of the approaching open sea. I couldn't remember how much I'd drank. I wasn't even sure what I was doing here.

Volodya returned with a plate of dried-out stale bread. "*Suchari*," he said.

"That's okay," said Laura. "We don't want any."

I looked at the plate and my stomach bulldozed into action.

"You will," said Volodya.

"Where's the bathroom?" I asked.

"The bathroom." Volodya paused for a moment, thinking, then turned to point. "Climb down these stairs, then turn right and go along the passage about twenty feet. Turn left, go down that set of stairs and turn right. Take a left at the end of the corridor, walk about a hundred and fifty feet—down to the other end of the ship—and there they are." He smiled apologetically.

"What?" I asked. "Where?" I needed a bathroom. I would need a bathroom continuously.

"Here, I'll show you."

"That's okay," I said. I wasn't sure I could walk anymore.

Laura moaned again and stumbled back out the door. "Let's go," she said to Volodya.

I lay down on the bunk, trying to focus on a chip of white paint as the cabin broke slowly into a spin.

Welcome, I thought, to Mother Russia.

I passed out.

Interlude

In the late 1970s through the 1980s, a group of American fishermen and businessmen teamed up with the Soviets to form one of the few joint Soviet-American companies in the world—Marine Resources Company. In this Joint Venture, Americans were to catch fish within the newly defined 200-mile limit, then pass them off at sea for the Soviets to process. To serve as translators, Marine Resources hired a dozen or so American speakers of Russian: university students, mostly, with a sprinkling of adult children of Russian immigrants thrown in. They were to live on board the Soviet trawlers and keep tabs on the amount of fish brought on board so that the fishermen would be properly reimbursed.

The relationship between Americans and Russians has tended toward volatility even at best, and fishermen everywhere are among the most independent, obstinate, and hard-nosed of people. In reality, therefore, the company representative's main function was to grease treads: ensure that the Soviets and Americans maintained a smooth working relationship. This could be a daunting task—a good representative needed a nimble command of both Russian and English, a strong streak of diplomacy, and perhaps most importantly, an endless capacity for alcohol. An occasional rep fell short on one or two of these requirements. More rarely, they lacked all three....

That's where, in the spring of '82, I came in.

Chapter Two
The *Izumrudny*

"THE *Izumrudny's* CAPTAIN is going to let me take his next two codends if I can get you over to him today." Captain Alex beamed, the smell of beer heavy on his breath. Three days after our convivial soiree in his cabin, I was finally mobile, but the captain was still four sheets to the wind. "Good deal, yes?"

A codend was the net used to transfer fish from the Americans to the Russians. A full codend was a mesh bag twenty-five feet long and seven feet in diameter; it contained perhaps twenty to thirty tons of fish. If it had also picked up a bit of junk on the ocean floor—a boulder, say, or a Volkswagen—it might weigh far more.

"You should be getting four codends for me in weather like this," I said, gripping the *Yegorova's* railing uneasily. The seas were rough that afternoon, with a brisk wind slicing the tops off the eighteen-foot swells as they rolled rapidly past.

"I know. We shouldn't be doing this." Captain Alex eyed a sea gull as it struggled to make headway against the wind. "The weather's pretty rough." He shrugged and belched.

I glanced at the approaching lifeboat. It had been bobbing toward us from the *Izumrudny* for the past half hour, several men busy bailing as the waves lapped up and over the sides. My taxi service to my new home. Even as it finally neared it looked downright tiny in the heavy seas.

"Let's not send me to the *Izumrudny* and pretend we did," I suggested.

"Ha ha," said Captain Alex. "Such a joker you are, Barbara. I will miss you." He nodded to one of his men and a rope ladder whipped down the side of the *Yegorova*, splashing into the water twenty feet below. The *Yegorova* yawed as a wave rolled underneath her, and the ladder suddenly hung ten feet above the water. A few seconds later the *Yegorova* had swung the other way, and the ladder trailed deeply into the water. I looked at the approaching lifeboat with even more trepidation. If the *Yegorova*, at 270 feet, was bobbing like a cork on the water, what must it be like on the fifteen-foot lifeboat?

"Captain Shevchenko wants to begin fishing very badly, and he can't do anything until you get aboard. Shevchenko is very... motivated," Alex said, enigmatically.

"What do you mean by motivated?" I asked, never one to let sleeping innuendoes lie.

There was a sudden crash and I glanced down. The *Izumrudny*'s lifeboat had rammed prow first into the *Yegorova* and was caroming off her side.

"Stupid fool! Watch it!" Captain Alex shouted.

"I am watching it," came a voice from below. "The tiller's stuck."

"Well, fix it then," said Alex, with impeccable logic. I gazed down, aghast. The lifeboat continued to slam into the *Yegorova*, grating along her side as the waves rolled it up and down. The end of a rope landed near the bow of the lifeboat, and a pasty-faced youngster grabbed and twirled it quickly around a hook, his fingers flying to avoid being nipped off as the prow bounced down in the swell and the rope pulled taut. The bow was now secured, but the stern still swung free.

A short, tow-headed man grabbed my duffel bag and threaded a rope through the handle, knotting it deftly. Good, I thought. I didn't want to risk losing a five-month supply of clothing. And I had several bottles of whiskey, gifts for the captain of the *Izumrudny*, nestled amongst the shirts. I'd sooner see the bag lowered than thrown.

"Hey, Barb, heard the *Izumrudny* was picking you up." It was Laura, still looking a little green. Her jaw dropped as the lifeboat pinwheeled in the swell. "You going down there? I wouldn't go down there."

The tow-head, ignoring the rope, threw my bag over the side. It crashed into a pile of boxes near the center of the boat. The men in the lifeboat looked up and began shouting. I didn't understand what they were saying. It sounded angry.

The *Yegorova* swooped down into a trough while the lifeboat bobbed up. The difference in height between the two boats was some fifteen feet, and it reversed every few seconds. With each new wave, the lifeboat slammed into the side of the *Yegorova*. A slip would land me in the surging water between the two boats, to be crushed on the lifeboat's next slam against the side of the larger vessel.

"Hold still. We can't have you going in the water." I glanced down as firm hands passed a belt around my waist. It had ropes attached to both the left and right sides, much like a tumbler's support belt. Two men took their places beside me, holding the ropes and grinning encouragingly. "Don't worry, we won't let you fall," said the shorter of the two. He was the one who'd thrown my duffel bag.

"Just wait'll you meet Shevchenko," said Laura, in English. "You'll hate him."

The men in the lifeboat looked up expectantly. I gulped and grabbed for the ladder, swinging myself over the railing. "Good-bye, Captain Alex. 'Bye, Laura."

"See ya later," said Laura. "Maybe."

Did fishermen do transfers like this all the time? Everyone seemed to expect it. Maybe it really wasn't too dangerous with the ropes attached. I concentrated on the wooden rungs of the ladder, slowing as I neared the bottom. I had to be careful to descend only to the high edge of the water line—otherwise I would be in danger of being crushed by the surging lifeboat on one of its periodic bashes against the *Yegorova*'s side. The problem was, one could never quite be sure exactly where that high edge of the water line was. One exceptionally large wave could quickly change expectations.

There. I'd reached a point on the ladder which seemed to be a few feet above the high water line. I glanced over at the crew of the lifeboat. They looked a little worried, bobbing up to almost my own level, then plowing down fifteen feet below me. I looked back up the *Yegorova*'s side. Laura watched with interest. Shifting on the ladder, I turned as best I could to face away from the ship and toward the lifeboat. The waves rose and fell—I waited for the lifeboat to shift in a little bit: to be right beneath and below me.

Now. I released and jumped, landing clumsily on the boxes. I'd done it—and was dragged immediately to the edge of the lifeboat, swinging helplessly into the air as the boat dropped into another trough. The crewmen on the *Yegorova* hadn't released their hold. I was being dragged off the lifeboat.

"Grab her! Let go, you fools!" Strong arms wrapped around me as the ropes suddenly released. I fell with a thud to the bottom of the boat, taking two of the crew down with me.

"Good show!" Captain Alex shouted. I wiggled around to look up. Laura gave a disappointed wave. The ropes fell away, and we were off, the motor sputtering as it revved up against the swell.

Being in a small boat in heavy seas is much like being seated in an Imax movie theater. You remain calmly seated, while before you, in gigantic living color, harrowing scenes unfold. Walls of water rolled ominously around us, bubbling and translucent, like sheets of molten glass. Then, suddenly, we crested a wave, and I looked down into deep, dark valleys and beyond to the hazy horizon, where the *Izumrudny* awaited us.

The waves were so large we scarcely seemed to move—for every few feet we edged forward, the waves rolled us back a foot. I wondered why the *Yegorova* and *Izumrudny* were so far apart, until I realized that, in this weather, no one was taking any chances that the two ships would collide. My seasickness, which had dissipated over the past few days, crawled back to life. I burped and swallowed resolutely. No time is a good time for seasickness, but I didn't want to meet the crew of the *Izumrudny* with the marks of a landlubber fast upon me. Actually, with our wild motion, I worried about getting on the *Izumrudny* at all.

At last we swung around the larger boat, seeking the relative calm of her leeward side. Crewmen lowered heavy block and tackle over the railings toward us. I sighed in relief. They were going to lift us aboard, boat and all. No more ladder climbs.

"Watch out!" The lifeboat lurched in the swell and a block swung by, dangerously close to my head. I dropped to the floor of the boat. Several others did the same. The men at the bow and stern tried to catch the heavy hooks and guide them through the steel rings at each end of the boat. Every time one man got a hook through a ring, the lifeboat bobbed up and it fell out.

"Ready," shouted the man at the stern. "Ready here, too," echoed a voice from the bow. The winches started, and I glanced back towards the front just as the bow hook fell out of the ring again.

"Stop!"

It was too late. The stern, still attached to the winches, began rising into the air while the bow continued to ride the wave. Down. I grabbed onto the edge of the lifeboat and hung on desperately as the stern rose higher and higher into the air. Boxes crashed past me, tumbling overboard. The heavy tackle loosed from the bow slammed into the man beside me with a meaty thud. "Stop, you goddamned perpetrator of unspeakable acts on your mother!" I heard, or words to that effect. "Stop!"

The winches ground to a halt and then, not a moment too soon, reversed. The lifeboat slowly regained a horizontal position.

"Let's try this again," grumbled the fleshy man at the stern. "And this time, watch what you're doing, Sasha."

Sasha grabbed for the hook, with an embarrassed glance towards me.

Within a few minutes the winches started again and we began lurching our way upwards, horizontal this time, rising a few feet and then falling a foot or so with a sudden, discomfiting jerk. I clung to my seat and examined the side of the *Izumrudny* from close range. It was coated with a dull, lumpy gray paint that bespoke a thick undercoating of rust. The lifeboat rose another notch, then thumped back down. A porthole appeared. I looked in, curious despite myself. A man looked back out, his bulbous nose inches from mine. We stared at each other a moment, both too surprised to react.

At last the boat ground to a halt and lurched sideways onto the davits. I peered out at the dingy gray decking of the *Izumrudny*. A group of serious-looking men stood huddled on the passageway beside the lifeboat. "Welcome," said a short man with grizzled hair and large, serious eyes. "I'm Captain Shevchenko, and this is my political commissar, Pavel Alexandrovich." He indicated a dapper little man with a bulldog look of aggressiveness.

"Welcome to the *Izumrudny*," said the commissar. "Welcome to Soviet life, striding forth under the banner of communism."

Uh oh, I thought.

"I told Alexei Vasilievich you shouldn't be transferred in this weather," said Captain Shevchenko with solicitude, "but he insisted." I looked at him questioningly as he continued: "Since we heard you were coming, though, we went ahead and told the American to set his trawl. He'll be hauling back any minute now. Would you come to the bridge and speak with him?"

It sounds as if I understood what the captain was saying. Actually, between Shevchenko's Ukrainian accent and rapid speech, the sound of the wind wailing past, and the omnipresent noise of the ship's engines, I understood only about half his words. I filled in the rest from context and guesswork. My gut twisted. I was all alone now—the only American on board. What if I had guessed wrong? I shouldn't even have to guess. What on earth ever led me to believe I could work as a translator?

"*Konyeshnuh*"—certainly, I said smoothly.

"You speak Russian beautifully," said the commissar.

I'd only said one word so far. "Thanks."

We headed for the bridge. The *Izumrudny* was a newer trawler than the *Yegorova*, slightly smaller and much more efficiently designed. The bridge was spacious, and large windows towards the stern overlooked the back deck: the main working area of the ship. One could stand on the bridge and see everything occurring both fore and aft.

"We're working with the *Hilo*." The captain stuffed a microphone in my hand. "Go ahead."

Go ahead and what? I wondered. I thumbed the mike hesitantly. "*Hilo*, this is the *Izumrudny*."

Static followed. I wondered if we were on the right channel. "*Hilo*, *Izumrudny* here."

"Well, fuckin' A," came a voice. "It's about time those bastards got you on board. I've been trying to tell them for the past half hour I'm hauling back, and they don't seem to understand." The voice paused while I turned to tell the captain they were hauling back the trawl.

"He's hauling back now," the captain interjected before I could say a word. "Ask him what his coordinates are."

"I don't know where the hell you are right now," the voice continued, "but you'd better get those assholes moving to these coordinates." He rattled off a string of numbers. "I don't think they know what the fuck's going on here. We've got some money to make."

"What does 'asshole' mean?" asked the commissar.

"Just a minute," I said to the commissar. Into the mike: "Could you say those numbers again, please?"

"What's the matter, you retarded or something? Get a fuckin' pencil next time, okay?" The voice repeated the numbers, more slowly this time. I repeated them in Russian to the captain.

"Tell him we'll be there in forty-five minutes," said Shevchenko. I relayed the information.

"Forty fuckin' five minutes," exploded the voice from the *Hilo*. "I can't believe this. What is this, a picnic? You guys are really something else. I could catch two more hauls in the time it takes you to get your idiotic act together."

"What's he saying?" asked Shevchenko.

"He's wondering if we could speed up a little bit," I said.

"Oh. Tell him we'll try."

"You should have set your trawl closer to the *Izumrudny*," I said into the radio. Call it creative translation.

The voice was silent. Captain Shevchenko reeled off a slew of orders, and the helmsman, a cauliflower-eared oldster with the broken nose of a pugilist, moved to comply. The drone of the engines deepened in pitch. We were under way.

Trawling can be seen as the maritime equivalent of flying a kite. The trawl itself is shaped like an immense butterfly net, and is played out behind the trawler at the end of two long cables. It flies through the water at a depth dictated by the cable's length and the weight of the trawl itself. Trawl doors are affixed to the cable just ahead of the great forward edges of the trawl. These are hydrodynamically designed sheets of steel that slice outward in the water, keeping the two sides of the trawl from collapsing in on each other. A series of floats and weights keep the top of the trawl's mouth from collapsing into the bottom. The very back of the trawl traps all the fish; it is the detachable codend, a sausage-shaped portion of the net attached to the rest of the trawl rather like a sock pinned to a pant leg.

The transfer of twenty to thirty tons of fish from one boat to another on the open sea is a risky business even in the best of weather. In foul weather it becomes particularly dangerous. In theory the operation is simple—the Americans reel their trawl aboard, funneling all the fish that have been caught into the codend at the back. This meshed bag is then detached from the trawl, cinched shut, and attached to a cable trailing off the stern of the Soviet trawler. Finally, the Soviets reel the cable back to haul the codend aboard their vessel.

In practice, however, the operation becomes much more complicated. The proper speed must be maintained by both vessels, as well as the proper distance and position relative to the wind and the wave action. The codend itself has to be released by the Americans at just the right moment, with just the right amount of slack in the Soviet's cable. The Soviets, in turn, have to ensure the codend was hauled aboard properly, particularly in heavy seas. Any deviation from the correct line of action can spell disaster: lost fish, fouled gear, an injury. Or a death.

The equipment involved in all this could cost a fortune—the *Hilo's* trawl was worth well over $20,000, and the ever-present possibility of a damaged or destroyed trawl required that a spare be kept on board, as well. Between the trawl gear, the electronics, and the boat itself, the cost of a well-fitted trawler could easily run into the millions—it was no wonder fishermen were so anxious to catch fish. It took a special kind of man to risk his money, time, and effort in that perilous gamble called trawling. Unfortunately, the kind of man it took was not often a very nice man.

"Would you like some tea?" I glanced up. A high-cheekboned individual with bushy, straight hair stood smiling with a glass in his hand. "I'm the second mate, Nicholai Alexandrovich. But just call me Kolya."

"I'd like some," I said. The bridge weaved in the swell, but my seasickness was much better than it had been.

Kolya handed me a heavy water glass filled with a tarry black substance. I held it gingerly by the rim—it was very hot.

"Some sugar?" I nodded. He turned and led me over to a small table which held a large steaming mason jar—the source of the tea—and a box of sugar cubes. I took a cube hesitantly from the box while Kolya poured himself a glass.

"Go ahead, have some more," said Kolya. He grabbed a handful of cubes and dumped them into his glass, then popped a few in his mouth. "Sugar helps build strong bones." He smiled again, more broadly this time, and revealed a set of stainless-steel teeth.

"This is fine," I said. I mimicked Kolya, rocking the glass to and fro to keep from spilling as the deck rolled beneath us, then took a gulp and grimaced. The tea was strong enough to tan leather. I watched while Kolya downed his steaming glass as if it were water.

The bridge was seedily luxurious: the walls were thick wood veneer, the floor a worn red linoleum with rounded troughs marking the patterns of standing and walking. A low ceiling diminished the brightness pouring in through the banks of windows to fore and aft, lending a boxed-in feeling, as if we were working inside a sandwich. The radio room took up the mid-section on the port side of the bridge; the chart room was to starboard. Miscellaneous pieces of equipment lay scattered about: several fish finders, with their seismograph-like scrolls of paper and wobbling pens; radios; speaking tubes; and unidentifiable pieces of machinery that looked like junk. An old radar detector with a worn eyepiece jutted from the floor like a mushroom. Dead center behind the windows to fore was the wheel where the helmsman stood, both hands firm on the polished wood.

"Hard worker, isn't he?" asked Kolya, glancing toward the helmsman. I nodded.

"Actually, we're on autopilot right now."

The helmsman took both his hands from the wheel and spread them in an expansive shrug, smiling. "I've got to do something to earn my pay," he said. His teeth were pointed, like fangs. He put his hands in his pockets and leaned back against an iron bar sticking up behind the wheel. The *Izumrudny* plowed ahead, undisturbed. I glanced around. The captain seemed to have disappeared, along with the commissar. Shevchenko hadn't seemed a bad sort. I wondered at Laura's prediction.

In the distance, the *Hilo* hove into view, surging heavily on the waves. At eighty-five feet, she was one of the largest American catcher boats. She seemed a miniaturized version of the *Izumrudny*, but she wasn't, of course. Below decks there were none of the crucial fish processing or storage capabilities of the larger Soviet vessel.

Kolya began giving orders to the helmsman as we closed in on the *Hilo*, circling ponderously around to come up on her port side as she wallowed in the waves. The codend at her stern slowed her movements in the heavy swell; at times the wind threatened to turn her broadside and capsize her.

"Here, you'd better use this." Kolya handed me a walkie-talkie. "You can stand by the back windows now and see everything." We moved over to the aft windows and watched the men on deck attaching buoys to a cable. The buoys would keep the heavy cable afloat; a special orange-colored buoy marked the end of the cable. Glancing to the side, I could see the *Hilo* as we passed.

"Looks like we're ready," said Kolya nervously. He reached down and turned a switch, then leaned over toward a microphone mounted on the wall as the loudspeakers on deck coughed to life: "Ready on deck. Cable's going out now." He thrust a lever forward and a winch hummed into action. The men grabbed the cable and began feeding it out over the edge of the stern ramp. It trailed, the brightly colored buoys tossing in the waves. We'd passed the *Hilo* now, and she eased in behind us, trundling as close as she dared to the cable. A man stood near the scuppers on the *Hilo*'s back deck, a grappling hook held loosely in his hand, ready to snag our cable by the end buoy.

"*Izumrudny, Hilo.*"

I jumped. It was the walkie-talkie. "*Izumrudny* here," I said. Shevchenko appeared as if by magic. Kolya looked relieved and stepped away from the windows.

"Slow down, goddamn it," the voice from the *Hilo* snarled.

"He asks if you could slow down a little," I said to Shevchenko. Shevchenko turned and nodded to the helmsman. "Cut her back a notch."

The *Hilo*'s crewman threw the grappling hook toward the cable trailing from the *Izumrudny*—a gust of wind tossed it back. The crewman ducked, then coiled the rope to try again. It still landed wide of the mark. The *Hilo* edged closer to the cable. Too close, though, and she could be pushed over by the wave action and foul on the cable. Too far away, and the crewman couldn't catch the cable with his hook.

Third try. The *Hilo*'s crewman snared the cable, then hauled it toward him as fast as he could, somehow keeping his balance as the *Hilo* reared and a wall of water washed over her deck. Another man waded into view, and as the edge of the *Izumrudny*'s cable came on board, both men grabbed and dragged it up to attach to the capron rope hooked into the codend dangling from the rear of the vessel. The *Hilo* slammed into a wave, and the deck disappeared momentarily in the swell. As the water washed back, the first man grabbed a sledgehammer secured to the gantry and took a swing at the pelican hook holding the codend to the *Hilo*. With a crack the hook flipped open and the codend floated free, attached now only to the *Izumrudny*'s cable.

The *Hilo* accelerated, fighting in the waves to roll out of the way. Their job was complete now. Ours had just begun.

I peered into the waters behind the ship. A hint of white flickered in the waves—the codend, floating just below the surface. I watched as the wind picked the tops off the waves, sheeting them back in glistening cascades of water. If anything, the weather was getting worse.

"*Hilo* here. Getting sloppy," came the voice, suddenly a little friendlier. "What's your name, anyway?"

"Barb. What's yours?"

"Jack. Guess our two boats'll be working together for a while."

"They've already assigned boats?" I asked, my heart sinking. Laura had told me this was a common practice after things shook themselves out in the beginning of the season. I hoped the *Hilo* wouldn't be assigned to us for too long.

"Yup. Well, got to go set my trawl. Give me a call when you get an estimate on that codend."

"Right." As soon as the codend came aboard, part of my job was to estimate how many tons of fish were in it. This was to be a difficult task: I'd never even *seen* a codend before, much less the type of fish we were catching—hake (also known to housewives as "whiting"). On top of that, it looked like I'd be working closely with Jack over the next months. I'd overheard some of the other American fishermen in the fleet talking with their reps over the radio. None of them had sounded as, well, irascible as Jack.

The codend arrived at the stern, and the captain slowed the winches as it began to ease its way up the stern ramp. Each time the stern of the *Izumrudny* rose into the air on the back of a wave, the codend was bent down to fold dangerously close to the propellers. The intercom connected to the far end of the deck picked up every sound: I could hear the heavy codend wheezing and popping in the swell, the torque exerted by the rolling action of the waves worsening the already heavy strain on the webbing.

The front of the codend edged over the stern ramp, and the captain stopped the winches as they began to whine with strain. He picked up the mike to the deck intercom: "Danielich, go ahead."

I watched in amazement as one of the men standing near the stern ramp leapt over the transom to land on the codend, fumbling at his belt for the hooks attached to the cables leading to the gantry above him. In seconds he had loosened the hooks and tucked them around the reinforcing cable strung through the front end of the codend. The *Izumrudny* slammed into a wave and water washed up and about, soaking the crewman as he clung like a limpet to the net. He shook himself, seal-like, and grinned up at us; then gathered himself and jumped lightly back over the transom as the deck bucked beneath him.

The captain waited for the stern to descend again before continuing to pull the codend on board.

The stern began to dip. Shevchenko applied power to the winches, playing them like a master puppeteer, anticipating the codend as it began to slip from one side to the other on its passage up the stern ramp; correcting, lifting, shifting. The codend groaned, water spurting from the meshes as the fish were compressed against the net. The bag began crawling onto deck, a seething twenty-five-foot-long, seven-foot-tall sausage of fish. The *Izumrudny* dove forward in the swell, and the codend slid fully on board, aided by the slope of the deck and the water's slickness as it licked up the stern ramp and out onto the planking.

"Let's go see what we've got," said Shevchenko. He grabbed another microphone and spoke into it: "Factory director to the deck, please."

We headed out a door beside the fore windows and traipsed towards the stern. The *Izumrudny*, I noticed, was in a lot better shape than the *Muis Yegorova*. No piles of rubbish lay around the walkways, and the cabin windows looking out on the passageway sparkled. The stark white and gun-metal gray paint had little of the rust found everywhere on the *Yegorova*. I grabbed a railing as the deck lurched, then pulled it away startled, my hand covered with sticky white goo.

"We just painted," said Shevchenko, glancing back. "Be careful."

"Right," I said, trying to rub the paint off unobtrusively as we passed the lifeboat. The goo spread onto my sleeve.

We climbed down several flights of stairs and emerged on the back deck. I eyed the codend as we approached. Tiny spurts of water erupted from the net: the last gasps of dying fish. Here and there an eyeball peered out at me, pressed hopelessly against the meshes. Ruptured membranes dribbled out, souvenirs of the explosive decompression the fish underwent as they were hauled abruptly to the surface. The codend oozed slime and muck, and it stank. It was disgusting.

A lardy individual with a full pompadour hairstyle joined our group. "Well, look what we have here," he said, rubbing his hands together. "The first catch of the season." He reached out to shake my hand. "I'm Gleb Vitalich, the factory director."

"Pleased to meet you," I said.

Gleb turned towards the codend and resumed rubbing his hands. "Nice bag. Very nice bag. Good start here."

"About how much do you think it weighs?" I asked. I'd been told to rely on the Russians until I developed a feel for making estimates on weight myself. There'd been trouble on other joint ventures with estimates—the Japanese, for example, had been caught underestimating catches by over a third through the use of secret storage compartments. Rather than estimating the Americans' tonnage from looking at the net itself, as the Russians did, they'd dumped the catch in holding tanks, siphoned a portion off, then measured exactly how "full" the tank was. Others—the Koreans, for example—had simply lied outright.

The factory director pulled at his chin, suddenly looking dubious. "Weighs?" he asked. "How much it weighs?"

"Yes," I said. "Could you give me an estimate?"

"An estimate?" The director looked at the captain.

"It's about twenty tons," said the captain.

"About twenty tons," echoed the director.

We stood back, watching, as deck crew workers shinnied onto the net, detaching some cables and hooking others in.

"Let's get the fish into the bunkers," said the captain. "This is not a good place to stay. If one of these cables breaks under tension," he made a popping sound, "it would take your head off—just like that." He snapped his fingers and smiled. We trooped back up toward the bridge. Shevchenko disappeared again.

Kolya manned the winches by the aft windows, and within minutes the codend swung into the air to spill the fish out section by section. Men with wooden sweepers began pushing the fish toward trap doors opened on the far edge of the deck. These were the entrances to the bunkers: the bins used to hold fish until the factory workers could process them.

I headed for the radio and opened my logbook: "*Hilo*, twenty tons, April 19th". My first entry. Taking a breath, I picked up the microphone. "*Hilo, Izumrudny* here."

A hesitation. "*Hilo* back." It was Jack's voice.

"I've got that estimate for you."

"It's about time."

"Twenty tons," I said.

There was a lengthy silence. "What?"

"Twenty tons of fish."

"I heard you the first time. Who are you trying to kid? That codend practically crawled up my stern ramp, it was so big. It was twenty-five tons if it was a pound."

I'd been told in my preliminary briefings that it was impossible for the Americans to guess accurately at the size of a codend as it trailed behind them in the water. Most of the codend remained underwater, like the bulk of an iceberg, and when the catch was small, the fish tended to spread out in the loose meshes, making the catch look larger than it really was.

"You don't know what the hell you're doing, do you?" he said.

Of course I didn't. "Give me a break, Jack," I said aloud. "The fish will be processed through the factory soon. Then we'll get the exact weight down to a tenth of a ton." Fishermen tended to be a little sticky about their initial estimate, I'd been told, because when more than one boat supplied fish, it was difficult for the Russians to process them separately. As a consequence, the fish were simply processed and the total true weight portioned out to the two supplying catcher boats based on the estimated weights. As the only catcher boat now working for us, however, Jack had no need to worry about this. Jack, I was learning, was just being Jack.

"All right," he said. There was an ominous tone to his voice. "We'll see. *Hilo* out."

"It's tea time, Barbara," said Kolya, coming up beside me. "You must be hungry. Here, Seryozha will show you to the officers' mess." He pointed towards the helmsman, who stepped away from the wheel and grabbed a bag from a box near the radio. Between Seryozha's fangs, broken nose, cauliflower ears, and multitudinous homemade tattoos, he looked like nothing so much as a hardened criminal.

He smiled, holding forth the bag: "This is for you, Barbara."

I took the bag, not knowing what to say. "Should I open it now?" I asked.

"If you'd like," he said, diffidently.

I glanced inside. The bag was stuffed with candy. "Thank you," I said. I was at a loss for words. Seryozha turned bright red, the tips of his cauliflower ears flaming. He turned and headed down a set of stairs just outside the chart room. I followed.

Russians hold an ambivalent attitude toward food. On the one hand, being overweight is not a national ideal, and young women in particular will go to horrifying dietary extremes to maintain a slender figure. On the other hand, a strong feeling exists that someone who is thin is also sickly: the very phrase "she put on weight" can also mean "she got well."

Food on the trawlers is served five times a day. There is breakfast, lunch, "tea," dinner, and a post-prandial snack around eleven in the evening. Since several of the company reps and fishery observers had come down with malnutrition the year before, a sixth meal had been instituted for them alone: the American breakfast, containing eggs, tomatoes, and other fresh produce. On the *Yegorova* I had sat with Laura and the observers and eaten the breakfast with a guilt-ridden conscience. I intended to put a stop to the practice on the *Izumrudny*.

The officer's mess aboard the *Izumrudny*, I discovered, was much like that of the *Yegorova*: a simple cabin filled with a long table. Duplicate pictures of Marx and Lenin spotted the walls. I entered the room nervously; a half dozen men sat towards the port side, talking.

"Hello," said one of the men, rising. "Pleased to meet you, Barbara. Have a seat." He indicated a spot on the bench across from him. I slid in to sit on the edge of the seat, and he sat as well, continuing. "I'm Oleg Pavlovich, the chief mate." He went around the table, introducing everyone. The names went by in a haze. "We're really glad to have you aboard. It gets a little tiring, doing nothing."

"Here, have some fish," said one of the other men, holding forth a plate. "First fresh fish we've had here in a while. It's great." My few days on the *Yegorova* had accustomed me to the idea of fried fish as the accompaniment for afternoon tea. Not that I'd been able to keep any down. "And don't forget your vitamins." He grabbed a bowl filled with cloves of garlic. One was expected to peel and eat them between bites of fish.

"Well, what do you think of the *Izumrudny*?" asked another.

"It's different," I said. In Russian the word also means strange.

The men laughed, then abruptly fell silent as Captain Shevchenko entered the cabin.

"*Priatnovo appatita*," he said. I cursed myself. The custom was to always wish everyone a pleasant appetite upon entering the mess. He took a seat at the end of the table. The waitress scurried in and poured him a cup of tea. The room remained silent. He reached over and pulled a piece of coarse bread from a basket in front of him. The bread, I noted, had swirls in it: the unused bread of the day before, ground and tossed into the new batter.

"That will be your assigned seat, Barbara," he said, smoothing some butter onto the bread and pointing with his chin toward where I sat. The other men examined their plates. Two of them excused themselves and headed out of the cabin.

The captain focused again on me. "Do you know what horsepower the engines here are?"

"No," I answered.

"Good." He took another bite of the bread and reached for the fish.

A man appeared at the cabin door. "Excuse me, sir, but could Barbara come to the bridge? The *Hilo* is calling for her."

"Of course," the captain said. I excused myself. Maybe I would go to tea when the captain wasn't there. I circled around the passageway to the foot of the stairs, then amused myself by waiting until the *Izumrudny* hit the top of a big wave. As she headed down, elevator-like, I floated up the steps, light as thistledown.

I grabbed the mike with a sigh: "*Hilo, Izumrudny* here."

"It's about time," said Jack, adding a few obscenities. "We're hauling back now. We'll have another load for you in half an hour."

"Fifteen and a half tons, Jack," I said.

"I heard you," came the peevish reply. "I can't believe it. You guys are a bunch of goddamned cheaters."

It was nine o'clock that evening, and the factory director had just given me the production figures on the first haul of fish. We were four and a half tons below the estimate.

"Some of the fish were crushed because the codend was bouncing around so badly in the heavy seas," I said. "And it wasn't as big as they'd thought to start with."

"If there were crushed fish there," said Jack, "they were crushed because it took you idiots so long to get here."

This required diplomacy. I'd never been very good at diplomacy. I racked my brains. On his own boat, insulated from contact with the Russians by both the radio and my own mediation, it was all too easy for Jack to be a royal pain. Something from an old psychology book nibbled—if

Jack met the Russians on board the *Izumrudny*, he couldn't very well think of them as faceless enemies anymore. What would happen, I wondered, if I introduced Jack to the Russians, face-to-face?

"Tell you what, Jack. Why don't you come over and take a look at the ship. You can see what we've processed so far, and satisfy yourself about the tonnage."

There was a long pause. Uh oh, I thought. What if Captain Shevchenko doesn't want him over here? I should have asked first. Me and my big mouth.

"All right." Did I imagine a gulp on the other end of the line? "When?"

"Just a minute." I turned to the chief mate. "Would it be all right if the captain of the *Hilo* comes over now for a little visit?"

The chief mate, a portly individual with a slick smile, suddenly looked serious. "Let me ask the captain." He headed out the door.

I glanced outside, waiting impatiently. With the setting of the sun, the schools of hake dissipated. The American catcher boats could no longer home in on them with their radar detectors. That was one of the advantages of fishing in the hake fleet off the coasts of Washington and Oregon—a little uninterrupted sleep at night. The yellow-fin sole and pollack fisheries in Alaska worked round the clock. I was tired enough as it was; I didn't see how anybody could exist on the two or three hours of constantly interrupted sleep that were the norm in the Alaskan fisheries.

Shevchenko appeared. "What's the matter?" he asked.

"The captain of the *Hilo* is having a little trouble understanding how the final factory figures are arrived at. And he would like to meet you," I said, not exactly lying. "Would it be possible for him to make a little visit this evening?"

Shevchenko's eyes narrowed. "What does he want to see?"

"Oh, the factory, maybe, and the trawl deck." I'd seen the factory on the *Yegorova*, but it hadn't been processing fish at the time. I wouldn't mind seeing the *Izumrudny*'s factory myself.

"I suppose that's all right," he said. "Tell him to come over." He turned away and headed down the stairs.

"You can come over now," I said into the mike.

"We'll be there in a few minutes," said Jack. "*Hilo* out."

"I'm pleased to meet you, too," I translated. Good, I thought, they're shaking hands.

Shevchenko turned. The commissar turned beside him, like a dog at heel. "Shall we get started?"

"Sure," said Jack. Meeting Jack had been a surprise. He looked a boyish twenty-five, with athletic good looks marred only by a slight paunch and jowliness about the chin line. He didn't look to have the pigheaded sense of certitude one associates with the true, died-in-the-wool ass. In fact, as he stood listening to the Slavic babble around him, he looked downright cowed.

We made our way quickly down flight after flight of stairs; the factory was on one of the lowest levels of the ship. As we descended, the stink of ammonia—the refrigerant used to freeze the boxes of fish—became stronger.

We passed at last through a series of low doorways into the icy factory area. Dim, naked light bulbs illuminated a large room filled with conveyer belts and clattering machinery. Wooden pallets lined the walkways as water sluiced by on the flooring beneath us. The captain led us over to several large tanks covered with a blackish slime. The tanks dripped constantly; water continuously flowed through them when fish were inside, making the fish easier to handle on the assembly line.

"These are the bunkers," Shevchenko said, pointing at a hole in the side of one of the tanks. "You can see the fish through here."

Jack moved over and looked carefully through the hole. Then he stood back, examining the bunkers from every angle possible. "Looks good to me," he said at last, scratching his head.

The captain smiled and moved on. "This is our cleaning line—an efficient operation, as you can see." A row of men stood at a conveyer belt, knives flashing as they cleaned fish and flipped them onto other conveyer belts. A woman stood near the end, scraping offal into a chute.

"Nina Alexandrovna here is one of our best workers," the commissar said. A young woman with pert features and bleached blonde hair, Nina was busy slicing the head off a fish. She did not look up. We watched for a minute; then the captain led us forward to a dark set of doors.

"This is where we do the freezing," he said, opening one of the doors. I peered into the darkness as a blast of frost enveloped us. Laura had told me the *Izumrudny* had lost a man last year, dragged overboard when his foot caught on an empty codend being returned to the Americans. They'd gotten him out within two minutes, but he was already dead, killed by the cold and the fear. They'd frozen him and kept him in the holds to take home.

This was the freezer where they'd frozen him.

"And now I'll show you the holds," said the captain, closing the freezer door. I hadn't been able to see anything in the darkness. We clambered down yet another flight of stairs and then through a small doorway into a large, frozen room. A stack of boxes stood in the corner: Jack's catch, cleaned and frozen.

"This is mine?" Jack asked. I had no need to translate the note of suspicion.

"Of course," the captain answered.

"Communists do not lie," said the commissar.

Jack headed for the corner, counting the boxes. My teeth began to chatter.

"It's twenty below zero here," said the commissar with feigned nonchalance. That put it at about minus ten Fahrenheit. The commissar's cheeks were beginning to look blue. I wondered if mine were, too. They'd never warned me about frostbite in Mrs. Holdsworth's third year Russian class.

Jack rejoined us at last and we headed out of the holds and toward the upper decks.

"Perhaps I can show you my cabin," said the captain.

"Okay," said Jack, as we headed back through the bridge. We trooped through the chart room and into a comfortable cabin with much the same finishings as Captain Alex's aboard the *Yegorova*. There was a big difference, however. Here only one bottle of vodka stood in the center of the otherwise empty table.

"Care for a drink?" asked Shevchenko, innocuously.

"I think I could use one," said Jack.

The captain reached into a cabinet and pulled out four tumblers.

"Oh, no," I interjected. "I'm working. I won't be able to translate very well if I drink too much." Actually, I was still feeling the effects of the last binge.

"Ah," said the captain, reaching back into the cabinet for a wine glass. "Then there will be champagne for the lady." He went through a set of curtains into what looked like a bedroom and emerged moments later with a chilled bottle of champagne. He popped the cork with a flourish, poured a glass for me, then liberally doused the tumblers with vodka.

"To the Soviet-American joint venture," he said, holding up his glass. The commissar immediately held his glass up as well. I translated.

"To the Soviet-American joint venture," said Jack. I watched as Shevchenko and the commissar kicked their glasses back. After a moment, Jack followed suit.

The captain poured another round. At least he's only got one bottle, I thought.

"To our successful working relationship," said the captain, and downed his tumbler once again. The commissar followed, a carbon copy. Jack took a breath and swigged the glass. His cheeks began to flush. I sipped again at my champagne. It was a good thing, I knew, that I was female. Women could pass on booze occasionally without looking like too much of a sissy. But for men—well, dead drunk is a good definition of Russian machismo.

"Looks like we're running low," said the captain. He poured the rest of the bottle, then disappeared with the empty into the bedroom, reappearing seconds later with another bottle. Oh no, I thought. Here we go again. The captain opened the bottle and continued pouring.

"To great fuckin' wads of money," Jack burst out, raising his glass.

"To friendship," I translated. The Russians lifted their glasses and smiled.

Shevchenko poured another round, and then another.

"These guys aren't so bad, after all," said Jack. "I think they're human."

I wasn't so sure. The commissar had just begun mouthing communist platitudes to no one in particular. The captain was busy getting another bottle.

"This is my first time out with the venture," Jack told me. "Looks like it's going to be a piece of cake. And by the way—no problem about the estimate." He spread his hands out in a magnanimous gesture and knocked his tumbler flying. "Oopsie."

Shevchenko smiled with everything but his eyes. "Care for another round?" he asked. The commissar jerked his head up. "Yes, I would." The captain silenced him with a glance.

"Of course," said Jack. He had a cornered look on his face, as if realizing, for the first time, that a trap had been sprung.

The captain poured another round. "To the proletariat," he proposed.

"To the proletariat," Jack repeated, after the translation. "What's a proletariat?"

The commissar began sagging in his seat.

"To hake," said the captain. Jack dutifully downed his drink.

"To capitalism," said Jack. I translated reluctantly.

"To communism," retorted the captain, as the commissar slid to the floor. Shevchenko shoved him under the table with his feet. Jack didn't notice. I sipped politely at my champagne.

"To friendship," proposed Jack, a subliminal plea for mercy.

The captain opened a new bottle, this time filling both tumblers to the brim. He grinned savagely—a killer on the loose. "To world peace."

"To world peace," repeated Jack, a look of determination on his face. He raised the glass and chugged the vodka, setting the glass down in triumph.

The captain tipped his glass in Jack's direction and swallowed the contents easily, setting his glass on the table. The two stared at each other. Shevchenko poured another round.

"To vodka," said Jack, and fell off his chair.

"To vodka," said the captain, and downed his drink. He set the empty glass on the table, steady as Gibraltar. "Call the *Hilo*," he said to me, rising. He picked up the bottle, stepping around Jack's body to head back to his bedroom. "Tell them to come and pick up their captain." He disappeared through the doorway.

The *Hilo* resumed fishing with us two days later.

Chapter Three
"You Know Too Much,
It's Time to Kill You"

I WOKE UP IN THE depths of depression. I'd spoken nothing but Russian for two weeks. Heard nothing but Russian, felt nothing but Russian—even smelled nothing but Russian: acrid detergent and rotten fish. I was sick of it. All I wanted was a burger and some fries from McDonald's and an uninterrupted night's sleep on something that didn't move.

Laura had warned me of this. Apparently all reps went through periods where they hated everything Russian, where even their comprehension of Russian faded, as if whatever power we used for peaceful understanding and coexistence temporarily burned out in the face of a brash and overwhelming intransigence. Laura blamed it on the ship's atmosphere: the tension of being in a new and sometimes hostile environment; the pressure of seeing the same, inescapable faces day after day.

She had a point, but I thought the problem went deeper than that. It was rooted in the Russian language itself.

Most European languages fall into what is known as the Indo-European language group. Let us say, for the purposes of solipsism, that English lies on a branch at the center of the Indo-European language tree. Crowded close to it, then, would lie the other Germanic languages: Frisian, Dutch, and German. Slightly farther away would lie the Scandinavian languages, then the Romance languages. Even farther away, the Baltic languages. Scattered around the outside of the tree, as far away from English as they could get and still cling to the tree, would lie Gaelic, Sanskrit, and last but not least, Russian. Russian is to English as Nome, Alaska, is to Miami, Florida. They may lie on the same continent, but man, are they different.

Sure, there are cognates, those lovely old proto-Indo-European words: whiskey, cognac, vodka, gin, (and even gin-and-tonic), cocktail, and bar. But don't hold your breath waiting for them.

Let's take the English "to bring." In German that's "bringen." Russian? "Nosit'" and "Nesti"—to bring by carrying, as opposed to bring by leading or rolling or driving or pulling or lugging, all of which have their own pair of verbs. And if you happen to be bringing something in instead of out, you'd better say so in Russian, even if you could care less in English. Actually, there are about twenty different prefixes you can stick onto that one simple verb, depending on what shade of meaning you want to convey. And if you're going somewhere in Russian, you'd better know exactly how you're going to get there. You can walk, ride, fly, climb, or crawl in Russian, but you can't just go—Russian doesn't have a word for it.

Where English has spelling as its bête noire, Russian has accent. An accent can slip from front to back to sideways, all depending on whether you're making it plural or genitive or dative or what-have-you. "Ah," say those of you acquainted with a second language, "but there are rules for these kinds of things." This is true. You are unwittingly quoting *Russian's First Rule*: "There is a Rule for Everything." However, there is a problem with this rule—a problem best articulated by *Russian's Second Rule*, which is: "For Every Rule, There is an Exception." Rules in Russian curl back in on themselves like some endless recursive nightmare, growing ever more convoluted and complex. For example, *Russian's Third Rule* is: "For Every Exception, There is a Rule."

When you study Russian in class you are introduced to these inanities slowly, with plenty of time to scratch your head and puzzle over them. Out on the boats they come at you in a constant barrage, with the background white noise of the ship—the rumbling of the engines, the ever-present shifting and swaying and rocking, the constant rattling and clattering of the machinery and things bumping into each other, to say nothing of the interruptions—making it difficult, if not impossible, to concentrate.

"We're setting now, Barb. This place is crawling with fish," said Jack. I looked again at the *Izumrudny's* fish finders. Jack was right. Blotches of ink scribbled their way onto the scroll of paper—sonar traces of the schools below us.

Fishing had petered out after the first few days I'd been aboard the *Izumrudny*. We'd been looking for fish off the coast of Oregon for over a week now, searching with our detectors through the plateaus and valleys of the ocean depths for the tell-tale signs of hake. For lack of anything better to do, the bridge crew and I had spent hours together staring at the screens. We'd never seen schools anywhere near this big.

"Just look at those dollar signs," Jack continued, as his trawl winches whined in the background. "It's enough to make your wallet salivate."

"What's he saying?" asked Kolya, impatiently.

"He's just being materialistic," I said.

Kolya nodded and looked back down at the finder. "I would be, too." The second mate, I'd discovered, was one of the few watch officers who took a serious interest in fishing. On Kolya's watch I could finally just sit back and do my job, translate. His shifts were my favorite times to be on the bridge, except when he was drunk and they wouldn't let him stand watch—or, worse, when he was drunk and they would. His only real problem was that he couldn't steer the boat worth a damn. I got nervous during transfers.

The other mates were inept at best: the chief mate had been, I gathered, a chief mate far longer than usual—he was capable enough, but only when he felt like it. He rarely seemed to feel like it. The third mate was hopeless: a non-stop talker with the liberated attitude of a twelfth-century Mongol. The fourth mate stood watch with the chief mate, as was the usual practice aboard the trawlers. He had little to do by way of actual work, but he was great to kid. When I corrected him at fumbled attempts at English, he would eye me, trying to understand whether I was teasing him or whether the whole English language was just completely screwy. He would often come up to me to spit out a short sentence in English, after which he would walk away to stand by himself, looking out a window. For a while I kept thinking I had unwittingly offended him, but then it dawned on me that it simply took him a couple of minutes of silent concentration to figure out his next sentence in English.

The first mate stood no watches at all. He was the political commissar. Technically, he was second in the chain of command behind the captain—senior even to the chief mate. In practice, he had a bare minimum of maritime training, and it showed. His responsibility was the crew's political "enhancement": spreading the gospel of Marx according to Lenin as modified by Stalin, Khrushchev, and Brezhnev. He also monitored the crew for signs of sedition and, I was to discover, contamination by foreign influences: me. Unfortunately, he showed an endless enthusiasm and ferret-like devotion to his task.

"Wow, look at that one," said Kolya, pointing to an ink blot the size of a silver dollar. The pen of the fish finder jerked again, beginning a trace of what looked to be an even larger school. We were cruising slowly directly ahead of the *Hilo*—Jack would be passing over these same schools within a few minutes.

I thumbed the mike: "It's even better up ahead of you, Jack. Some really thick schools up here."

"Great," said Jack. Relations between the *Izumrudny* and the *Hilo* had improved a little since our tête-a-tête in the Captain's cabin. I wasn't so sure, however, whether I liked Jack nice any better than I'd liked Jack nasty.

"What've you got here?" Shevchenko appeared at my elbow. Kolya drifted imperceptibly away.

"Some big schools. The *Hilo*'s setting right now."

"Is it?" The captain scratched his belly, sweating from a self-imposed workout on the walkway just aft of the bridge. Several of the men exercised daily with the weights and chinning bar located there. I'd begun sneaking out there myself, although using a jump rope on a weaving deck can be a bit of a challenge.

Shevchenko bent down to examine the paper more closely. "How long did you say Jack has been fishing?" he asked.

"Eleven years."

"Eleven years." Shevchenko laughed. "He's not fishing, he's rinsing his net. This is feed."

"What's feed?" I asked.

"Small fry. You know, little fish the bigger fish feed on."

I looked back down at the paper. The pen scratched frantically at the paper, sketching out yet another large school. "How can you tell?"

"It's circular, for one thing. Hake schools don't look like that—they tend to be more irregular looking. See how the edges look hazy? Hake schools show up with crisp edges. And the school's very low in the water." He pointed to the jagged line indicating the ocean floor. "In these depths, at this time of day, the hake tend to school up mid-water." His finger moved back up on the paper to smudge the ink.

"Oh," I said. Jack had spent hours bragging about his hundred thousand dollar fish-finding equipment, with the latest in computer technology showing every aspect of the ocean floor and the fish below on a giant color monitor. It was hard to believe he could be wrong. Still, the captain had fished this area for hake long before the Americans. "Should I tell Jack?" I asked.

"If you'd like." Shevchenko sauntered towards the door.

Kolya drifted back, shame-faced. "Actually, I was just going to say it looked like it might be feed."

"Of course, Kolya. And my mother wears army boots."

"Does she?" Kolya asked, curious.

I picked up the mike: "*Hilo, Izumrudny* here."

"*Hilo* back."

"Captain Shevchenko says he thinks what we're seeing on the screen is feed."

"Captain Shevchenko is full of shit."

I improvised, since the captain had already left. "The captain says he is not full of shit."

"Well," said Jack, flustered, "I mean, tell him I think he's wrong."

I paused again. "The captain says we'll see."

"Damned straight. We've just hit another big school. We'll start hauling back in another minute or so."

Jack had only been trawling about five minutes. The usual tow lasted anywhere from half an hour to three hours. He must really think he's hit it big, I thought.

I grabbed the walkie-talkie and headed with Kolya for the railed passageway just beside the bridge, eager to see what came up in the nets. "The winches have started," said Kolya. He handed the binoculars to me and I scanned the *Hilo*, cruising slowly a thousand yards sternwards and to port. Water sheeted off the twin cables as they surged from the spray behind the American boat, winding up over the deck and onto the winches.

Kolya and I waited impatiently at the railing. Depending on the length of cable, it could take anywhere from ten to twenty minutes of hauling back for the bright orange trawl net to begin emerging from the water. It would take another ten minutes to get the trawl itself aboard, and only then would we be able to get a good look at the codend.

Kolya pointed at last. "There's the trawl."

"Let me see." I wrestled for the binoculars.

The brilliant orange trawl came sharply into view. Even as I watched, more of its hundred-yard length floated to the surface. I zeroed in on the tail end. Was that the codend bobbing there? I fiddled with the focus. It was too far away to tell.

The trawl reeled slowly on board. Sandy and Ed, Jack's two crewmen, stood carefully minding the net, pulling and tugging at the trawl as it was pulled aboard to ensure it fed properly onto the huge drum just aft of the bridge superstructure. Kolya grabbed for the binoculars.

"Do you see anything?" I asked.

"Can't tell. Can't tell." He adjusted the focus.

"Let me see, Kolya," I pleaded.

"Mine," he said, slapping my hand away.

"Any fish?" I asked.

He sucked in a breath, then handed me the binoculars. The codend had just arrived at the *Hilo*'s stern. As I watched, it flipped up onto deck and twirled up and around the trawl drum—empty. The junior-sized fish had slipped through the large meshes of the trawl, leaving nothing behind to funnel into the codend.

I lifted the walkie-talkie: "*Hilo, Izumrudny.*"

There was a very long pause. "*Hilo* back."

"Do you want an estimate on that codend?"

"Fuck you," said Jack.

We spent several more days in the area off Coos Bay, Oregon, scratching up a few tons here and there, but finding in the main only immense schools of feed—young hake, mostly, with some herring and even some jellyfish thrown in.

The Pacific hake, *Merluccius productus*, also known as whiting, spends late winter and early spring spawning off the coast of central California. It then migrates back north, where it masses in great schools all the way from northern California to the Gulf of Alaska from spring to early autumn. Hake is like gold—once you find a vein or a pocket, there's a good chance there's more nearby. But it's the finding in the first place that can be difficult. Each year has its own peculiarities. The hake may school up around fifty fathoms one year—around two hundred the next. Fishermen all have their own ideas about where to look for the fish; good fishermen aren't about to let you know what those ideas are. But water temperatures play a part, of course, as well as the path of the California Current, and even the amount of sun falling on the water that particular day.

Our fleet consisted of five Russian trawlers and eight American catcher boats. The American lead representative, in consultation with the Soviet fleet director, decided to split the fleet to maximize search capabilities. The *Alexandrovsk* and *Tigil* headed to the far north, to search the shallow waters off Washington state. The *Mramorny* and *Muis Yegorova* would continue the search off the coast of Oregon.

The *Izumrudny* would head south, towards central California. And I would get to take a bath....

I'd been taking spit baths for the past few weeks, sticking my head under the ice-cold tap of my sink every few days to rinse off as well as I could. In the long run it had been a losing proposition, although I was certainly far cleaner than anyone else aboard. I'd known something was afoot one morning when I spotted Gleb, the factory director, in the hallway with a towel, wet hair, and a rosy pink brightness to his cheeks. "*S lyokhkim parom*," he'd said, happily. "With light steam?" I'd wondered. And then it hit: it was shower day.

Every ten days or so the captain turned on the ship's hot water for baths. In the rush of my first few days, I'd missed the last cycle. Today, apparently, was bath day again.

The showers reminded me of nothing so much as the decrepit facilities one sometimes finds in second-rate campgrounds—the white paint peeled by the steam, the walls showing eruptions of rust and crud from years of use. Heavy wooden pallets kept the bather off the floor, and a filthy and torn plastic curtain kept a little of the water off clothing stacked on the ledge outside. The water, desalinized ocean water, was rusty and discolored.

The men had an additional perk on bath days—the ship was equipped with a steam bath. There were only six women, counting me, in a crew of eighty-five, so the men basically had dibs on the sauna. Russians enjoy steam baths in a thoroughly masochistic fashion—they roast themselves silly, then take ice cold showers and beat themselves with branches. Occasionally, they go a bit overboard. Irena had told me about the man on the *Kontaika* last year who had taken a steam bath while plastered and had fallen asleep with the heat turned on high. They'd found him parboiled early the next morning.

But if the showers were bad, the toilets were worse. For starters, there *was* no toilet—there was only a filthy flat catch basin on the floor with a hole in it. Two rusted and encrusted plateaus rose off the bottom of the basin—places to stand slightly above the squalor in order to do one's business over the reeking hole.

The hole itself was an excellent wave indicator. Every time the waves rose over ten feet, it surged. I could always tell how high the waves were when I got up in the morning by whether or not I got goosed when I hit the toilet—a whole new way to start the day.

Completing my business was never a simple matter. In heavy seas the floor bucked wildly while I attempted to squat. All the while, obscene looking goop lapped at my drooping trouser legs. I was hesitant to grab at the walls for support—they were pitted and corroded with urine and unmentionable matter. As for toilet paper—I'd been warned to bring my own from shore. Russian toilet paper would put Ajax to shame as an abrasive, and there was hardly ever any in the head, anyway.

This morning, I'd been happy with just a little hot water to wash in. Then I'd taken a half hour out and washed my clothes by hand in the sink in my cabin. There was a laundry on board—Irena had taken my things a few times and returned them nicely folded. But the soap the Russians used had eaten a hole in one of my pairs of jeans, and my shirts had been faring poorly as well, so I'd stopped letting Irena take them. Besides, not only was the soap strong, but it also left an oily residue, so that the clothes felt dirty even when they were clean. And it stank with an odor that overpowered even the cabbage in the kitchen and the fish rotting out on deck.

But now, after an easy day of showering and lounging as we traveled south, it was time for me to begin my usual evening's translation duties.

"Individualism's all right," said Major Burns, "as long as we all do it together."

Canned laughter echoed through the officers' mess. It was eight o'clock—just after dinner, and the cabin was filled nearly to bursting with curious Russians. Two days before, the radio operator had rewired the ship's two television sets so they could receive American broadcasts. Now I generally found half the crew watching television in the officers' mess after dinner each evening, and the other half squeezed in front of the TV in the tiny radio room on the bridge. First up on the screen this evening was an old rerun of "M.A.S.H.", and as translator, I was temporarily the most popular person on the ship. Last night the men had been in a delirium of excitement over a beauty pageant; Shevchenko had pronounced the program "very nearly sex itself," although that hadn't prevented him from watching every minute of the two and a half hour program with everyone else.

"This "M.A.S.H." is disgusting," murmured Shevchenko beside me, his eyes glued once more to the screen. The episode was a set piece on homosexuality; the reaction: a hushed silence. Although homosexuality had at last been officially recognized as existing in the Soviet Union, it was still illegal: such things were not considered tasteful for a public forum.

A commercial came on, and I left off translating. The men were spell-bound, anyway. Maidenform bra commercials need no translation.

Simultaneous translation is a difficult art even for those who speak both languages like a native. A good translator stays about a sentence be-hind; the better to see the full thought, and rearrange it, if necessary, for proper grammar in the target language. You need an accurate, facile memory for that kind of thing, as well as a ready command of the vernacular. As a simultaneous translator, I was a washout, but since I was the only transla-tor within a hundred miles or so, nobody complained.

"Barbara, come with me," whispered the captain in the darkness. We clambered over seated bodies and out of the darkened cabin. A feminine hygiene commercial had popped onto the screen—nobody even noticed our leaving.

"Would you care for some tea?" he asked as we reached the hall.

"Sure," I said. I knew what that meant.

We hesitated briefly as the captain knocked on the commissar's door; the key rattled inside as he answered. The commissar was the only one on the ship who kept his cabin door locked, and he kept it locked constantly, whether he was inside or out.

"Pavel Alexandrovich, would you care to join us for some tea?"

"Of course." The commissar disappeared for a second, then reap-peared with his set of keys and carefully locked the door behind him.

The commissar and I were, apparently, expected. Inside the captain's cabin Irena was just putting out a plate of fried potatoes and some oil-drenched cold slaw. A dish of caviar stood beside a basketful of bread. Fresh tomatoes lay in a bowl, sliced and seasoned. A teakettle sat off to the side, and, in the middle of the table—a bottle of vodka.

"Pavel Alexandrovich and I have been learning some English in our spare time," said Shevchenko. "We thought maybe we would practice it a little this evening."

Oh well, I thought, as good a reason as any for a party. Things had been a little dull lately, with no fish coming on board.

"Have a seat, Irena," said the captain.

Irena sat, smiling at me. We'd gotten to know each other after a fashion; she was rather shy. I liked her. As the senior stewardess, she looked after me and my cabin, just as she looked after most of the officers, particularly the captain. Only this morning I'd caught a glimpse of her ironing the captain's shirts in his cabin. Irena's work days ran from about 5:30 in the morning, when she began setting up for breakfast, until about 11:30 at night, when she finally finished washing up after the late evening tea. All this with never a break for months on end. Of the five women in the crew, she had one of the easier jobs—the cooks had even longer hours. And if the deck crew's work near the turbulent waters of the open sea seemed perhaps more dangerous, a bounding kitchen full of steaming pots and pans and vats full of boiling oil was no safe haven, either.

"How do you say '*vint rulyevovo upravleniya*' in English?" asked the captain, setting out glasses: smaller shot glasses this time.

"Huh?" I asked.

"You know," he said with a shade of impatience. "*Vint rulyevovo upravleniya.*"

There was no way around this one. Apparently it was something I was supposed to know. "Would you spell that, please?"

Shevchenko spelled it and poured a round. We downed our shots. Irena's cheeks flushed an immediate rosy red.

"Excuse me for a minute," I said. I had a glimpse of the commissar looking befuddled, then I was out the door and down and around the hallway to my cabin.

"*Vint rulyevovo upravleniya*" I muttered to myself. "What in the hell does '*vint rulyevovo upravleniya*' mean?" I paged through my dictionaries.

Third dictionary. Third try. There it was: *vint rulyevovo upravleniya*. Controllable pitch propeller. Hell, I thought. What's a controllable pitch propeller?

Back I went to the captain's cabin. "Howdy," I said, in English.

"What does 'howdy' mean?" asked the commissar. He pronounced it "khow dee."

"It's like hello, but a lot less formal."

"Khow dee," said the commissar. "Khow dee."

"How do you say '*vint rulyevovo upravleniya*'?" asked the captain again, as if I'd never left.

"That's 'controllable pitch propeller,'" I said, nonchalantly. "Why?"

"Would you write that down please?" asked the captain.

I wrote it down. Sounded like that was it for tonight's English lesson. A far cry from Captain Alex's "Give me five" on the *Muis Yegorova*.

"What's your slang word for Coast Guard?" asked the commissar.

I thought for a minute. "I don't know. But we've got slang words for policemen. Like 'narc'—it's a derogatory term for a police officer who investigates narcotics violations."

"We don't have 'narcs' in our country," said the commissar with a straight face. "We don't have any illegal drugs."

The captain poured another round and we all drank.

"Do you believe in God, Barbara?" asked the commissar.

"I'm not really sure, to tell you the truth."

"Here," he said. "This may help you." He reached behind to a shelf and handed me some literature: an English edition of the Soviet Union's constitution and some more leaflets. The captain handed me another fistful of brochures from a lower shelf. I felt like I'd just been attacked by a group of Hare Krishnas.

"Oh well," said the captain, apropos nothing. "They gave him a year." In Russian it rhymes: *"Nu vot, dali yemu got."*

"What does that mean?" I asked. "They gave him a year?"

The captain smiled mysteriously and poured another round. "You Americans believe the strangest things," he said. "I had to laugh about that news brief." The captain was referring to the evening news we'd witnessed the night before. "They were saying sugar was bad for you. Everybody knows sugar helps build strong bones."

"If it helps build strong bones, why does everybody here have such rotten teeth?" I asked.

Shevchenko ignored me. "It's all a distortion. Like the films they showed of the Poles rioting. If that really happened, I'm sure it was because the Poles were paid to riot."

"Whoever's paying the Poles must have an awful lot of money," I said, dubiously. There'd been thousands of people in that footage.

"Do you know how many Russians were killed in Poland during World War II?" asked the commissar.

"No, but I'm sure a lot more Poles died."

"Barbara," said Irena, her first words of the evening. Her eyes were bright from the vodka. "Do you have a Sears catalog?"

"No, sorry." I wondered if the Strategic Arms Limitation Treaty had been negotiated with the aid of Sears catalogs.

The captain poured another round. We mulled our drinks quietly for a moment, then downed them.

"Why do the Americans hate Negroes?" The commissar renewed his onslaught.

"Most Americans don't hate Negroes," I said. "There are just a few who do, and they make it worse for everyone."

The commissar looked unconvinced. "What about the Jews. How many Jews do you have in America?"

"I couldn't really tell you. Are there many in the Soviet Union?"

"Actually," the commissar said in a holier-than-thou tone of voice, "we have a separate state set aside for them in Siberia. But hardly any of them live there." His voice lowered to an intense whisper: "They're clever little bastards and like to live in warm climates."

The captain gave the commissar a warning look and he fell silent.

It was time to change the subject: "Do you have a phrase in Russian for 'a hair of the dog that bit you'?" I asked, explaining the sense that a morning shot of whatever you'd drunk the night before could help stave off a hangover.

All three Russians burst into laughter. "No," said the captain, "but it's a great concept. How did you say that in English?"

"A hair of the dog that bit you," I said slowly.

"A khair uf the dogk that beet you," said the commissar. I nearly fell off my chair. The commissar's mellifluous and suave Russian had disappeared into a cacophony of butchered English.

"That's right," I said.

The captain poured another round. "I noticed," he said, "you exercise every day."

"Not every day. Sometimes I'm too lazy. And you can't really do that much on the ship." It had taken me a while to adjust to not being able to do my daily two mile jog.

"Back on shore I run a mile every day," said the commissar proudly.

"That's not too bad," I said, "considering."

The captain burst into laughter and the commissar looked embarrassed.

"Spies have to stay in good shape," said the commissar.

I nearly choked as I downed my glass. I came up gasping for air. "What?"

"You were in the army. You were a captain."

So that explained the suspicion. They knew about my military history. But where had they learned about *that*?

"Everybody makes mistakes," I said. I'd been a lousy military officer. "Captain Grim is very well liked by her subordinates," my evaluations had said. "Captain Grim speaks her mind." The kiss of death, in military parlance.

"We have ways," said the captain. He looked into his drink and smiled. "Oh well, they gave him a year."

"What does that mean?" I asked again in irritation.

"It means they gave him a year. In the camps," said Irena. The captain shot her a dirty look, but she was looking down at the tablecloth. "The saying goes: 'They gave him a year, but he got out early with only twelve months.' " She had a distant look in her eyes, as if she were remembering. "Have you ever heard of Stalin?" she asked.

"Of course." I'd noticed a picture of him on the captain's wall.

The captain looked surprised. "You have?"

"Yes." I tugged at the tablecloth and continued. "Did you know Stalin was responsible for the deaths of at least twenty million people during his purges?"

"Have you ever known anyone who lost somebody during those so-called purges?" he scoffed.

"Yes," I said. "Most of my teachers lost at least one member of their family."

"Oh," said the captain. He'd thought he had me. "Well, as you say, everybody makes mistakes."

"How can you believe that communism is a good system when such terrible things can happen under it?" I probed.

The captain glanced at Irena, looking uncomfortable. "What we have now is not communism, it is socialism. That's why we have problems. When the whole world is communist, there will be no problems."

"Maybe it's time to go get some sleep now," I said, standing. Irena stood as well.

"Goodnight." We shuffled out the door, leaving the captain and the commissar looking at the bottle of vodka.

"Barbara," said Irena, glancing back down the hallway as the captain's door snicked shut. She came close and spoke in a low whisper. "There's another favorite saying the captain has. He just doesn't say it around you."

"What's that?" I asked.

"*Slishkom mnogo znat', para ubivat'.*" The rhyme tripped gently off her tongue. "You know too much, it's time to kill you."

Chapter Four
The *Hilo*

"WE SHOULD BE GETTING a codend from one of the other catcher boats," said Shevchenko. His lower lip stuck out petulantly. "I want you to call Leonard up and tell him that our boat should be getting the next codend that the Americans catch. Not the *Muis Yegorova*. Leonard's doing a lousy job of deciding who gets what fish."

"You want me to criticize Leonard, or just offend him?" I asked. Leonard was the head representative, the "lead rep" who was in charge of all the fleet's American representatives. He made all the decisions about which Russian processor got the Americans' catch. The *Muis Yegorova*— the flagship of the Soviet fleet—had already taken fifty tons today; the *Alexandrovsk*, the *Mramorny*, and the *Tigil* weren't far behind. Having just completed the thirty hour run up the coast from California, our ship had taken exactly nothing. And it would be several hours before the *Hilo*, our assigned catcher boat, would be ready to hand us over a codend—they hadn't even set their trawl yet. Shevchenko was angry.

"Say whatever you'd like, but it's not fair. You notice Leonard makes sure *his* ship gets the most fish." Shevchenko turned and stalked off the bridge.

The captain was right—it probably wasn't fair. But he needed to complain to the Russian fleet commander. There was nothing I could do. Unfortunately, the fleet commander also had a vested interest in the flagship receiving the most fish, since he was aboard her. It was a little easier to complain ineffectually to me than to be seen as a whiner by his boss.

"*Muis Yegorova, Tigil*," came a voice over the radio. I scooted closer to the receiver, recognizing the voice. It was Dave, the *Tigil's* rep. We'd met briefly during the two-day training session we'd had at the Marine Resources offices before we'd come out to sea. Why would Dave want to call the flagship? I leaned a little closer, curious.

"*Yegorova* back," came Laura's familiar voice. "Hi, Dave."

"Hi. Is Leonard around?"

"Hang on a sec," said Laura, "he's in the can."

There was a long pause, then: "*Tigil, Muis Yegorova*, Leonard here. What can I do for you, Dave?" Leonard had a thick New York accent that seasoned even his Russian.

"Let's go to channel thirty-three," said Dave.

"Meet you there," said Leonard.

The fishermen, we'd been told, could not receive channel thirty-three, so the reps used the channel to speak without the fishermen listening in. This conversation sounded as if it might be interesting. I reached forward and switched the radio dial to thirty-three. There were a few seconds of static, then:

"What's the scoop, Dave?" Leonard's voice.

"We're having a problem. Our catcher boats have been double bagging on us."

Double bagging meant fastening two codends together, so that you had a fifty foot instead of a twenty-five foot long bag. Fishermen could catch double the amount of fish, but there was a problem: the bag could weigh upwards of fifty tons. It was often very difficult, if not impossible, to get such a heavy codend aboard the Soviet vessel. Then too, the fish became compacted in the net by its own weight, so that much of it was crushed and unsuitable for processing.

"This is the third time they've done it," Dave continued, "and the captain's very upset. The fish has been in really bad shape. We've processed it, but we're afraid it might not pass the food grade inspection later on. And we've already broken two winches getting the bags on board. I've asked them to stop, but you know how that goes."

"Yeah," said Leonard. "Actually, we've been having the same problem with our catchers. I think it's about time to put a stop to this. Just because the *Jackdaw* has been getting away with it, everybody wants to try it, even though the product quality is lousy. Anything to make a few extra bucks."

"You'll talk to *Jackdaw* then?" Dave sounded relieved.

"Sure. Don't worry about it. *Yegorova* out."

"*Tigil* out."

I switched back to eight, the fleet channel.

"*Jackdaw, Muis Yegorova*." Leonard's voice. He paused. There was no reply. "*Jackdaw, Yegorova*."

"*Jackdaw* back." The American's voice sounded reluctant.

"Percy, good buddy. Hear you've been double bagging."

"Just workin'," said Percy. "Just trying to catch fish while they're here." He was right—the hake that swarmed beneath us now hadn't been here when we'd searched the area last week, and could be gone again tomorrow.

"You're ruining the fish," said Leonard, mildly. "No more double bagging."

"Who cares what the fish looks like?" said Percy. "It's all going to Africa or Asia or something like that anyway. *They* don't care."

Most of the company's product ended up being sold to third world countries. The American market for hake was slim, although sales were better when it was labeled "Pacific Whiting, Imported." Even the Russians, far better fish eaters than Americans, weren't too keen on keeping the company product for use in their country, both because hake wasn't an especially tasty fish and because quality control on the joint venture was questionable at best.

"You may not care what the fish looks like, but the Russians do. If too high a percentage of their product is bad, the whole crew gets fined."

"My heart bleeds," said Percy.

"So will your pocket book if you don't quit double bagging. And any of you other guys listening here—no more double bagging. It's unacceptable," Leonard said, his voice suddenly sharp. "*Muis Yegorova* out."

I sat for a moment, comfortable on my wooden perch by the radio. I glanced once more out the window. In the far distance I could see another Soviet trawler—the *Yegorova*?—coming slowly around on a smaller American boat. A few hundred yards to starboard was the *Hilo*, the men hard at work on deck as they prepared to set the trawl. I'd be glad to see them get it in the water. It might improve Shevchenko's temper.

It was taking the *Hilo*'s crew a lot longer than usual to get their trawl into the water. I sauntered over to the bank of forward windows. The *Hilo*'s two deck crew workers, Sandy and Ed, were hunkered over a piece of webbing. I reached for the binoculars resting in a case near the sill. What were they working on?

Sandy appeared through the lenses. He was threading a shuttle in fluid, practiced motions through the white cotton webbing of a codend. I adjusted the focus, straining to see. Sandy looked up and grinned at Ed, then dropped the net, finished. Both men picked up the heavy webbing and began dragging it toward the stern. The codend looked inordinately large and unwieldy.

The *Hilo* was double bagging. I slammed the binoculars back in their place and was at the radio. If the captain of the *Tigil* had been very upset about the quality of double-bagged fish, there was no telling what Shevchenko would do. Hadn't Jack heard Leonard on the radio? Everyone was always supposed to be tuned in to the fleet channel.

"*Hilo, Izumrudny* here." I hesitated, waiting.

"*Hilo, Izumrudny.*" I waited again, longer this time.

"*Hilo, Izumrudny.*" No answer. This was the first time Jack had not answered.

The bastard. Jack had overheard Leonard's conversation, and he wasn't about to be told not to double bag when he was already setting up to do it.

"What's up, Barbara?" It was Kolya, fresh on watch.

"I think the *Hilo* is double bagging. He won't answer."

"That's not good," said Kolya, pulling on an ear. "The captain will be very upset."

"He's already upset," I said.

"I know," said Kolya. We both stared glumly out towards the *Hilo*. Ed and Sandy were taking their positions by the gantry.

I thumbed the mike uselessly: "*Hilo, Izumrudny.*"

The trawl doors splashed off the stern of the *Hilo*.

"Well, Barb, tell the Skipper there he'd better be ready for a big one. We've got a double bag this time," said Jack. I could hear the sly grin in his voice.

"Why didn't you answer?" I asked. "I've been calling you for the last hour." It was useless to even ask, but I couldn't help it.

"I've been having a little trouble with my radio this morning. Why?"

"Leonard just told the *Jackdaw* they're not supposed to double bag anymore. Nobody's supposed to double bag anymore."

"Gee—sorry I didn't get the message. I'm afraid we'll have to pass this one to you now, though. You guys ready?" I stared at the radio, grinding my teeth.

"*Izumrudny, Hilo.* You there, Barb?"

I didn't answer. Kolya turned to me, eyebrows raised. "The *Hilo*'s ready," I said. "Better tell the captain it's a double bag."

"I'm not telling the captain," said Kolya. "That's your job."

"*Izumrudny, Hilo,*" said Jack.

"*Izumrudny* back." The huge codend trailed in the water behind us, slowly being winched aboard.

"We've got a problem," Jack said. "One of my men, Sandy, is hurt. A pelican hook snapped back and hit him in the face. He may have a concussion. I'm not sure. He doesn't look so good."

A pelican hook is the heavy-duty, long-handled hook and bar affair that holds the twenty or, in this case, forty or fifty ton codend to the American boat. It withstands enormous pressures and, when released, snaps back with tremendous force. Being slammed in the face by the handle would not be pleasant. In fact, it could be deadly.

"Do you want to call the Coast Guard?" I asked. If worst came to worst Sandy could always be evacuated by air.

"No. I can't afford to lose him right now. We've got work to do. But maybe you could have your doctor take a look at him."

Each Soviet trawler had a doctor aboard. That is, they were called doctors. Actually they were more like medics, with perhaps a few months of medical training. I'd been introduced to the *Izumrudny*'s doctor and had not been overly impressed. But then, it's hard to get the measure of a man when he's drunk.

"Just a minute. I'll talk to the captain." I turned to Shevchenko, standing beside me by the bank of aft windows. "One of Jack's men has been hurt. Maybe a concussion. Jack would like to know if our doctor would take a look at him."

"You shouldn't have let him set with a double bag," said Shevchenko again.

"Up yours," I said earnestly in English.

"What?" said the captain suspiciously. He glanced at me, then turned his attention back to the controls. "Maybe Jack should call the Coast Guard."

"He doesn't want to do that yet. Can we send the doctor over to take a look at him?"

"The doctor. Oh. Him. Yes." Shevchenko didn't sound very enthusiastic. He turned and motioned towards Kolya. "Get Bondarenko. One of the Americans has been hurt—maybe a concussion. Tell Bondarenko to get ready and be at the lifeboat." Shevchenko turned back to me. "We'll send the doctor over as soon as we get the codend on board."

"Okay," I said.

Shevchenko concentrated on the controls before him. "This is strange." His hands played over the winch controls. "The bag isn't flying double, and it isn't flying single." His head tilted to the side, as if cocking an ear somehow helped him feel the drag on the ship and the strain in the cables.

"*Yob tvoyu mat'*," he said, with sudden savage intensity. Much Slavic swearing pertains to things you wouldn't want done to your mother. This was no exception. "*Yob tvoyu mat'*. This is a sinker."

A sinker was a codend with no natural buoyancy. Rather than ride the waves just beneath the surface of the water, sinkers fell like stones deep into the water as soon as the Americans released them. The strain on the Soviets' winches and cables was far greater than usual—the bags had to be pulled aboard against the force of gravity as well as the drag of the water. Usually a codend was a sinker because the fish in it had been badly crushed, so that the air leaked out of their air bladders. Occasionally codends were sinkers because something heavy had been picked up in the net. Either way, it was not good news. Below me on deck I could hear the winches whining with strain.

"*Yob tvoyu mat'*," repeated Shevchenko. The whine increased. He slammed the controls to a stop and grabbed the mike in front of him: "Danielich, do you see the codend?" Danielich, I'd been told, was the senior trawlmaster—the head of the deck crew.

We watched as Danielich craned his head over the stern side of the transom: "Yes. It's just reached us."

"Increase speed," said Shevchenko to the helmsman. "Gently. Gently." He was fearful of the codend wrapping around the propellers. Greater speed would push the codend back away from the ship.

Shevchenko once again applied power to the winches, trying to ease the codend up and onto the stern ramp. It was a good thing the weather was calm today—I wasn't sure the winches could take the additional torque of any wave action.

The cable stopped as the whine of the winches turned to a screech.

"Danielich," said Shevchenko. "Quickly." Danielich turned and motioned, and in a flash, a man scrambled over the edge and down to the codend. At least, I assumed he was down on the codend—it was still too low on the stern ramp to be visible from the bridge. I could see the long cables that led to the gantry above, quivering and shaking as they were hooked into the reinforcing straps on the codend. The man reappeared and Danielich nodded back up at us.

Slowly, almost tenderly, the captain began easing the heavy codend on board. Even with four winches, two overhead and two forward, the machinery screamed with strain. "Goddamn that American," said Shevchenko. "Goddamn this goddamned codend."

The front of the codend crept up and over the edge of the stern ramp. Then it stopped dead as the winches jammed.

"*Yob tvoyu mat*" Shevchenko repeated monotonously. He reached for the mike. "Danielich. Wet the deck."

Danielich nodded and two men grabbed a hose as big around as a football. Water streamed out of it as a third man tugged at a large stop-cock. The men aimed the hose toward the deck, slicking down the raw, dry wood in front of the codend.

"Enough," said Shevchenko. The men turned off the hose.

Shevchenko once again eased power into the winches. They hummed, then whined, then screamed. The codend didn't budge. He eased back on the winches. "Danielich. Have them cut the side of the codend. Carefully—we don't want to lose too much."

The last desperate measure. If he lightened the load by dumping some of the fish, he should be able to get the codend aboard. We watched as the man slipped back down the stern ramp and disappeared again.

"Goddamned American," said Shevchenko in a monotonous undertone. "Goddamned codend." We waited impatiently.

"What's going on down there?" Shevchenko asked.

"He can't get the fish out," came Danielich's voice. "It's packed in too firmly. We'd need a jackhammer."

"*Yob tvoyu mat*'," said the captain once again. "Get him back out of there." Danielich turned and spoke. The man crawled back up the stern ramp.

All eyes turned to the captain as he stood, his slight yet masterful figure tensed in frustration. He stared at the front of the codend, as if he could force it aboard by sheer strength of will. His shoulders twitched as he gathered himself, reaching forward once again to the control levers.

"*Yob tvoyu mat*" he said again, and hit the levers.

The winches screamed, the cables sprung to a whistling tautness, and with a terrible groan, the codend jerked into motion. A ragged cheer went up from the crew. "*Molodets*," exclaimed Kolya. Good show.

The captain stood tense, the tendons in his neck still taut, then relaxed suddenly, leaning back with his hands loose on the controls. "It wasn't so hard." He looked smug.

Then, one of the overhead hawsers gave way, cracking like a cannon overhead as the whole ship shook. Danielich and the others threw themselves onto the soaking deck—anything to avoid the whip-like cable as it thrashed with mad relief from its strain.

On the bridge, we stood in silence while the broken cable quieted to dangle at last from the gantry.

"Goddamned codend," said Shevchenko, "Goddamned American."

The codend was fully on board now. The front end bulged with fish—all so badly crushed I couldn't even make out an individual body. The second codend had been attached incorrectly, somehow, so that it had twisted in the water and no fish had funneled into it at all.

The deck crew picked themselves up, covered with a muddy slime. Indeed, everything was being covered with a muddy slime as great gouts of the stuff spewed from the front part of the codend.

"Goddamned codend," Shevchenko intoned once again. We made our way off the bridge and down to the deck, stepping carefully to avoid the foul smelling sludge. One of the crew workers was already hosing down the side of the codend. Another began pulling at the rope "zipper" that held what was actually a large slit in the webbing together. Normally, once that zipper was pulled, the fish flowed out of the codend in the stream of water from the hose.

The rope of the zipper came free, and nothing moved.

The crewman took a knife and began cutting into the webbing, extending the opening around the zipper. The net would be repaired later—the only concern now was getting the fish out.

The full force of the heavy hose smashed again onto the exposed layer of fish.

Still nothing moved.

The man with the knife clambered to the top of the codend and began jumping on the fish. A clump fell out—an oozing, black mass—nothing like the iridescent and still-flipping hake I had seen in previous tows.

The captain picked up a filthy clump to examine it, then threw it down in disgust. "This is hamburger. Mincemeat. It's not fish. There's no way to process something like this. I don't even want to try—I don't want this sludge all over our conveyers. Danielich!"

Danielich hurried over from the entrance to the bunkers.

"This is shit. I want it back overboard. Now." My heart sank. It was bad enough dealing with Shevchenko. Now I'd have to deal with Jack as well. He wouldn't be happy to hear we were going to throw his fish overboard.

"It'll take a while. We'll have to saw the codend in two and dump it by halves."

"Do whatever it takes." He turned to me, his face flushed with anger. "Goddamned American."

"Is the lifeboat ready yet?" I asked, as innocently as I dared. "We need to see about that crewman."

We trooped back up the stairs to the lifeboat. The chief mate stood by with several men.

"Where's the doctor?" asked Shevchenko.

"He's coming. He can't find his keys."

"Can't find his keys?" roared the captain. "He's had a half an hour."

The chief mate looked meek. "He's trying to find them right now."

"Well, go help him then, by God," the captain thundered. The chief mate disappeared down a companionway.

The captain turned to me. "Goddamned doctors." He stalked off.

I headed for the radio.

"You're fuckin' *what?*" screeched Jack. His voice had a hysterical edge to it, like a mother whose baby is about to be hit by a train.

"It has to go overboard, Jack. The second codend didn't fill—it just flipped a bunch of silt into the first one. And the first codend was so full all the fish were crushed. There's no way you can process it. You can't even get it clean."

"Don't joke with me," said Jack, his voice filled with menace.

"I wish I were. I'm sorry. There's nothing I can do."

"You little jerk. This is all your fault. If you had half a brain in that pea-sized head of yours you'd have talked the captain into keeping it."

This was getting to be a bit much. I didn't have to take it. I could feel my blood pressure shift into high gear as I flipped back to the fleet channel: "*Muis Yegorova, Izumrudny.*"

"*Yegorova* back. Hi, Barb." It was Laura.

"Laura, I'd like to speak with Leonard," I said in Russian.

"I think he's taking a shower right now."

Great. "I don't care if he's naked. I need to talk to him."

"Oooh," said Laura. "I'll be right back."

I waited impatiently as the minutes went by.

"*Izumrudny, Muis Yegorova.* Hi, Barb." It was Leonard.

"*Poshli na tritsat' tri*," I said. Let's go to channel thirty-three. I wanted to let it all hang out in English, and I didn't want Jack overhearing.

"*Poshol*," said Leonard. I reached forward and changed the channel.

"What's up?" said Leonard, in English.

"To tell you the truth, I'm getting a little tired of working with Jack. He just double-bagged his codend, after you'd told everyone not to. The fish came up crushed and filthy, and now he's angry because my captain wants to throw it overboard. To tell you the truth, Jack's been an asshole to work with since day one."

"Oh," said Leonard.

"I don't like being cussed out, either. Especially when I don't deserve it. I've been getting it from both sides here."

"Oh," said Leonard again. I could see he was going to be a big help.

"I've got to go," I said. "Apparently one of Jack's crewmen was injured. Jack cusses us out even when we're sending our doctor over to take a look at his man," I said indignantly. "The guy's a real prick."

"Well," said Leonard. "Maybe we'll see about switching the *Hilo* off with another boat. You could work with someone else for a while."

"Fine," I said. "*Izumrudny* out."

The chief mate was back at the lifeboat. The doctor was nowhere to be seen.

"Where's the doctor?" I asked, still angry.

"He's coming," said the chief mate. "He still can't find his keys."

I headed for the infirmary. The doctor stood alone in the middle of the wide, white cabin. He looked up at me and grinned apologetically.

"I know they're around here somewhere." He tugged at a drawer. It was locked. "Well, I guess they can't be in there."

I shot him a look of raw hatred.

He stood scratching his head. "Ah," he said, turning to notice my stare. His face became intent. "I think I may know where they are." He opened a cabinet and began pawing through its contents. "Aha," he said, pulling a medicine bottle out triumphantly. He unscrewed the top and fished around in the container, pulling a set of keys from the yellowish fluid inside. He rinsed them quickly in the sink. "Just give me another minute or two. I'll be right out."

I headed back for the lifeboat. Now the chief mate was gone. The remaining two men stood relaxed by the lifeboat. The one nearest me winked. "Hi. You must be Barbara. I'm Gregori."

"And I'm Yuri," said the second. We shook hands.

"What do you do?" I asked. I tried to relax a little.

"Not very much," said Gregori. He smiled—a broad, gentle smile.

"We're the deck crew," said Yuri. "Part of it, anyway. We've seen you on the bridge."

I'd seen them too, now that I thought about it—they were on the deck crew's morning shift.

"Are you finally ready, Barbara?" It was the chief mate. He had the doctor by the scruff of the neck and was quick marching him to the boat. The doctor clutched a large black bag, looking confused.

"Let's go," I said, my ill humor instantly back in place. We all piled into the lifeboat, and within a few minutes were at the *Hilo*, floating two hundred yards off the *Izumrudny's* bow.

"It's about time you got here," said Jack in greeting. He and Ed leaned over and hauled me from the lifeboat onto the *Hilo*. Beside me, the doctor heaved his bag onto the *Hilo*'s deck. There was a suspicious sound of breakage as he crawled clumsily after it. "Where's the patient?" he asked, standing and wiping his hands on his pants. The chief mate remained in the boat with the two crewmen. Gregori peered at the American boat, fascinated.

"This is Doctor Bondarenko," I said, by way of introduction. "He'd like to know where Sandy is."

"This way," said Jack. He led us through a spacious galley and into a dark cabin. Sandy lay quietly on a bunk in the far corner. He held a bloody cloth to the side of his face.

"Can he speak?" asked the doctor.

"Can you say anything?" I asked.

"Yeah," said Sandy. I could barely make out the word.

"Let's see what we have here," said the doctor, in a bedside manner known the world over.

"Would you take off the cloth?" I said in English.

Sandy pulled the cloth away from his face and I winced. An ugly, bloody gash ran from the right side of his mouth all the way up to his hairline, and the whole side of his face was swollen in a deep, mean-looking purple. He looked like he'd been hit by a train.

The doctor bent down and jabbed at Sandy's jaw. "Does this hurt?" he asked. I translated.

"You besh your fuckin' ass it hurts," said Sandy.

"Yes," I said in Russian.

Bondarenko stood back, his diagnosis complete. "He needs to come back to the ship with us. That cut needs to be sewn up. Other than that he looks okay."

"Aren't you going to check him for a concussion?" I prodded.

"Ah, concussion. Yes." Bondarenko leaned back down and stared into Sandy's eyes. Sandy stared back, looking dazed.

"No. There's no sign of concussion. But we'd better get him sewn up." The cut had started bleeding again after Bondarenko jabbed it. Blood dribbled down Sandy's cheek and onto the pillow.

I turned to Jack. "The doctor says we should take him back over to our ship. He's got the equipment to sew him up over there."

"All right," said Jack sullenly. "I hope this doesn't take too long." Sandy groped his way to his feet—I offered my shoulder for support as we made our way slowly out to the back deck. The chief mate sat stolidly in the lifeboat, a bored look on his face. Gregori still busily ogled the deck.

"We have to take Sandy back over to the ship," I said. "The doctor can sew him up there." The chief mate nodded.

"I'm coming along," said Jack.

We struggled to get Sandy into the lifeboat. Even in calm seas, there was quite a bit of motion between the two boats; for Sandy, it was very rough going. At last we took our seats, Sandy in the middle, with Jack and I propping him up on either side.

"You okay?" I asked, as the lifeboat's motor thrummed to life. Sandy's skin was pale and clammy. He looked ready to pass out.

"I'll make it," he said huskily. "Don' worry abou' me."

Jack's lips were pursed together in a sulky frown. I looked past him to the *Izumrudny*. She'd drifted to lie a hundred yards north of us. I could see the gantry winches working as Jack's codend was wrestled around on the deck.

"I don't appreciate being called an asshole," said Jack, suddenly. I glanced back over at him in surprise.

"What do you mean asshole?" I asked. How would Jack know I'd called him that?

"And I especially don't like being called a prick by some mealy mouthed little college kid." He leaned around Sandy as he spoke. His face looked evil.

Sandy moaned.

"You get channel thirty-three," I said stupidly.

Jack's mouth worked as he wrestled with his conscience. The need to boast won out. "You bet I get channel thirty-three. I keep one of my radios tuned there all the time. Costs a little more for the setup, but what you find out makes it worth it." His voice turned into a snarl. "Let me tell you something, you little commie loving..."

Sandy moaned again between us, then slumped. We both reached for his sagging body.

"...company *rep*. Nobody just up and throws my fish overboard. Nobody. You tell your captain that."

We were swinging around the *Izumrudny* now, bouncing in the chop past her stern. "If you want to tell the captain that, you can tell him yourself." I pointed to the *Izumrudny*'s stern ramp, not fifty feet from us. We had an excellent view of the steep, rusty steel slide. Above, on the very edge of the back deck, Jack's codend rose into the air. Clumps of fish began pouring out of the bag and down the slick ramp, tumbling haphazardly into the ocean.

Jack's eyes moved from me to the fish, his face turning an apoplectic red. Faster the fish tumbled, and still faster, until the whole filthy mass had streamed in stinking abandon into the sea.

The doctor leaned forward in his seat facing us. "Is he all right?" he asked, nodding toward Jack.

"He's terribly worried about his crewman," I said dryly in Russian. I leaned around Sandy's body to smile at Jack.

Twenty-five stitches later, the doctor said Sandy would be as good as new, given a few days of recuperation. Jack took the doctor at his word and kept Sandy working for another two weeks, until the *Hilo* had to go back into port.

I never saw Sandy again. He saw a doctor in Coos Bay and was hospitalized for fifteen weeks with a broken jaw, crushed cheek and chin bones, and neurological damage resulting from a concussion.

Chapter Five
At the Threshold

"LEONARD ON *Muis Yegorova* calls you," said the fourth mate in his valiant English. He had a horrifyingly serious look on his face. "No take codend now. No! Take away! No take codend—too much fish!"

"What's the problem? Is the factory down for repairs?" I rubbed my eyes and blinked. It was fast approaching noon, but the bridge crew had awakened me three times last night between midnight and four—twice when the new watches came on shift to find out what the situation was ("How should I know? I'm sleeping."), and once when the *Jackdaw* had called to find out what the factory weights for their fish had turned out to be. And I had gone to bed late anyway—I'd spent the evening celebrating International Labor Day with the deck crew. May Day is a great Soviet holiday (no one could believe Americans didn't celebrate this "International" day). I was tired now, and I had a blockbuster headache.

The chief mate emerged from the chart room. "The factory isn't down. What makes you think there's a problem?"

"Sasha says we've got too much fish."

The chief mate shot an amused look at Sasha, who turned away, embarrassed. "The only problem with comrade fourth mate here is that he's got factory shift tonight, and at the rate we're getting fish on board, he's going to have to pull it."

I reached for the radio. "*Muis Yegorova, Izumrudny.*"

"*Izumrudny, Yegorova.* Hi, Barb."

"Hi, Leonard. What's up?"

"Two things. First off, I need you to pick up a codend from the *Golden Hope*—the *Mramorny* is having some engine problems and can't take the tow."

I grinned at Sasha.

"Secondly, I guess your captain's told you your observer should be there any minute. Go ahead and take him aboard before you get the *Golden Hope*'s codend."

"Our observer's coming *now?*" I said. The captain had said nothing about it.

"Yes—he came out with the *Hilo*. Shevchenko's known he's been coming ever since they left Coos Bay two days ago."

Oh. Why hadn't Shevchenko told me? "That's great!" I said. "Roger, wilco, and all that crap." Someone to speak English with on board the *Izumrudny!*

"Have fun," said Leonard, "*Yegorova* out."

"Hey, the National Marine Fisheries observer is coming!" I exclaimed to the bridge crew.

"We know," said the chief mate. He didn't look happy.

I thumbed the mike again. "*Hilo, Izumrudny.*" The *Hilo*, I knew, was supposed to have a replacement skipper, Charlie Brendo, while Jack took a vacation. Charlie, thank God, was reputed to be a nice guy who was easy to work with.

"*Hilo* back. You must be Barb."

"Yes. You must be Charlie."

"That's right. I've heard a lot about you."

I'll bet he had. "Seems you've got an observer for us aboard. Where are you?"

"That's a rog, kiddo. If you'll look behind you, you'll see us coming up your stern ramp."

I leaned around the corner of the radio room to take a peek at the stern. The *Hilo* was about two hundred yards astern, gaining fast.

"Here comes the *Hilo* now," I said to the chief mate.

"Oh boy," he said, unenthusiastically.

"And we have to pick up a tow from the *Golden Hope* right after we get the observer."

"Great," said Sasha. He looked very unhappy.

National Marine Fisheries Service observers were assigned to nearly every trawler in the Joint Venture. They were expected to monitor the fish coming aboard for a variety of scientific purposes. They also ensured that the Russians stayed within their allotted quotas and did not keep unlicensed fish, such as halibut or salmon. If communism had done nothing else for the Russians, it taught them to fear bureaucracy. Unlike the Koreans, who had in the past been inclined toward using kidnapping, rape, and death threats to keep their observers in line, most of the Soviet captains would do almost anything to ensure their observers never found a problem. Still, the observers were understandably nervous. The Fisheries Service even had a code word, which, when used innocuously by an observer in one of their weekly transmissions, would summon the Coast Guard. These code words were heavily guarded secrets that changed from year to year. Reps, being employees of the Soviets, were not privy to the code words, but Laura, who seemed to have ways of finding out just about anything, had already confided that this year's secret code word was "thumb." I wondered how one could use the word thumb in a transmission about fish and have it be innocuous.

Rumor had it that all National Marine Fisheries observers were weird. As Laura had put it: "What person in their right mind would want to spend two months throwing up and cutting off fish noses in this filthy dump when they don't even speak the language?" As a cultural experience, it rated on par with cleaning radiation-contaminated nuclear waste.

I was getting much more comfortable with the Russian language, but still, my month of linguistic solitude had made the thought of another English speaker, whatever their vocational predilection, entrancing. "Come on," I said to the chief mate, and headed out the door.

"Call the captain," said the chief mate to Sasha. He headed after me.

It was a mild, breezy afternoon, with a faint haze in the sky that made it hard to pick out the line of the horizon. I squinted down toward the *Hilo* as it approached. A tall, lanky man stood alone on the back deck, a pile of bags beside him.

"That must be him," I said, pointing.

"Yes," said Shevchenko, sliding up beside me. "Unfortunately."

Ropes went down, and in seconds the *Hilo* was fast at our side. A heavyset man emerged from the wheel house as we let the rope ladder down. "Yo, Barb. I'm Charlie," he shouted. He pointed to the lanky man: "This is Ben, your observer."

"Pleased to meet you," I yelled. I pointed to Shevchenko: "This is the captain." The three nodded at each other as the crew let more ropes down. Charlie and the observer tied them to the bags and they were hoisted aboard. Next, the "tumblers belt" went down. Charlie grabbed it and fastened it about Ben's waist. Ben looked up and smiled: "Ready or not, here I come." He clambered up on the *Hilo*'s gunwales and made a flying leap toward the rope ladder.

He missed. Suddenly the two men beside me hauled frantically at their ropes, trying to keep Ben from going into the water. Ben clawed at the air; flipped neatly upside-down. He made a swipe for the rope ladder as Shevchenko and I grabbed at the ropes, trying to help haul my fellow American upward.

Ben's feet appeared over the railing. The man nearest me grabbed for a boot. It came off in his hands and fell down into the water.

"*Yob tvoyu mat'*," said Shevchenko. We manhandled the feet around, pulling Ben awkwardly over the railing and plopping him down on the planking.

Ben sat for a moment, feet splayed out on the deck before him as he glanced up, panting. "Pleased to meet you."

"Welcome aboard," said Shevchenko. "An entrance like that calls for some tea, does it not?" he inquired.

"The captain wants to know if you'd like a drink," I translated.

"Uh," said Ben, looking uncertainly up at us. "Yes, I think I would. Maybe we could get my gear put away first."

Ben's cabin was on the aft side of the political commissar's. It faced the back deck, just under the outlet chimneys of the fish-meal furnace. It stank.

"Home sweet home," I said, breathing through my mouth. Ben appeared unfazed, or perhaps overwhelmed.

"Been taking many salmon lately?" he asked.

"No," I lied. Actually we'd been taking fifty or sixty silvers and chinooks in each haul down in California, beautiful three-foot fish. Dead, each of them: killed by the net. I had watched sadly, my mouth watering, as crewmen tossed them overboard to rot in the water. If the Coast Guard caught anyone purposely keeping even one, they would heavily fine the captain and crew and rescind their license. Of course, if anyone had known how many salmon we were catching accidentally, we would have lost our license anyway—we were only allowed so much "incidental" catch, and if we exceeded the low limits set on most species except hake we would lose our fishing rights altogether.

Now the observer would be strictly monitoring our daily catch. No wonder the crew wasn't too happy to have him aboard.

"This your first time out?" I asked.

"Yes," he said, shoving some large blue baskets toward a corner. He set his suitcase with a thud on his bunk. "How long have you been here?"

"Two months." I watched as Ben opened a suitcase and withdrew a lumpy black plastic bag.

"Present for the captain," he said, tapping the bag and glancing at me. His face held a mixture of excitement and embarrassment.

"We'd better go," I said shyly. Now that I was finally around another American, I didn't know what to say.

The captain, the commissar, and an innocuous single bottle of vodka waited in the captain's cabin.

"Welcome to the *Izumrudny*," said Shevchenko, rising to extend a hand. "Glad to have you on board."

"Glad to be here," said Ben, as I translated. Ben had the usual "translatee's" problem—should he look at me, since he was speaking to me, or should he look at the captain, for whom the speech was intended? He compromised, eyes flickering nervously between us. "Does anyone here besides you speak English?" His glance settled momentarily on me.

I shook my head. "A few phrases here and there, nothing much, though."

"Would you like," said the commissar in his fractured English, "a khair uf the dogk that beet me?"

"What?" asked Ben. His eyes widened.

"Um, I've been teaching them a few words of English."

"I see," said Ben.

There was a knock on the door and Danielich stepped inside.

As senior trawlmaster, Danielich would work with Ben on deck on a daily basis. Apparently the captain wanted to break the ice between the two.

"Hello," Danielich said gruffly, doffing his cap. He spoke Russian the way a hillbilly speaks English—I could barely understand him. He was no more than about five foot seven, but burly, with muscles like an aging weight lifter's and hands the size of hams. With his weather-beaten features and grizzled hair I'd taken him for nearing sixty. Irena had told me he was forty-two.

"Have a seat," said the captain, twisting the lid off the bottle of vodka. Ben and I shifted over to make room. Danielich sat, looking uncomfortably out of place, like a child called to the principal's office. The commissar set out shot glasses while the captain poured.

"Here's to faithful observance of all regulatory requirements," said Shevchenko, raising his glass.

"Hear hear," said Ben. We all raised our glasses. The captain, the commissar, Danielich, and I downed our shots with practiced motions. Danielich gave a loud and satisfied belch and wiped his mouth with his sleeve.

Ben looked doubtful. "You just drink this stuff straight?" he asked.

"When in Rome," I said. "It's not bad cold." The Russians liked to keep their vodka at freezer temperatures—it did take the edge off.

"Okay," he said, his voice still unsure. He tilted the glass back and came up choking. "Strong," he wheezed. Danielich, beside him, began pounding him heartily on the back. Shevchenko had the bottle out and was already pouring another round. We hesitated while Ben recovered his breath.

"To the National Marine Fisheries Service," said Shevchenko.

We drained our glasses once again. Ben looked as if he'd been kicked twice by a mule.

"Have you been working as an observer for a long time?" asked the captain.

"I'm majoring in fisheries at the University of Washington," said Ben, "but this is the first time I've ever been to sea."

Shevchenko's eyes wrinkled into a smile. I knew Shevchenko well enough to know what that smile meant. Fresh meat. He poured another round.

"I've brought a present for you," said Ben, suddenly lifting the black bag. He looked guiltily at me as I translated. "This is what the fishermen said I should bring," he added in a low voice.

"I hope it's booze," I said. "Or a Sears catalog."

"Thank you," said the captain. He took the bag and opened it, pulling out a stack of magazines and a number of small cans. He stared at the cover of the top magazine, his gaze growing chilly. "This is not acceptable," he said.

Danielich leaned over, riveted. I glanced at the magazine. A naked woman sat smiling astride a bright orange motorcycle.

"This is against the basic tenets of Soviet socialist behavior," said the commissar. "I'm afraid I'll have to confiscate this." He grabbed the stack of magazines and stuffed them back into the bag, placing them under his chair.

"What was all that about?" asked Ben.

"I think the fishermen gave you a bum steer," I said. "Things on this boat are pretty strict. Pornography is illegal."

"Oh, I'm terribly sorry," said Ben, his face turning red. "It's not something I ordinarily, uh, you know, read. But Charlie said it would be hot stuff over here."

"What's this?" asked the commissar, picking up a tin.

"Chewing tobacco," said Ben. I paused. "It's tobacco which you chew," I said finally in Russian.

The captain looked faintly nauseated. "Really?" he inquired.

"What are you supposed to do with it?" asked Danielich.

"You put it in your mouth and chew it," I said, "but you're not supposed to swallow it."

The commissar looked skeptical. Danielich reached for a tin and opened it, sniffing suspiciously. "Looks like dirt," he said. All three Russians looked up to stare at Ben, who wilted visibly.

"Does the phrase 'lead balloon' ring any bells with you?" I asked. Apparently Ben had yet to learn that most fishermen hate observers. Maybe the *Hilo*'s replacement captain wasn't really as nice as everybody'd been saying. In fact, I could probably get to like the guy.

"Here's to good intentions," I said in Russian, raising my glass. "Remember, Ben is unschooled as to the basic tenets of Soviet socialist mankind."

The captain and Danielich raised their glasses. We downed our drinks.

"Barbara, please come to bridge." It was Sasha again, on the ship's intercom.

"It must be the *Golden Hope*," I said. "We were supposed to pick up a codend from her." I got up and headed for the door. "I'm sure you can make do without me."

Shevchenko grinned wolfishly.

"Hey, Sunshine, how goes the war?" asked Gary, the even-tempered skipper of the *Golden Hope*.

"Just fine, dreamboat," I said. I eyed the deck before me. The chief mate was nowhere to be seen, and the deck crew was busy playing football with a buoy, kicking it with wicked abandon and pelting one another with fish. Sasha, the fourth mate, nervously guided the *Izumrudny* to come up on the *Golden Hope*'s starboard side. He had somehow, in the half hour since I'd seen him last, shaved his head: he was now as bald as an egg.

Gary's voice crackled over the radio once again: "You're making my day, picking up this codend."

"No problem. We can always squeeze a little room for *your* fish on decks." Gary was that oxymoronic rarity: a capable fisherman who was also an amiable family man. I enjoyed working with him.

"Let's go to ten," Gary suggested.

"Meet you there," I said, reaching forward to change the channel. Most radio contact during the actual fish transfers did not take place on the fleet channel. There was too much of a possibility that either one speaker or another would be "walked over"—have someone else key in their mike and talk while they were talking. The Soviets were especially guilty of this—to them, the English conversation usually found on the fleet channel was just so much gibberish.

"You there, Sunshine?"

"Right here," I said. An overpowering scent of alcohol suddenly enveloped me. I glanced beside me as the chief mate took his position at the winch controls. Apparently he'd been having a little party of his own. We exchanged knowing grins.

The chief mate grabbed the mike to the deck intercom: "All right, you guys, knock it off and get the fish out of the way. We've got a cable to go out."

The men kicked the buoy-*cum*-football into a corner. Two of them began pushing fish out of the way, while a third, Gregori, started pulling the heavy cable out toward the stern ramp. With the flotation and marker buoys already attached, it was ready to go. The chief mate powered the winches as Gregori fed the cable off the stern ramp.

"Cable gone," I said, in that familiar non-speech of rep rap.

"Gotcha." The *Golden Hope* eased in behind us.

"*Yoda*, This is the *Tigil*," came Dave's voice suddenly over the radio. Apparently the *Tigil*'s rep and his catcher boat, the *Yoda*, had switched to channel ten as well.

"*Yoda* back," came a mournful voice.

"It looks like that last tow was about two and a half tons," said Dave. A pittance, compared to what most of the fleet caught.

"Golly." There was a long pause. "Maybe we'll do better next time." I'd heard about the *Yoda*. Maybe they wouldn't do better next time. Even when the fishing was hot, as now, they never seemed to catch much of anything. Gary had told me that Elmer, the *Yoda*'s skipper, had had a hernia for the past month, but that he refused to go into port to have it fixed. Elmer also liked to tipple.

"I hope you do better, too," said Dave. "But I just talked to Leonard. He says you're going to be working with the *Izumrudny* instead of us for the next week or two."

My internal warning mechanisms sprang to full alert. Sounded like Dave had been doing some dickering with Leonard behind my back to foist the lowly *Yoda* off onto us. Shevchenko would have a fit. Nobody wanted to waste their time working with the *Yoda*. I'd have to talk to Leonard after this transfer.

"Oh, all right," said Elmer. "Who's the rep on the *Izumrudny*?"

"Her name's Barb. You'll like her, but her captain's an asshole."

Well, that summed things up neatly.

"*Yoda* out," Elmer drawled. He drew out the 'o', so that *Yoda* sounded like a wail.

"*Tigil* out." Gary and I were left alone once again on our channel.

We were fast upon the *Golden Hope* now. I could see Gary's two deck crew workers, Brian and Bob, standing at the scuppers. Kolya and I referred to them as the human deck cranes—they were brothers who stood six-foot seven each, with shirt-popping muscles that left the Russians nudging each other in awe.

"You got any bread today, Sunshine?" Gary asked.

"Sure," I said. "Hang around after the tow and we'll hand you some." Despite the occasional use of rehabilitated bread dough, the Russian bread was delicious—rich, chewy, and flavorful—and baked fresh each day. Most American boats on the joint venture never bothered to bring bread from port, preferring to get it from the Russians when they ran low.

The *Golden Hope* edged in behind us, and one of the brothers snagged the heavy Russian cable and pulled it aboard as if it were a piece of string. Both men tied it off rapidly, then Brian hit the pelican hook and the cable on deck before me sprung into aching tautness, singing as the full weight of the codend came against it.

"All yours now, Sunshine," said Gary. The *Golden Hope* slowed, edging in behind the codend to follow it like a snuffling mother cow.

"Gary'd like some bread," I said to Sasha. He nodded and headed off toward the stairs. The chief powered the winches, and the codend began working its way toward the stern ramp. Within a few minutes, it was aboard. I headed aft, Sasha at my heels with two crusty loaves of warm bread.

"Good tow," I shouted. The *Golden Hope* bobbed not ten feet away from our stern while Brian stood lightly on the bow. He caught each loaf easily, football fashion, as Sasha tossed them over. "Thanks," he yelled. "When're you coming to visit?"

"Soon, I hope." I caught a glimpse of Gary waving from the bridge as the *Golden Hope* veered off. "Good luck with the next one!" I yelled, cupping my hands. Brian tucked both loaves under a bulging arm and waved.

"How many religious believers are there in America?" asked the commissar, pouring himself a cup of cold tea. Unfortunately, four o'clock—tea time—was also the time Jim Baker and his evangelical ministries program appeared on the only channel our television received. I'd quit translating the show several days before, but the tearful praying and prominent pictures of a blond, blue-eyed, and haloed Jesus needed no translation. The show always seemed to raise a blood lust in the commissar. This was the third day in a row he'd started off a conversation with the same question.

"I don't know how many believers there are in the States," I answered, plopping a piece of fried hake onto my plate. The tablecloth was wet, so that the plates stayed in place without sliding. "How many believers are there in the Soviet Union?"

"Very few," said the commissar. He broke off a piece of bread and slathered it with butter. "We don't have superstitions like that." I raised my eyebrows. Classifying Christianity as a superstition seemed a bit lacking in diplomacy to me. And officially, the Soviets might not be superstitious, but the crew of the *Izumrudny* sure was. Two days ago Irena had sat me down and read my fortune, explaining that her fortune telling wasn't as good as a real gypsy's. The men watching us had been amazed to hear that gypsies didn't roam our country. ("You know," Gregori kept saying, "they're really obvious—the women wear long decorated skirts.") Earlier this morning the chief mate, along with Sasha and Igor, the helmsman, had caught me whistling and had nearly sprouted feathers. Whistling at sea is generally considered *very* bad luck—it attracts ill wind. One also could not straddle the threshold of a doorway or bring bananas on board. In fairness, however, Americans were not much better—the *Hilo* had waited until precisely 12:01 a.m. to head back to the fleet the previous Saturday, since it was bad luck to leave on a Friday. And the *Golden Hope* absolutely forbid black suitcases.

"What about people who leave your country and resettle in a new country? What do you call them?" the commissar asked. He speared a piece of hake and then smeared hot red tomato paste from a ceramic bowl over his fork.

"Emigrants, I suppose," I said. "Why? What do you call them?"

"Traitors," said the commissar, smiling as I fell into his trap.

I looked back down at my plate.

"Do people walk the city streets at night in your country?" asked Fyodor, a tall (for a Russian), craggily handsome redhead who was the assistant factory manager.

"Not usually." I began a long-winded explanation of urban America, trying to present a balanced, honest appraisal of the crime scene. Fyodor listened intently. "That's funny," he said as I finished. "I guess you have a lot of reasons for not going for walks at night. In some countries it's just not the custom."

You win some, you lose some. I cut my hake into quarters. Then I split each piece, carefully picking out the bones. Today there hadn't been much more than a half hour between the time we caught the fish and fried it. Even if hake was one of the least expensive fish, because of its soft flesh and low oil content, I still thought it tasted pretty good. The only way I didn't like hake was in soup, when the fish heads with their staring eyes floated to the top of the bowl.

Fyodor and the commissar, the last of today's tea crowd, excused themselves and rose. Irena, standing as usual by the door, stepped forward to take their plates. I sat pat—Irena and I often stayed to gossip after tea.

"You haven't eaten anything again," she said, reaching over to grab my plate of shredded fish. "You're turning into skin and bones. It's just not healthy."

Irena was right, I really hadn't been eating very well lately. Between the incipient seasickness and the greasy food, I just hadn't been hungry. Last night I'd made a new personal record, finding three large pieces of bone in one forkful of hamburger.

"I'll bet I weigh a lot more than you do," I said. At five-foot nine, I was a good six inches taller than Irena.

"I'll bet you don't," she said.

"How much are you willing to bet?"

"Tell you what. If you win, you have to go to the movies tonight," Irena said.

That didn't sound very fair to me. I'd been avoiding the nightly movies, and Irena knew it. The last one I'd seen had been a Georgian film about a joint Soviet-American climbing team. I couldn't understand a word, and had been very disheartened until the fourth mate had asked me to translate what the Americans were saying: the sound quality had been so poor I hadn't even been able to tell that the so-called Americans really *had* been speaking English.

"Okay," I sighed. "Well, how are we going to prove this?"

"Just a minute," she said, carrying the last of the plates into a small room just off the mess. She washed and rinsed them quickly, then dried her hands and took off her apron. "To the factory," she said. Off we went, down the steep stairs, through the living quarters, past the entrance to the engine room. On beyond the door to the factory, where ammonia stung my eyes and nose. Down to the very bowels of the ship—to the fish-meal plant.

Fish meal came from the offal of the factory-processed fish. But not all the offal was processed. Otherwise the holds would be filled with cheap fish meal, to be used for fodder and fertilizer, rather than the more valuable processed fish. The unused scraps were piped overboard, to become food for the ravaging gulls that hovered constantly about the *Izumrudny*. The processed offal was essentially burned dry—most of the American fishermen swore they could tell a Soviet processor from miles away by the stink of fish-meal processing, although, to be sure, the fish rotting on deck added its own reek to the mixture.

The fish meal packaging room reminded me of a barn, with great burlap bags full of meal lying about like bags of grain. On the starboard side of the room hung a large chute where workers fed fish meal from the kilns into the bags. The air itself seethed with a powdery dust. As we entered the room, two workers looked up, their hair fluffy with fish meal. Beside them, near the chute, stood a large weighing scale.

"Me first," said Irena. The two factory workers crowded over. "What's going on?"

Irena got on the scales. "We're settling a bet." She wiggled the weights back and forth, settling the bar at last to horizontal. "Fifty-five kilograms," she pronounced. "Now you."

"I'll bet Barbara weighs less," said the taller of the two workers. Irena gave him an ugly look.

I climbed onto the scales. "Remember," I said, "I've got boots and heavy clothes on." I had to run outside all the time and Irena didn't.

Irena shifted the weights until the bar slowly teetered to horizontal. "Fifty-eight kilograms. Ah hah—you have to go to the movie tonight!" she said triumphantly.

"I didn't think Barbara would weigh so much," said the other worker. "That's a surprise."

The intercom erupted suddenly in the musty dimness: "Barbara, would you please come to the bridge? Barbara, to the bridge."

"My page," I said. "Gotta run." I headed out the door, glancing back to see Irena scooting the weights to the side of the bar, eliminating signs of our presence.

My lobbying efforts with Leonard had been unsuccessful; we were going to have to work with the unpopular *Yoda* for the next week. As compensation, we'd also work with Charlie on the *Hilo*. We were about due for a tow from Charlie now—hence, most likely, the page. I wondered absently how Ben was faring as I made my way to the bridge.

"Where were you?" Pasha fumed. He handed me my walkie-talkie. I switched it on, ignoring him. Pasha had been interrupting me constantly lately, and was rapidly becoming one of my least favorite people. "*Hilo, Izumrudny.*"

"*Hilo* back. Go to ten, Barb."

I switched channels. "Where are you, anyway? I just got to the bridge."

"Look out your front window. I'm at eleven o'clock."

I glanced behind me toward the bow. There was the *Hilo*, awash in the heavy swell.

"We're having a little trouble here," Charlie continued. "The automatic trawl gear has broken, so we've been doing everything by hand. And we found a big rip in the side of the net. It'll take us most of the night to repair."

"We've got a fair bit of fish here," I said, "so it's..."

"What's the new observer's name?" said Pasha.

"Can't you see I'm talking?" I said to Pasha, irritably. Back into the mike: "So it's not too big a problem if it takes you a while to set again."

"*Izumrudny, Yoda.*"

What did Elmer want? "*Izumrudny* back. Hi, Elmer."

"Leonard told me you were on this channel. We're hauling back now. We'll be ready for you in about five minutes."

Great. It would be at least a half an hour before we were finished with the *Hilo*.

"What are your coordinates?" I asked.

Elmer reeled off a string of numbers and I translated them for Pasha.

"That's about seven miles from here," said Pasha. A forty-five minute run. Well, the *Yoda* would just have to wait.

"We'll be there as soon as we can, Elmer. It'll be a while, though."

"That's just fine," said Elmer in a quivering voice.

"*Izumrudny, Yegorova.* You there, Barb?" It was Leonard's voice.

"*Izumrudny* back." Now what?

"You'll need to pick up the *Golden Hope*'s trawl again. The *Mramorny* is still having problems."

"I hope he isn't ready..."

"We're having fried potatoes at dinner tonight," said Pasha. "It's one of my favorites."

"Pasha, *will* you quit interrupting?" I hissed. "I hope Gary isn't ready yet," I repeated to Leonard. "It'll be over two hours before we can get to him."

"He's ready now," said Leonard.

"I've got a big bag here, Barb. I'm afraid it might be ruined if I wait too long." It was Gary's voice.

"You sort it out, Barb. I've got a function to attend," said Leonard. Probably tea, I thought. I was beginning to worry. We had a lot of fish on deck already. With Charlie's tow we'd have even more. If Gary had a big haul I wasn't sure how we could handle it. "What are your coordinates, Gary?"

Gary read off a string of numbers. I translated again, and Pasha figured for a moment. "The *Golden Hope*'s about five miles from here."

"Toward the *Yoda*?" I asked.

"No, the other way. The *Yoda*'s north. The *Golden Hope*'s south."

Great. We were supposed to pick up three codends simultaneously—twelve miles apart. "Elmer, how much fish you got there?"

"Oh, four, maybe five tons." He was probably pushing two.

"We'll take Gary's tow right after Charlie's, then we'll head for you, Elmer," I decided aloud. "By the way, if we're going to be working with you and Gary most of the time, I'd appreciate it if you two wouldn't set so far apart."

I glanced back toward the bow. We were now rapidly approaching the *Hilo*. She was at the ten o'clock position now, not more than a hundred feet to port.

"When do you think you'll be here?" asked Gary.

"We should be there..."

"Why don't you ever drink *kompot* at dinner, Barbara?" asked Pasha.

"Pasha, will you *shut up*," I exploded. "I'm trying to work, here. Can't you see I'm talking on the radio?"

"Well," said Pasha airily. "If you can't do two things at once, you should be working at a different job. That's the trouble with you women. You can't concentrate very well. I can talk on the radio and easily do several other things at the same time."

I wrapped my hands tightly around the walkie-talkie. "We should be there in about another hour, Gary."

"Jesus Christ, are you guys trying to ram us?" Charlie's voice. I glanced back out the front window. We were heading directly for the *Hilo*. Pasha followed my glance and his eyes widened in horror. "Full starboard!" he cried to the helmsman.

The helmsman glanced up and froze, then spun the wheel madly clockwise. The *Izumrudny* continued unchecked. "She's not responding!"

"Charlie," I yelled into the mike: "The steering's out. Get out of the way!"

Pasha dithered. "Try again," he yelled.

"I told you, she's not responding!" said the helmsman. The *Hilo* was dead ahead. I felt as if I could reach out and touch her.

"Stop. Full engine stop!" Pasha screamed. He ran for the wheel as the *Izumrudny* faltered and suddenly slowed. I heard a door bang open. Shevchenko bounded onto the bridge.

Charlie had turned hard port. I raced to the front set of windows and braced myself against the sill. Forty feet. Thirty. Twenty. Would we miss him?

We slivered past the *Hilo*. I ducked out to the side balcony, looking down on Charlie's pale, strained face as the *Izumrudny*'s momentum carried us by. I slipped back onto the bridge.

"Chief mechanic to the engine room," the captain was saying into the ship's intercom. He headed down the stairs toward the engine room, as light on his feet as a dancer. Shevchenko had drunk close to a bottle of vodka that I'd seen already today, but he acted cold sober.

Ben lurched his way out of the chart room from the captain's cabin with Danielich close on his tail. "Hey, wa's goin' on here?" he asked.

"We're having a problem with the steering," I said.

"Oh," Ben said, considering. "I think I'll go lie down." I remembered my first few days at sea and felt a pang of pity. "Can you find your cabin okay?"

"Sure," he said. "No problem." He started down the stairs, then stopped and got down on his behind as the *Izumrudny* began climbing a wave and the stairs trimmed up to stand nearly vertical. He bounced down the rest of his way on his butt, singing.

Danielich and I looked at each other. "It was a good croak," he said. "Croak" in Russian is slang for "to get drunk."

"Why don't you and Irena stop by my cabin this evening? We'll croak some more." He tapped the side of his neck meaningfully in the curious Slavic gesture which means "get soused."

"Sure," I said. Why not? Maybe it would get me out of the movie. And I liked Danielich—I'd spent many a pleasant hour helping him fix nets on deck, after he and Gregori had shown me some of the simpler knotting techniques.

"What's going on with your steering?" Charlie said.

I turned back to the radio: "They're trying to figure it out right now. I'll let you know as soon as I find out anything."

Pasha was standing by the speaking tube connected to the engine room. "What's going on?" I asked.

"Don't worry your pretty little head about anything, Barbara," he said. "We'll have it fixed soon." He reached over to pat my shoulder.

"Get your goddamn hands off me," I snarled. "And tell me what the fuck's going on."

His startled eyes met mine: "They're working on the problem. Actually, I don't know what's wrong."

The ship began to shake, and suddenly I heard the distant thrum of its engines. "Pasha," came a voice through the speaking tube. "Take her slow dead ahead. See if she responds."

The *Izumrudny* responded, and within a few minutes we had eased back around the *Hilo*. A half hour later we were under way toward the *Golden Hope*, and I headed down for supper.

"Looks like you're becoming a real sailor now, Barbara," said Shevchenko. He ladled himself some fish soup from the steaming tureen before him. "You haven't gotten sick at all today, have you?"

"No," I said. I was beginning to feel pretty cocky; despite the worsening weather, I'd been feeling just fine. It looked as if I was finally beginning to adjust to life at sea.

"*Priatnovo apatita*," said the commissar as he entered the room. He glanced around and zeroed in on me. "Barbara, so you're feeling better. We've made a sailor out of you at last." He, too, looked surprised.

"I guess you have," I said, sitting up even more cockily.

Something in Irena's station crashed to the floor as the *Izumrudny* lurched into a trough. I watched as the factory director, seated opposite me, slid slowly away from the table as the floor tilted beneath us. He scooched his chair back to the table, picked up his bowl of soup, and slurped noisily. "Is the steering in good shape now?" I asked.

A large fish head floated to the surface of the captain's soup, its mouth gaping. The captain rammed it back down under a potato. "The steering's fine. No problems at all," he said, glancing around the table. I followed his gaze. Everyone suddenly examined their soup bowls. "By the way—we can't take any more fish this afternoon."

"What?" I put my spoon down. "We're heading toward the *Golden Hope* right now to pick up their codend."

"We can't take it," he said, grabbing a crust of bread and stuffing it into his mouth.

Across from me, the factory director spat a chunk of bone onto his plate with a loud "ptui." I looked back at the captain. "Why?"

"Too much fish," he said, through a mouthful of bread. "We've taken too much fish already today."

"What do you mean?" I said. "We've only taken forty tons so far today." We'd taken seventy tons three days ago.

"We can only process so much," said Shevchenko. "That's the way it is."

I scooted around the edge of the table, excusing myself and standing. "I'd better tell *Golden Hope*," I said. "Somebody's got to take his fish. You should have told me this before."

"You're a real sailor now." Shevchenko smiled through his bread.

On the way to the bridge I stopped off at my cabin and threw up in the sink. Through the paper-thin walls I could hear the chief mate next door doing the same thing.

"It's ridiculous for Shevchenko to say he won't take fish now," said Leonard. "Let me talk to the fleet commander; he's right here. He'll talk some sense into your captain."

"All right," I said doubtfully. "I don't know what's gotten into him. He's never said a word about too much fish before. Good luck."

"*Yegorova* out."

"So you and Irena had a weighing contest," said Kolya, drawing up beside me with a glass of tea in his hands. "Who won?"

"Irena did," said Seryozha, smiling at us from behind the wheel. "She weighed three kilograms less."

I stared at Seryozha. How had he found out about that, and so quickly? The old saying was right—there are no secrets aboard ships.

Seryozha switched on the automatic pilot and poured me a glass of tea; then we gathered around Kolya to look at some pictures he'd brought of his wife and children. Kolya missed them immensely.

The shortwave radio in the chart room sputtered to life and Kolya twisted sharply around, listening. It was the *Yegorova*, calling us. I smiled. The Russians used the shortwave in preference to VHF marine band for lengthy ship-to-ship conversations. It was also the radio the Soviet fleet commander preferred using. Kolya disappeared into the chart room, then emerged seconds later to page Shevchenko.

"It's the fleet commander," said Kolya, as Shevchenko pounded up the stairs. "He wants to talk to you." Shevchenko turned to give me a suspicious look, then stepped into the chart room.

"When's the steering going to be back in good working order?" I asked Seryozha. I suddenly understood Shevchenko's problem.

"Nobody knows. They've got it temporarily fixed, but it could go out again at any time. They're having trouble with the main shaft."

Bingo. Shevchenko didn't want to take more fish aboard for fear of losing maneuverability in the middle of the operation, as had happened with the *Hilo*. But he hadn't wanted to admit anything was wrong. Screwy way, I thought, to run a ship.

I set my watch and turned to gaze out the window. The sun was just sweeping its way out of the sky. It really did set extraordinarily quickly: the time between when the lower edge of the orb hit the horizon and disappeared altogether took, by my watch, an average of one minute and thirty-seven seconds.

So very little time.

The sky filled with a luminescent molten silver, shading gradually to yellow, then orange, then burning, angry red. Kolya came out of the chart room. "Fifteen degrees to port," he said to Seryozha. "Full speed."

"What's happening now?" I asked.

"We've got to pick up the *Golden Hope*'s codend," said Kolya, as if it were the most obvious thing in the world. I heard a door slam off the chart room—the door to the captain's cabin.

It took us another half hour to get to the *Golden Hope*. After we took his battered codend aboard we headed for the *Yoda*, an hour and a half away, while I fulfilled my promise to Irena and took in the evening's movie. It was an old war film—they were nearly all old war films—much spliced, and distinguished only by the fact that the hero bore a suspicious resemblance to Leonid Brezhnev. I was glad to see it end.

"*Yoda, Izumrudny*," I called, having climbed once again to the bridge. I could see the *Yoda*'s running lights growing near our port bow.

"*Yoda* back," Elmer warbled.

"We're coming up off your starboard side. We should be in position in another minute or two."

"Fine," said Elmer. He was being such a good sport about us being late that it made me feel guilty. I just wished he could catch more fish.

"How are you fixed for bread?" I inquired.

"We could use some."

I turned to Kolya. "Could we get a couple loaves of bread to pass over to the *Yoda*?"

"No problem," he said. Seryozha grabbed the phone to call the galley.

We took Elmer's codend aboard without incident, and Kolya and I trudged down to the deck for an estimate.

"It's maybe a ton," said Kolya. We gazed at the sodden, pathetic lump of mesh. Danielich strode up to join us. He looked singularly chipper in the yellow deck lights.

"Can't we call it three tons?" I asked. "Even if it doesn't turn out to be that..."

"It won't," said Kolya.

"...we could sort of steal a little from Gary and Charlie's tows. They're so big it really won't make a difference." I looked up and out toward the *Yoda*, drifting aimlessly—sadly, almost, off our stern. Her prow looked punched-in, as if it had rammed something and been inexpertly repaired.

Irena appeared beside us, a bulky plastic bag in her hands—the bread. She wore her standard short-sleeve dress; I wondered that she didn't freeze in the windy cold of the evening.

"See if you can get some more plastic bags from him," she said. The Soviets couldn't get plastic bags.

"Elmer, you have any plastic bags you can send us?"

"No," came Elmer's shaky voice.

"Oh well," I said. "You want to come on up and get your bread?"

"Sure. About how many tons you think we have there?"

"Three," I said. I'd sort it out later. We walked over to the railing and the little *Yoda* heeled over to bob in the chop ten feet away from our stern. A crewman made his way around to the bow, and Irena threw him the bread, a straight shot into his arms.

He missed. The bread tumbled into the water.

"No problem, Elmer," I said into the walkie-talkie. "It's wrapped in plastic."

"Okay," said Elmer. His crewman grabbed a boat hook and the *Yoda* began making passes at the bread.

Danielich looked meaningfully at Irena and me and tapped his throat.

"Let me go put my stuff away," I said, looking out into the darkness. It was nearing midnight. "I'll be down in a few minutes."

The *Izumrudny* made a long, slow turn and the *Yoda* grew smaller and smaller in the distance, still circling.

You had to worry about a catcher boat, I thought, when they couldn't even catch bread.

Danielich's cabin, a little larger than most, was painted a nauseating sea green. Irena and I crowded in and sat at a tiny table with a huge scorch mark in the middle. When making tea the Soviets tended to use heating elements which would have given safety officers anywhere goose bumps: the wires had a flammable cotton insulation—when they had any insulation at all, that is. The heating elements were meant to be dangled, red hot, into a mason jar of water.

"What was that?" I said. I'd heard a mysterious twitter above the background noise of the engines.

Danielich blushed. The twitter sounded again, coming from a closet just beside the open porthole.

"That's my bird," he said gruffly. He got up and opened the closet door. Inside, in a box with soft rags, nestled a little sparrow.

"He lost his way," said Irena. "Danielich is taking care of him for a few days until the storm passes and we get closer to land."

I'd seen such birds occasionally—sparrows and finches and other tiny birds blown from shore out to sea. They hovered around the ship, lost and alone among the trailing crowd of ruthless, strident gulls. The deck crew liked to leave pieces of bread out for the little creatures, trying to keep them alive until they found strength and a lucky, shoreward wind to fly back to land.

Danielich reached in to stroke the sparrow on the top of its head. It blinked its eyes sleepily. "Go back to sleep, little one," he said softly, and shut the closet door.

"What are they saying?" asked Ben. I'd run into Ben emerging from the bathroom up in the officer's quarters while I'd been putting my things away. He'd looked miserable, so I'd invited him down; we'd propped him, semi-comatose, in a corner of the cabin.

I explained about the bird while Irena poured tea. Danielich reached under his bunk and with great ceremony pulled out a bottle of Stolichnaya. Ben's face shaded toward the color of the cabin walls.

"Just have some tea," I said solicitously.

"How can you drink all this alcohol?" he asked.

"I didn't stay with you in the captain's cabin," I pointed out. "Besides, you get used to it. It's the Soviet way of life."

Ben took a sip of tea and coughed, choking. "I don't know which is worse, the vodka or the tea. This stuff would take the hair off an ape."

I laughed as a knock sounded at the door. In a wink Danielich had the bottle back under the mattress. Gregori, the deck crew worker, peeked in. "Feel like a little entertainment?" he asked.

"Come in, you ass," said Danielich affectionately. "And lock the door behind you." Gregori slipped in the door with Yuri and Katya, the cook, behind him. Gregori carried a huge accordion.

Danielich brought the bottle back out again. I drained my tea, feeling the acid churn its way down to begin tanning my stomach. Danielich poured a round and we drained our glasses.

"What would you like to hear?" asked Gregori.

"How about a lullaby?" asked Irena. "For the little sparrow." Gregori tugged at the straps holding the heavy instrument to his body and softly began to sing:

Sleep, my baby, my beauty,
Lullaby, lullaby,
Silently the clear moon watches,
Your tiny cradle, my love.

Gregori's voice was deep and pleasing; his fingers moved gently over the keys while his arms wove in and out. He sang verse after verse, and we all listened, mesmerized, until he'd finished.

Danielich poured another round, finishing off the bottle. "Here's to Gregori's silver throat," said Yuri. We drank.

"Hey, Katya," said Gregori, "You've got the keys to the pantry. Can't you see about maybe getting a bottle of champagne for us?"

Katya, who'd been silent so far, flushed pink. "You know the commissar said there was too much drinking going on. It's strictly forbidden. I'm not allowed to take anything."

Yuri and Danielich leapt into the fray. "Oh, come on, Katya. One little bottle won't hurt. He won't even miss it. Pretty please?"

"No," said Katya. "I can't. They'll find out."

"No they won't," said Yuri. "Come on."

"I just can't," said Katya, standing. "We're not allowed to."

"Sure you can," said Gregori.

Katya unlocked the door and left, looking very upset.

Gregori launched into a rollicking tune, his fingers dancing over the keys:

Wildly do I love you, darling,
My soul is filled with thee.
I am pining, I am afire,
Love did strike so hard at me!

Ben sipped at his tea, looking as if he was beginning to recover a little. I translated for him.

"Would Ben like to hear some good jokes?" asked Gregori.

"Sure," said Ben.

"What is 150 yards long and eats potatoes?" Gregori said. I translated and Ben looked intrigued. "I don't know."

"A Moscow queue waiting to buy meat."

Ben laughed.

"What is the state of transition between capitalism and communism?"

Ben shook his head.

"Alcoholism."

There was another knock at the door. Yuri rose to unlock it.

Katya entered, a brown, bottle-shaped paper bag tucked under each arm.

"Katya!" said Gregori. "I knew you could do it."

Katya smiled prettily. "No more, now."

"Oh, no. This is plenty," said Danielich, winking at me.

Danielich busied himself opening another bottle while Gregori started another joke: "They ask a Soviet theoretician to explain some different styles of painting. 'Expressionism,' he says, 'is painting what you feel. Impressionism is painting what you see.' Then they ask him what socialist realism is." Gregori wound back to deliver the punch line.

I didn't understand it.

Gregori looked at me expectantly. Hell, I thought, loathe to interrupt the flow of conversation. I gave a forced laugh and improvised: "I didn't understand the punchline, but here's where you laugh."

Above: An American stern-ramp trawler. *Below:* A typical Russian "RTM" type stern-ramp trawler.

All photographs courtesy of the author.

View from the back deck of the Russian trawler. The process of taking a codend aboard is just beginning. The cable is being fed off the stern ramp.

A continuation of the codend-taking process. A codend has been attached by the Americans to the end of the cable, which is now being hauled back aboard the Russian vessel. The men are removing buoys from the cable.

The codend is now aboard and is being dumped into the bunkers.

Fish being pushed down toward the bunker (the hole on the right). Notice the "work-to-watch" ratio: one man working to three men watching. From left to right: Yuri and Gregori (members of the deck crew), "Danielich," and "Gleb."

On the left is "Danielich," web-mender extraordinaire.

The author is standing atop a mountain of fish on the deck of the *Izumrudny*.

Kolya, second mate of the *Izumrudny,* working on the bridge.

Rocking to the beat of Queen—hauling a codend aboard the *Chasovoi* at 2:00 a.m. on a quiet Bering Sea.

It's party and picture time aboard the *Chasovoi*. No matter how intoxicated Captain "Yuri" may be, he never appears for a picture without a tie. The remains of a typical banquet are on the table.

Looking down onto the back deck of a typical American trawler rigged to fish yellow-fin sole on the Bering Sea.

Above: The author with the deck crew of the *Chasovoi*. The ill-fated puppy Rosella is seated on the author's lap. *Below:* To Russian-American friendship.

Ben gave a good-natured guffaw.

"Could you both sing a song for us in English?" asked Irena.

Ben and I looked at each other. "Uh, do you know any songs?" I said.

Ben looked stumped. "How about 'A Bridge Over Troubled Waters'?" he suggested at last.

"I don't know the words," I said, "but I can hum along."

We muddled our way through the song, and then another, working away at the champagne and swilling syrupy tea. Gregori went through another spate of jokes, and then sang another round of songs, including "Clementine" and "Way Down upon the Swanee River." Katya and Irena accompanied him with gusto. They seemed to know more English songs than we did.

"Have you ever heard," asked Danielich, "why we do this when we mean drink?" He tapped his throat again, cupping his hand to snap his index finger against the side of his Adam's apple with a hollow thump.

"No," I leaned forward. "Why?"

Danielich lowered his voice. "I suppose you've heard of Peter the Great?" he asked. I translated for Ben, nodding.

"Peter wasn't content to leave the building of Leningrad—St. Petersburg, as they called it then—to just his workers."

"He couldn't," Gregori interrupted. "They kept dying."

"Well, yes, there's that," Danielich admitted. He took a healthy slug of tea; we'd finished the champagne. "Anyway, Peter was supervising the foundation for the fortress when a huge storm came up."

"Leningrad was very swampy," said Katya.

"So when the storm came up," Danielich continued, "everything began to flood. Peter was trying to rescue some of the workers..."

"He couldn't have *all* of them die," said Irena.

"...when a wave of water washed over them, sweeping Peter off his feet and washing him toward the river. One of the workers, standing on higher ground, saw what was happening and leapt into the water. He was a very strong swimmer, and he managed to pull Peter to safety."

"The rest probably just died," said Gregori. Danielich poked him and Irena and Katya giggled.

"In gratitude for the worker having saved his life, Peter offered him whatever he desired in the kingdom. Of course, the worker knew exactly what he wanted: a free pass so that anywhere he went in the kingdom, people would have to give him all the booze he asked for."

"The prototype of the model Soviet citizen," said Yuri.

"So Peter had a great pass made up, complete with seals and stamps and signed by every sort of official, including, of course, himself. The man took the pass and spent a week in his cups, hitting every bar he could find. Then he lost the pass."

"Men are worthless when they are drunk," said Katya.

Danielich grinned. "Aren't we, though? Anyway, the worker went back to Peter, told him he'd lost his pass, and asked for another."

"So Peter had another pass made up, with all the same signs and seals and signatures. The man took it, went off, and got drunk again. Within a week, he'd lost this pass, too. Back he went to Peter: 'I lost my pass again,' he says."

"Peter looked at the man and said, 'This time I'll give you a pass you'll never lose.' And he had another great pass made up—this time in wrought iron at the end of a rod. When the man came back to pick up the pass, Peter branded it on his neck." Danielich tapped his throat again. "Right here."

"Of course the man couldn't speak after that, so from then on, whenever he wanted to drink, he'd just go into a bar and tap his throat," Danielich thumped his throat a last time, with emphasis. "Just like this."

The Russians laughed as I finished translating. Ben looked appalled. I yawned despite myself and glanced at my watch. It was a quarter to three.

"It's probably time to go," I said. I stood, holding onto the side of the wall: the seas were picking up.

We headed quietly out the door, heading up the long stairways toward the deck. Danielich and Gregori followed—their factory shift was due to begin in fifteen minutes and they needed to get their protective gear from the team room just off the deck.

"Could I see their working quarters?" Ben asked.

"What on earth do you want to see the team room at nearly three in the morning for?" I asked. I was tiring fast.

"This'll probably be where I work most of the time," he said.

Gregori and Danielich stepped into the small, dark cabin just off the fore part of the deck while Ben peered over their shoulders to glance inside. I grabbed at a rail on the winch casing outside the cabin as the *Izumrudny* slammed into another wave and began riding up on the swell. The deck began to tilt ominously, the bow rising higher, the stern sinking lower and still lower, until suddenly it seemed I was looking straight down the nearly perpendicular deck into water swirling, dark and mean, directly below me.

"Tell Ben not to stand in the threshold," came an irritable voice from inside the team room. "It's bad luck."

Bad luck, nothing. I was about to fall overboard.

"What's he saying?" Ben asked, standing in the middle of the threshold. One hand rested on the inside edge of the heavy hatch, with the other braced across the door frame on the steel sill.

"Don't stand in the doorway," I said, trying to tighten my grasp on the railing. I glanced back down the deck to the propeller-roiled waters below. Were we going to keep climbing this wave forever?

"What did you say?" Ben asked. I wrapped my arms still tighter around the railing and glanced over at Ben just as the heavy steel hatch on the team room doorway bumped loose from its latches and began to swing shut.

"Watch out!" I yelled.

It was too late. The heavy door, aided by gravity, swung ponderously down, catching Ben's hand and squeezing it like giant pliers against the hinges.

Ben screamed and Danielich bolted into view, pushing against the heavy door with all his might.

"Get his hand out, get his hand out!" Danielich yelled. Gregori appeared, pulling at Ben's hand. Ben screamed again and began flailing at Gregori. Danielich gave a great thrust against the door, Gregori pulled again, and Ben reeled away from the door, cursing.

The *Izumrudny*, as if satisfied, began settling back to horizontal. Ben tucked his hand up against his body, his face suddenly strained and white. I released my grip on the railing and galloped over the now perfectly horizontal deck toward Ben. We hustled him into the team room and sat him amidst a pile of overalls covered with fish scales and entrails.

"Let me see your hand," said Danielich. Ben cradled his hand for a moment longer, then extended it.

The inside of the palm was bruised and bleeding—scraped raw by the rusty edges of the door frame. But it was Ben's thumb that had caught the brunt of the pressure between the door and the hinge. It was already a dark and ugly red throughout its length, with swelling that seemed to grow even as I watched.

"Is it broken?" I asked.

"I don't know," said Ben in a hoarse voice. "It hurts like hell, though. Is there any kind of doctor on board?"

"Yes," I said hesitantly. This was not the time to discuss the Soviet's true medical capabilities.

Gregori fetched the doctor, who wrapped and bound Ben's hand. There was little else we could do, so we took him to his cabin and then went our separate ways.

I was tired. Too tired to think; certainly too tired to sleep. So I sat at my desk and gazed outside toward the bow. The hawsers sang in the wind: a lonely, endless drone. Suddenly, a flash of lightening lit the entire sky, and a thunderclap went off like an explosion, shaking the ship. I leaned forward to open the porthole, and wind swirled into the room. It had just rained, and the front deck before me glistened in the darkness, slick and smooth. The air was fresh with ozone and rust. Off in the distance, perhaps five miles, the lights of several boats shone brightly—so brightly they seemed on fire.

I looked into the darkness until I could barely see. Until my legs fell asleep, until the winds chilled me to the bone. Then I stumbled to my bunk to lay, eyes wide, in the dull glimmer of the ship's running lights.

Chapter Six
"As the Processor Turns"

I PRIED MY EYES open uneasily. Something was wrong, very wrong. I lay on my bunk, listening. The usual rumble of the ship's engines hummed beneath me, and next door I heard the clatter of dishes as Irena set plates out in the officers' mess. I checked my watch: 6:05 a.m.

I lay quietly, tired, but loose and relaxed. I'd always had trouble getting used to the way the bunk rocked back and forth beneath me as I tried to sleep in heavy seas. No matter how much I snuggled into a secure position, the next wave always tilted me askew. The pitching—a front-to-back seesawing motion—didn't bother me so much, but the yawing from side-to-side, constantly threatened to flip me, so that even asleep I had to keep my muscles tensed to remain in one position. Sometimes the yawing and pitching motions would combine in one energetic swooping roll—at those times I flew from one side of the bunk to another. Even with the heavy sideboard to restrain me, I'd nearly been thrown out of the bunk several times. We'd had heavy seas so much lately that I'd gotten used to it, although it hadn't been easy.

That was it; it was calm. Too calm. I got up and crossed to the porthole, glancing out to see nothing but empty, fuzzy grayness.

We were in heavy fog. I strained my eyes, but couldn't even make out the bow straight ahead of me, not thirty feet away. Turning my head, I could see the shapeless outlines of a man standing at the starboard railing about fifteen feet away, turning to peer back and forth into the mist. I dressed quickly and headed for the bridge.

"It looks like a catcher boat, maybe half a mile from here," Kolya was saying as I came up the stairs. He was bent over the ancient radar gear, his eyes fastened to the worn eyepiece. "It's definitely heading away."

Shevchenko grunted. Unshaven and dressed in a tee-shirt and gray cotton sweat pants, his hair was wild and his eyes bloodshot. He looked as if he'd been drinking all night. In fact, he probably *had* been drinking all night. I followed his gaze toward the bow; the fog had thinned momentarily and the watch came into view—three men, one to the starboard bow, one to the port, and a final one at the prow—each scanning the sector in front of him. The man at the prow suddenly disappeared as the fog thickened.

Kolya glanced up and saw me. "Barbara, we can't raise the *Hilo*. You want to give it a try?"

"Sure," I said. "Can we work in this kind of weather?"

"I want fish," said Shevchenko. "We can work." He walked over to peer into the radar.

"*Hilo, Izumrudny*," I said, and paused.

"*Hilo, Izumrudny*." No answer.

"*Yoda, Izumrudny*."

"*Yoda* back."

At least someone was out there. "Morning, Elmer. I guess we're supposed to be working with both you and the *Hilo* today."

"What are you talking to the *Yoda* for?" Shevchenko muttered in the background. "It's just a waste of time."

"The trawl got twisted when we set this morning," Elmer said in his quivering voice. "It's going to take us a while to get untangled."

The *Yoda*'s usual luck. I relayed the information.

"Ask him if he's seen the *Hilo*," said Kolya. I translated.

"No, I haven't," said Elmer. "The fog's pretty thick here."

"Charlie told us where he was going to have the *Hilo* set this morning," I said to Shevchenko. "He should probably be somewhere near those coordinates now." I fished around for the notes I'd jotted down late yesterday when we'd taken Charlie's codend. "Here we go."

Shevchenko took the paper. His eyes shifted to the side for a second as he calculated. "That's about a mile and a half northwest of here." He turned back to the radar, pausing to tweak a knob. "That could be her right...there." He straightened. "Seryozha—set a course on 270 degrees and hold her steady as she goes."

Kolya, I noticed, was standing by the front bank of windows, his eyes flicking back and forth to check the men on the bow. He bent his head, eyes still on the bow watch, to speak in a low voice into the receiver of my walkie-talkie; communicating, I presumed, with men stationed at the *Izumrudny*'s stern. I shivered and went out the salt-stained wooden door to stand at the port-side railing.

Where the seas had been heavy and wild only hours before, now they were calm and silky smooth, as if the weight of the fog itself had pushed them into oily flatness. And the ocean sounded different, somehow, echoing with muffled silence as if I were trapped in a padded cell. I stretched a hand out, feeling the tiny droplets of the thick vapor condensing on my skin. I'd never seen fog so thick in my life. I hoped I never saw it again.

Since I'd joined the *Izumrudny*, more Soviet trawlers had arrived from Nakhodka, until we now had eleven Soviet and sixteen American vessels in the fleet. The hake sign had been very concentrated of late, so that the fleet had been rubbing elbows in a very small area. Fishing was difficult enough even with full visibility. Several times we'd had to veer sharply to pull away from a bank of two or three American boats, all plowing in a solid line straight into our path as we tried to pick up a codend from yet another catcher boat. With this fog, fishing would be a nightmare. I shivered as the damp coated my glasses and began to seep through my jacket, and went back inside.

No one was at the radar as I entered, so I leaned over for a quick look. Kolya had shown me how it worked; the radar sweep showed as a rotating line on the circular screen. As it revolved, the radar targets splashed into momentary brilliance that faded as the line passed. One would think radar would make travel in fog relatively safe. In practice, many of the smaller boats barely showed on the screen, and spurious shadows of waves and the ghostly imprints from the old equipment itself made for a very fuzzy picture of a world already obscured.

I counted nearly twenty-five targets on the screen. Some of them were almost invisible—tiny gnats fluorescing and fading with a metronome's regularity as the sweep circled the screen. Salmon trollers, most likely; unaware with their own lack of gear of the danger lurking about them.

"*Tuman*—fog," said Shevchenko beside me. I straightened and turned as he took a sip from a glass of tea, eyes focused outside. "You know, in all the years I've been at sea, it's the only thing I'm really afraid of." He moved away to lean against the fish finder. I stared after him in surprise.

Kolya took a turn over the radar. "We should be getting close," he said. His hands gripped the polished handles of the old equipment, knuckles white.

"Tell everyone to be on the alert," said Shevchenko. "Take her dead slow, Seryozha." The *Izumrudny* slowed to a crawl.

"We're too close now. There's no more target," said Kolya. The Soviet radar couldn't resolve at close range. "We should be coming on her any second." We all looked out the windows, anxiously scanning the mist. The slower we went, the longer it would take to find the *Hilo*, but any increase in speed upped the risk of collision. Even at very low speeds the *Izumrudny* took hundreds of yards of clear water to slow to a stop—clear water we wouldn't have if we came suddenly upon the *Hilo* from the wrong angle. It was as if we were feeling around a dark closet for a rattlesnake.

Nothing. And still nothing. Shevchenko ordered the *Izumrudny* into a slow series of turns, crisscrossing the area. The fog, if anything, was growing thicker. I strained my eyes, gazing off the starboard bow, then glanced at the radio, then looked off to port.

Nothing.

And then: there she was, looming from the mist so close it seemed I could reach out and touch her.

"The *Hilo*," I gasped, pointing.

"Stop!" Shevchenko ordered. Seryozha pulled back on the throttle and the *Izumrudny* slowed as we began to glide past the American boat. "Good girl, Barbara," he said approvingly. "You'll be a sailor yet."

"*Hilo, Izumrudny*," I said into the radio. The *Hilo* drifted quietly. She didn't answer.

"They're sleeping," said Shevchenko. "But we can take care of that." He strode over to the edge of the chart room and pulled a short chain dangling from the ceiling.

A massive blast nearly deafened me; the fog horn. Shevchenko held the chain down a good thirty seconds, a look of satisfaction on his face.

"That should get their attention," he said. "Try them now."

"*Hilo, Izumrudny*," I said again, and paused.

"*Hilo* back," came a tired voice. "Is that you, Barb?"

"No, it's Elizabeth Taylor," I said. "Where have you guys been this morning?"

"Um. Let's just say it's been amateur hour over here. Sorry about that. Let me get the crew up and we'll get started."

"What's he saying?" Shevchenko asked.

"I think he overslept." I stumbled, trying to give the flavor of Charlie's apology. "It has been the 'hour of inexperience'," he says.

Shevchenko laughed at my clumsy translation.

"I'm sorry," I said, "I wish I spoke a little better Russian."

"Don't apologize," he said, still laughing. "You speak Russian very well. You have no idea how bad some of the translators are out here. The rep on the *Karenga* speaks Russian about as well as I speak Urdu. And I don't," he said, turning once again to scan the fog, "speak a word of Urdu."

Actually, Shevchenko was, for once, just being nice: I was frequently guilty of mistranslation. Just yesterday I'd been joking that we'd have to start eating more rockfish: taking more to the galley instead of the freezer, but in Russian it came out, "We should put more rockfish inside the halibut instead of in the refrigerating mechanism." The day before that I'd made the pronouncement that we should put pizza dough in our soul (*dukh*) instead of our oven (*dukhovku*).

The bad thing about these kinds of mistakes is that, inane though they were, they wouldn't hit me immediately. The Russians would just look at me a little strangely after I came out with my line of nonsense, and then change the subject. It wouldn't strike me until hours later what I'd really said. This untimely realization of mistranslation happened so frequently that I had a name for it: the delayed dumbshit reaction.

I turned to gaze back out the window. The *Hilo* had disappeared again into the hollow grayness.

I wondered how Ben was doing.

"I'm not sure if it's broken or not," said Ben, looking glumly at his thumb. It had swollen so much he'd been forced to remove the bandages. The nail hung loose from the purple, pussy mass. He looked drugged from lack of sleep. "I'm not sure what to do. I mean," he looked up at me with serious eyes, "this is my very first day on the job as a fisheries observer. This is my *career*. What are they going to say if I tell them I've injured my lousy *thumb*, for Christ's sake? What if I go back into port and it's not broken; it's just sprained or something? I'll be a laughing stock. I'll never live it down."

"Look —can you work the way things are right now?" I asked.

"I don't think so."

"There you are, then."

"I'll think about it," said Ben.

"Okay," I said. Ben needed proper medical care, and we both knew it. I was just glad Ben wasn't a Russian. Laura had whiled away an afternoon's radio gossip telling me the story of the captain of the *Maltseva*. A glass reading gauge had exploded in one of his seaman's eyes; the captain had refused any outside medical care, insisting the seaman was fine. The *Maltseva*'s rep found out the man *wasn't* fine; indeed, that his injuries had become severely infected. She called the Coast Guard, who forcibly evacuated the seaman for medical treatment. He went blind anyway, although the doctors said it would have been a simple matter to have saved his sight if he'd been treated right away. Nothing had ever happened to the *Maltseva*'s captain. The rep, however, was immediately accused of drug abuse. (She had glazed eyes and smiled a lot, said the report.)

"Barbara, please come to bridge," rasped the intercom, in English.

"Gotta go," I said to Ben. "There are always catcher boats heading back into port. If you decide to go in, let me know."

"I can't go in without informing headquarters," said Ben unhappily.

"Your mother's going to be staying with us for *two* weeks?" came Linda's dismayed voice. Linda, the lead observer in the fleet, was in her fourth season on the Joint Venture. Her boyfriend, Rick, was the observer on the *Alexandrovsk*. The two held daily conversations on "restricted" channel thirty-three.

"I'm sorry, sweetheart, there was nothing I could do about it. Mom's not really that bad. The time'll go by before you know it."

"Before *you* know it, maybe. You're a jellyfish when it comes to your mother. You know how she browbeats me."

"You're just a little oversensitive, that's all."

"Oversensitive!..."

"Anything interesting going on?" It was Shevchenko.

"It's Linda and Rick," I said. "Same old thing." Shevchenko knew about the torrid romance. In fact, most of the fleet tuned in to channel thirty-three from ten to eleven in the morning, when Linda and Rick held their daily conversations. The crew of the *Krakatoa*, I'd discovered, had even made a tape recording of the excerpted conversations, entitled "As the Processor Turns": "Join us next week to see whether the pair will spend their break at Linda's parents', or whether they will spend the week alone together in lurid Arizona."

I sat by the radio with that uneasy feeling of boredom that only idle nervousness can bring. It was still foggy, and the fleet waltzed in a constant, careful dance as we maneuvered about each other in the small area which had shown signs of hake. It was like having a full dress ball in a coat room with everyone wearing frosted glasses. Twice we'd narrowly avoided a tiny salmon troller, and once we'd nearly rammed the *Jackdaw* as she swerved to avoid yet another boat. Now I was afraid to leave the bridge even to go to the bathroom—I might miss that one frantic call in English that would warn us of an impending collision.

I reached up to switch the channel of my secondary radio. In fog like this I always kept my main radio tuned to the fleet channel. During normal weather I often didn't bother. Actually, most of us reps had "off" channels we hung out on: I usually worked with my catcher boats on channel ten; the *Tigil's* rep, Dave, liked six, and Laura worked on twelve. After a while it became second nature to know that if, say, Randy on the *Karenga* didn't answer on the fleet channel, he could probably be found on channel eleven. In the fog, however, nobody took any chances—we all kept one ear cocked to channel eight for immediate accessibility.

"Just how late do you think the transport vessel is going to be, anyway?" came a voice over channel seven. It was Emily, the assistant lead rep, who was spending the week on the *Karagach* taking over for the vacationing Glenn Jones. The transport vessel offloaded the Soviet factory ships when their storage reached capacity.

"Three days if we're lucky. A week if we're unlucky," said Leonard. This was interesting news. I knew our holds were beginning to get full—just how full, of course, Shevchenko wouldn't say. Looked like there might be trouble coming.

"Here, Barbara, I brought you some lunch." It was Seryozha, bearing a plateful of oily fish and coleslaw.

"That's awfully nice of you," I said. It *was* nice, but it was also a smart thing to do—now they could be sure I'd stay on the bridge through lunch.

"Could you ask Charlie for an update on his coordinates?" Kolya asked.

"Sure." We'd been looking for Charlie for the last half hour while he was hauling back.

"*Hilo, Izumrudny*," I said on channel eight.

"*Hilo* back," came Charlie's voice.

"How about an update on your position?"

Charlie reeled off another string of numbers. I checked my notes. He'd barely moved from his last position. I passed the numbers to Kolya.

"We just looked there," he said irritably. "We'll try again." He ordered Seryozha to bring the *Izumrudny* around.

"If we end up waiting too long for the transport vessel, we might as well send some of the reps in for a break," Leonard continued on channel seven. "We're beginning to need it." I nodded in silent agreement. *I* was beginning to need it. Official company policy was that no rep would be at sea for more than two months without some sort of break on shore. I'd been out a little over two months now.

"Could you send me in first?" laughed Emily.

"I think we might be able to..." Leonard paused. "Jesus H. Christ. Oh my God." His voice broke off.

"What's happening?" asked Emily. Leonard didn't answer.

"*Muis Yegorova, Karagach,*" came Emily's voice. "*Muis Yegorova, Karagach.* Leonard, are you there?"

"Emily?" came Leonard's voice. He sounded shaky.

"Yes. What happened?"

"God, we just came out of the fog an arm's length from another ship. Jesus, that was a close one..."

Behind me I could hear a commotion, but I stared at the radio, spellbound by Leonard's voice.

"...I think it's the *Izumrudny.*"

Gee, that's funny, I thought. We're not close to anyone right now, except, hopefully, the *Hilo.* I turned to take a glance out the front windows.

The *Muis Yegorova* loomed like a brontosaurus off our starboard bow.

"Reverse engines!" Shevchenko yelled. "Hard port!" Seryozha thrust the throttle back and spun the wheel with all his might. The *Izumrudny* lurched violently as the *Yegorova* plowed past just off the front of our bow, going so fast I could almost feel the wind skating off her. I grabbed the edge of the radio casing and hung on, frozen and staring.

It was the *Muis Yegorova*'s very speed that saved us. She nipped past the *Izumrudny* just as we cut into her wake, missing her two hundred and seventy foot length by bare inches.

A stream of angry Russian began spewing from channel eight: the *Muis Yegorova*, calling us. Shevchenko grabbed the mike and began shouting back. From a linguistic point of view, it was a fascinating look at the richness of the Russian vernacular.

I turned to gaze outside. The *Yegorova* was already gone, swallowed up by the mists. We were alone again in the fog.

My eyes began automatically to search again through the fuzzy dimness.

"No, Pasha!" I said. The man seemed to be deaf and blind, as well as stupid. "You need to zigzag back and forth in front of him. Like this." I drew a wavy line in front of a boat on a sheet of scrap paper.

The heavy fog of the morning had cleared around noon, leaving cloudless blue skies and a fleet scratching for the dregs of the great shoals of hake that had swarmed the area in the last few days. The trawls had slashed the heart out of the schools, and the remaining fish were wary and flighty. They hadn't yet had a chance to regroup, so the fish finders showed only small schools scattered here and there: "hake fuzz," as the fishermen called them. Only Gary on the *Golden Hope* seemed able to find good amounts of fish, steadily coming up with twenty-five ton bags even as the others were lucky to come up with ten. I wondered about his secret, and so, obviously, did some of the other fishermen; the *Plunkett* and the *Barroom* followed the *Golden Hope* everywhere, setting right beside him as he set, hauling back when he hauled back. Those two did even worse than the others—most of their tows were only five to seven tons.

Fortunately for us, Leonard had assigned the *Golden Hope* to the *Izumrudny* for the day, since the *Hilo* had been having still more problems as the morning wore on. Charlie had begun laying out his trawl only to discover yet another huge tear that they'd somehow missed while repairing the net the night before. Then the automatic trawl had gone out again, and their engine had stalled. With the *Hilo*'s problems, and since the *Yoda* could scarcely be counted as a catcher boat, we had been in dire straits until Leonard had shifted boats. Now, with fifty tons from the *Golden Hope* aboard, Shevchenko was top skipper for the day among the Soviets. He wandered about the bridge looking smug: only the sprightly sparkle in his eyes revealed that he was still drunk.

"I need you to check for fish with your finder off my starboard bow, Barb," crackled Gary's voice over the radio. "Could you get the mate to move the *Izumrudny* in that direction?"

"I've been trying." This was the third time Gary had asked me to try to get the *Izumrudny* to search a particular spot. We'd failed each time—wandering instead off behind the *Golden Hope*, far out of reach of her trawl. At least Gary was still nice about it, unlike some of the other fishermen I'd been working with.

"I'm afraid the mate's attention span is subliminal," I said. "I think he just doesn't like to turn the boat." I turned to Pasha once again, pointing in exasperation toward the north. "*That* way, Pasha. He wants you to look *that* way."

"But there could be fish in this direction," Pasha said.

"But he can't *get* here from there!" I exploded. "He's trawling the other way."

Pasha ordered the *Izumrudny* slowly about.

The battles had been growing heated on the bridge lately as the fishermen had berated me for not having the *Izumrudny* where it should have been to help guide them to the fish. Even when the fishing was good, it helped to have us bird-dogging out in front, checking with our fish finders for the greatest concentrations of fish. But none of the mates, with the exception of Kolya, seemed to understand that checking beside or behind the American catcher boats didn't help at all. The catcher boat had only about a thirty degree front span in which it could turn, and *that* was the area that needed to be checked. Time and time again the chief mate and Pasha had told me, in response to a fisherman's request, that they didn't need to be told where the *Izumrudny* should be. They were experienced fishermen, they explained, and already *knew* where the *Izumrudny* should be, regardless of what the Americans requested.

Actually, the chief mate and I had been on the outs for over a week when, in a fit of frustration, I'd told him it was a good thing he'd told me he was an experienced fisherman, otherwise I would have thought he was a dishwasher. I was also irritated at his habit of showing up drunk on watch; several times I had to tell him to shut up and get out so that the fourth mate and I could work unhampered. This week we were once more good friends, but we both circled carefully around each other—I was careful to imply that obviously an experienced fisherman might want to be in a certain place, and he was careful to assert that he thought so, too. I also only called him on about half of his excuses for doing nothing. The captain was the only one who seemed to be able to drink all day and still work the same as ever, save for a certain sprightliness of demeanor, a medicinal breath, and a set of bloodshot eyes. I'd found it interesting to watch him laughing and joking at evening parties, and then turn instantly into The Captain when the phone rang.

"Look at this!" Pasha exclaimed, pointing excitedly to the fish monitor. A huge school began tracing its way onto the screen; a school that had somehow managed to elude the nets. It wouldn't today, I thought.

"*Golden Hope*, *Izumrudny*," I said.

"*Golden Hope* back."

"You might want to angle about ten degrees over to your right." With all the other fishermen in the area, I wasn't going to make it sound too enticing.

"Thanks, Sunshine." The *Golden Hope* began veering slowly to the right. The *Plunkett*, a hundred yards to Gary's port, began veering as well.

"It's a good thing for the *Golden Hope* that I'm out here looking," said Pasha. I broke my pencil and bent to pick up the pieces before they rolled away.

"Hi, Barb." It was Ben, looking like something we'd dragged up off the ocean floor. His hand was loosely wrapped in bandages.

"What's the word?" I asked.

"I think I'd like to go into port, if only for peace of mind about whether my damned thumb's broken or not."

Shevchenko wandered onto the bridge, walking past us to scowl at the fish monitor. He pulled the paper out, examining the large school Pasha and I had just seen. "Does the *Golden Hope* know about this?" he asked, turning to Pasha.

"I've been running a zigzag pattern in front of Gary, trying to spot fish for him," Pasha said in his most professional manner. "I just found that school a few minutes ago. I had Barbara tell him about it."

I seethed silently.

"Good," Shevchenko grunted. He dropped the paper and walked over to Ben and me. "So you tangled with a door, eh, Ben?"

I translated and Ben looked embarrassed, his face a study of flustered pink on pale white. "Yes. I've decided to see if I can get a ride into port and have my hand checked out. I'll be sending a message to the National Marine Fisheries headquarters to let them know I'll be in for a few days. Who should I give it to—you or the radio operator?"

"To me. I'll give it to the radio operator." The radio operator, I knew, could communicate with the American mainland by means of telegrams transmitted in Morse code. With Morse, it didn't matter whether the operator could speak English or not. All maritime radio operators knew Morse code.

"I'll get it ready right now," Ben said. He turned to stumble toward the companionway.

"I think his hand is broken," I said to Shevchenko. "Or at least his thumb. He doesn't look very good to me. I wish there were something more we could do."

Shevchenko watched as Ben disappeared. "There might be." Did I detect a note of compassion in his voice? "Pasha!"

Pasha leapt to stand in front of Shevchenko: an obedient, groveling puppy. "Yes, sir."

"Get the commissar. Send him to my cabin."

"Yes, sir."

Shevchenko eyed me for a moment, his face expressionless, as the radio crackled again: "*Izumrudny, Hilo.*"

"*Izumrudny* back. Hi, Charlie."

"Barb, I'm afraid the *Hilo* is falling apart. We can't seem to get the automatic trawl straightened out, and the hydraulics are giving us so many problems I've decided to call it quits and head into Astoria. We should be able to get whipped back into shape in a couple, two, three days."

"Sorry to hear that," I said. "Do you think you could take Ben in with you? He's injured his hand and he needs to get it looked at."

"No problem. It'll take us another couple hours to get the engine going again. I'll give you a call as soon as we're ready to go."

"*Izumrudny* out," I said. I walked over to the telephone on the radio room wall and called Ben's cabin.

"Hello?" said Ben, somewhat hesitantly.

"It's just me. You've got a ride into Astoria in a couple of hours with the *Hilo.*"

"Great." He didn't sound enthusiastic. "I'm just finishing off the telegram. I'll get packed."

"Roger dodger," I said, hanging up. I leaned down to pour some scalding tea from the mason jar on the small table in front of me. Kolya had just come on shift and, as always, tea had been put on to boil first thing.

"What does that mean—'Roger dodger'?" asked Seryozha.

"It's kind of like 'okay'," I said. All the Russians in the fleet used the English word "okay." As a generic affirmative it couldn't be beat.

"Roger dodger," said Seryozha, rolling the r's. I grinned.

"*Izumrudny, Golden Hope.*"

I scrambled for the radio. "*Izumrudny* back."

"We're hauling back now." Gary's voice sounded different, somehow. Happy.

"We'll slide your way."

"See you in a few. *Golden Hope* out."

"He's hauling back now," I said to Kolya.

The *Izumrudny* went into a ponderous turn and we slowly began easing up to the *Golden Hope.* Within minutes the great steel trawl doors emerged from the water, signaling the arrival of the trawl itself at the *Golden Hope*'s stern ramp.

"Trouble," said Kolya, scanning the water. He reached for the binoculars and, after a few moments, handed them to me: "Nice trouble—he's caught too much fish."

I focused in on the water behind the *Golden Hope* and gasped. The entire length of the trawl, perhaps three hundred feet of webbing, had floated to the surface, crammed with fish. There was probably a hundred tons or more of hake there, with silvery white bellies flashing through the webbing.

"What will the *Golden Hope* do with so much fish?" I asked, glancing at Kolya.

"What can they do?" He shrugged. "They'll have to cut them loose."

I looked back at the trawl. Trawling, I knew, produced a shameful amount of wasted fish, but I'd never really understood just how wasteful until now. Even though most of the fish were still technically alive in the net, their air bladders had expanded as they were lifted to the surface, emerging from the mouth, gills, and anus like membrane balloons to float and prevent the fish from resubmerging. I'd frequently watched such fish flounder at the surface until they'd been picked to death by the ravaging gulls. Now another eighty tons of hake would become bird food. What a terrible waste.

"Good thing the net didn't split," said Kolya. We watched as Brian and Bob started winding the mouth of the trawl onto the reel. It didn't get very far before being stopped by the mass of fish packed into the trawl's midsection. Brian shinnied around the edge of the gantry and climbed down to the trawl net. To my amazement, he stepped out and suddenly began moving away from the boat, walking on water as lightly and firmly as if he'd found God.

He walked on the trawl itself: an undulating path of trapped, bloated, gasping, dying fish. A hundred feet out, Brian bent down near where the codend hooked into the body of the trawl proper and began sawing at the meshes. In a few moments, hake began floating free of the net, and Brian scampered back up the trawl toward the stern ramp, stopping once to jump into the air and kick his heels together.

"Looks like you guys did okay," I said into the radio.

"We try," said Gary modestly. The trawl began again to move slowly on board, winding up and around the giant reel.

Suddenly the webbing seemed to disappear in the water. I grabbed for the binoculars and focused in to see a wall of fish washing out from where the trawl had been.

"Damn," said Gary mildly over the radio. It was the first time I'd heard him swear.

"What happened?" I asked Kolya.

"The trawl's exploded," he said stoically as an immense line of fish began floating toward us. "Let's just hope the codend itself has held together." I scanned the binoculars back and forth past the *Golden Hope*'s stern. Gary was winding the remnants of the trawl on board as fast as he could, hoping to keep the fish from floating out of the codend, if indeed the codend was still intact.

Something was moving in the water behind the *Golden Hope*: the codend, still whole. It approached the boat rapidly. Thirty tons, I thought, if it's a pound.

"We'll be ready in another five minutes or so, Sunshine," said Gary. "We were lucky."

"I'll say."

"The trawl's in pretty bad shape, though. I think we're going to be out of commission here for the rest of the day putting things back together."

"That's too bad." Shevchenko wouldn't be very happy to hear about that. Since we already had more tonnage today than anyone, there would be no way he could talk Leonard into giving him another catcher boat to make up for the loss of the *Golden Hope*, and with the *Yoda* still out of commission and the *Hilo* heading back into port, that meant no more fish today.

"It's going to take Gary the rest of the day to get his trawl fixed," I said to Kolya.

Kolya nodded, looking serious. "I'd better tell the captain."

Shevchenko walked onto the bridge, a strained look on his face.

"Captain," Kolya began.

"Not now, Kolya," said Shevchenko. He turned to me, thrusting a paper into my hand: "This is Ben's radio message to headquarters."

"Yes?" I asked.

He pointed to a word on the message. "Does he really mean to say that?"

I looked at the word. It was "thumb," as in: "I've injured my thumb and will be going to port to have it examined."

"I suppose he meant to say 'thumb'," I said. "Why?"

Shevchenko looked horrified. "Isn't there a synonym he might use?"

Then I remembered. "Thumb" was the code word for "Emergency—Coast Guard assistance required immediately."

"Um, maybe he didn't really mean to use this word," I said. "Let me go ask him." I slipped down the stairs to Ben's cabin, message in hand.

"Ben," I said breathlessly as he opened his cabin door. "Did you really mean to use *this* word in your transmission?"

"What's that? Thumb? Yes. Why?"

I hesitated. I wasn't supposed to know what I knew. For that matter, I thought suddenly, how did Shevchenko know?

"Isn't that your emergency code word?"

Ben looked shocked. "Oh my God, yes it is!"

"Maybe we could change it to hand or something."

"Yes." Ben grabbed the paper and scribbled the offending word out, replacing it with "finger." "There, that should be better."

I trotted back up the stairs and handed the message to Shevchenko. "But I thought you didn't know any English?"

"I don't," said Shevchenko. He glanced at the message, looking relieved.

"Looks like no more fish today," I said, explaining the *Golden Hope*'s situation. "It's going to take Gary the rest of the day to get the net fixed."

Shevchenko thought for a moment. "It doesn't have to take him the rest of the day, you know."

"What do you mean?"

"We have some excellent web men on board. Maybe Gary could use a little assistance."

"I can always ask," I said.

Danielich gazed with awe at the *Golden Hope*'s video machine.

"It's called Pac Man," said Bob, toggling a lever as I translated. "And you try to keep the little man from being eaten." We watched the screen, and Gregori's fingers shifted in sympathetic reaction. He was dying to try it.

"We'd better get busy," said Danielich regretfully. A brief tour of the boat had been in order as we had arrived, but it was time to get down to business. We walked back to the deck and Gary pointed out the damage to the trawl. Danielich nodded. He'd been to sea most of his life—he needed no translation. He grabbed a handful of net and began working back on the trawl, searching for the kernel of the explosion from which to begin piecing the shreds of webbing back together. Gregori and Yuri bent down beside him. In moments the three were busy knotting twine through the torn netting, creating meshes where they had been destroyed, healing rips and tears. On the other side of the deck, Brian and Bob set about the same task.

"How about a cup of coffee?" It was Gary, mug already in hand.

"Thanks," I said, reaching for the cup. We watched Danielich and his crew silently for a while.

"That old codger really knows nets," said Gary admiringly. Indeed, it seemed as if the net was being reborn even as we watched. "At this rate, we'll be back fishing within an hour."

I nodded and gulped my coffee. Even Maxwell House outshone the Russian dreck.

"Heard you had a little run-in with old Jack on the *Hilo*."

I nodded again, glancing over to Gary. He was sparsely bearded and sported a spare tire about his midriff—most of the American skippers did. It was no wonder: they lived at the helm, fortified by coffee if the boat was dry, by whiskey if it wasn't. They had little sleep and almost no exercise— the deck crew had the tough task of hauling gear. The only thing there *was* plenty of was food. Most skippers snacked their way through the repetitious setting and hauling back of the trawl, nibbled through the nervousness of not finding fish, noshed while they passed the trawl off to the Russians, munched through the boring trip to the fishing ground, and gorged themselves on the celebratory (or despairing) way back into port. All this was not to mention the hearty three meals served daily: eggs, steaks (a surprising number of fishermen wouldn't eat fish aboard their boat), bacon, pies, cakes, and cookies of all descriptions. In short, a nutritionist's nightmare.

"Been meaning to talk to you a little about Jack," Gary said. He lifted a plump arm and took a sip from his coffee. Under the fat, I noted, Gary still looked as if he sported a good set of muscles. I wouldn't have liked to tangle with him.

"Can't really say these kinds of things over the radio, but I'd kind of steer clear of Jack if I were you. He can be just a *leetle* temperamental."

I raised my eyebrows.

"Couple of months ago he bought his wife a brand new Porsche for her birthday. He found out last week his wife was cheating on him," Gary paused and took another sip from his coffee, staring vaguely at the deck. "He took a sledge hammer to the car."

I shivered. What had I said to Jack last time I'd seen him?

"Not that Jack's that much worse than any of the others out here. It's Gunnar up in Alaska you really have to be careful of."

I'd heard of Gunnar. Last year he'd gotten riled and taken a few pot shots at Leonard with a twenty-two.

Danielich motioned to me and I went over to translate as he explained what he needed.

Forty-five minutes later, the trawl was as good as new and we were back in the lifeboat, heading for the *Izumrudny*.

"You ready?" Shevchenko yelled down at us. I'd been wondering why we hadn't been hoisted aboard yet. Now I knew.

Ben's legs appeared over the side, then the rest of his body. His arms flopped limply. Apparently the commissar had served double duty as ship's anesthetist. Ben was definitely feeling no pain, and literally at the end of his rope. The Russians lowered him quickly down into the lifeboat, where Danielich cradled him like a baby in his lap.

I thumbed my walkie-talkie: "*Hilo, Izumrudny.*"

"*Hilo* back,"

"We've got your passenger ready."

"Fine. Haul him over."

Ben wriggled and Danielich propped him against the seat. "You okay?" I asked. The lifeboat did a swooping roll and Ben vomited over the side. My walkie-talkie crackled to life:

"Barbara, is this you?" asked a voice in Russian.

"Of course it's me," I answered, irritated. The Russians hardly ever spoke to me on the radio. "Who are you?"

"Barbara, I need to know where my cabin is." It was the mellifluous voice of the political commissar, overlaid with more than a soupçon of vodka.

"Go ask Shevchenko," I said, glancing guiltily at the others. I turned the radio off.

Ben stopped retching and leaned back into the boat. "I just want to die."

"Ask him how his hand is," said Danielich. I translated.

"It's the only part of me that doesn't hurt." Ben looked at his bandaged hand for a moment and then leaned back over the edge of the lifeboat.

Charlie's deck crew workers plucked Ben out of the lifeboat. "Don't worry," shouted Charlie from the back window of the wheel house. "We'll take *very* good care of him." Ben gazed piteously at me—I remembered the incident with the *Playboy*s and the chewing tobacco and wondered what Charlie had in mind.

In moments we were off again: "Where are we going?" I shouted to Danielich over the sputter of the motor. He shrugged and pointed to the chief mate.

"To the *Alexandrovsk*," said the chief. "We're picking up a few supplies and exchanging films." The Soviets had only a limited supply of movies, and they exchanged them with the other ships in the fleet at every opportunity.

I settled back to enjoy the ride. I rarely had an opportunity to leave the ship, and as far as I was concerned, today the lifeboat could keep right on going across the Pacific.

"Look, a sunfish," said Danielich, grabbing my arm. The name was apt: sunfish enjoyed basking on their sides just below the water's surface, soaking in the sun's rays like the most lascivious of nude bathers. I'd seen them before, but never so close. The sunfish rippled in the waves, a sturdy, two-foot round, black-and-yellowish discus. Then it was gone.

The sea today was populated with hoards of jellyfish that had appeared from nowhere like a swarm of locusts. The deck crew hated them—they clung to the nets like so much snot and gummed the machinery at every turn. But I loved watching their clear, nearly luminescent bodies bobbing past, catching glimpses of their tendrils as the waves washed up, like evanescent windows on the underworld of the sea. A log drifted past, a gaggle of common murres perched in a cocky row along its length.

We neared the *Alexandrovsk*, the chief mate gunning the engine to swing the boat around in a dashing curve that ended with us paralleling the larger boat. I ducked as ropes were thrown down, and in seconds we were fast.

"Halloo, Barbara."

I glanced up, searching the faces.

"It's me—Matt." A friendly, bearded man smiled and waved—Matthew Hanley, the *Alexandrovsk*'s rep. I'd never met him, but I'd talked to him over the radio. "Why don't you come up and visit for a few minutes?" he said. "It'll take them a while to get everything sorted out, anyway."

Why not? "Sure," I said. Matt's face disappeared and a rope ladder flipped down toward us. I climbed aboard.

"Pleased to meet you," said Matt, helping me over the railing. "It's good to see another American."

"I'll say." I'd been wanting to meet Matt—I'd heard a lot about him. Every great once in a while, a linguist comes along who is a Stradivarius among more pedestrian fiddles, or at least a Cremona. Matt was a member of that select breed—he spoke Russian like a native, although he'd learned Russian as an adult.

The "normal" path to a solid second language in modern day America is through four years of study at your handy dandy local institute of higher learning. Based purely on my own highly suspect observations, about 50 percent of students find the mental contortions of Russian grammar simply too mind-boggling to deal with. Of those who *could* handle the grammar, about 70 percent had tin ears—their Russian was heavily accented, almost incomprehensible, at least to a Russian.

That left perhaps 15 percent of the student population capable of learning to speak this second language well. Let us say you are in that elite group. You slave away, spending hour after tedious hour memorizing vocabulary lists, practicing unnatural grammatical formulations until they become natural, and twisting your mouth to perform arcane verbal gymnastics. You are proud of your prowess, and eager to make use of your hard-earned skills. So you do something stupid, like pick up a copy of *War and Peace* to read, or, even worse, strike up a conversation with your neighboring Russian émigré. If you're smart, you give up your language study at that point. If you're not, you go on to graduate school and *really* begin to learn the language.

But through all this, you at least have the consolation of knowing that your fellow students, if they've gotten this far, are slaving away just as you are—studying until three in the morning to cram for that final exam; carrying vocabulary cards on the bus; taping verb conjugations to their bathroom mirror. You have that consolation, until you meet someone like Matthew Hanley.

Matthew had taken to Russian like pollution took to the Great Lakes: with all-pervasive, deadly ease. From highly reputable sources (well, all right, Laura), I'd heard that Matthew had an exceptional memory; where I spent an hour becoming truly conversant with a list of, say, forty vocabulary words, he had only to read such a list once to know everything on it. He'd read every Russian dictionary he could obtain, and knew Russian slang and colloquial usage better than most Russians. A natural mimic, his accent was flawless. Matthew was a human sponge for Russian, indeed, for any language he dabbled in. Although I'd read about people like him (the pages of adventure novels are frequently populated with his ilk), it was disheartening to find that he actually existed.

Matthew, however, had carried his passion for Russian to questionable extremes. He'd switched religions from staid Lutheran to mystical Russian Orthodox, took on a Russian mistress wherever he went (for their language abilities, or so he said), and of course, was well on his way to complete alcoholism.

"It's my birthday today," said Matt, leaning heavily against the railing, his eyes bloodshot and shiny. "The party's beginning in about another half hour, after we take a tow from the *Plunkett*. Why don't you stay?"

"The lifeboat will be leaving in a few minutes. And we're due to take one more tow from the *Golden Hope* today."

"Nyet problem," said Matt. "You can do the transfer from a distance." He meant having me listen in on the radio as the transfer took place, with the *Golden Hope*, the *Izumrudny*, and myself all monitoring one channel. Whenever Gary needed the *Izumrudny* to do something, he'd tell me in English, then I'd get right back on the radio to repeat the request in Russian for the *Izumrudny*'s benefit. Officially, transfers at a distance were not allowed—it was slower, and in an industry where fatal accidents could occur in the blink of an eye, slower meant more dangerous. It also meant there was no "impartial" observer watching the transfer to determine liability if something untoward should occur. In practice, however, transfers at a distance took place all the time; as the working relationship between the Soviets and Americans solidified, the transfers had become, for the most part, routine. Many a rep had been known to monitor a transfer with party noises going on in the background. These boats also had a suspicious number of accidents.

"I don't think Shevchenko would be too happy if I stayed."

"Shevchenko can shove it up his ass," said Matt pleasantly. His face split into a wicked grin: "Your captain has been busting his butt to be top boat so he could be first at the off-load vessel when it arrived this evening. The *Izumrudny* is nearly full now—another haul should just about top it off. But the off-loader's been delayed, so now Shevchenko's going to have to sit around for a week or so while everybody else fills up."

"How do you know?" I asked. "Shevchenko hasn't said anything."

"He wouldn't. But he used to work with my skipper. Under him, actually. They hate each other. I'll bet my captain talks to me a little more than yours does." He straightened. "Want a quick tour of the ship while you're here?"

"I don't know," I hesitated. It looked like the *Izumrudny*'s lifeboat was getting ready to go again. Matt followed my gaze.

"They've still got the cabbages to load. Come on." He thudded down the passageway toward the bridge and I followed, glancing behind me toward where Danielich stood, lowering the last of a pile of boxes down to the lifeboat.

The *Alexandrovsk* was a "routine mother" like the *Izumrudny*, and, I quickly learned, much like her right down to the stink in the air and the bilious black smoke and floating bits of fish entrails in our wake. We ended up in Matt's cabin—a more spacious affair than mine, where Matt pulled a beer from a small refrigerator, popped the top, and handed it to me.

"I should think the lifeboat'll be leaving any minute," I said.

"It left ten minutes ago," Matt said. "We told them the skipper had authorized you to stay."

I took the beer, temporarily at a loss for words. "Shevchenko will just send the boat back over when he finds out I'm not on it," I said at last. Whatever else he was, Shevchenko was as much a stickler as I was about me being on the bridge whenever a transfer took place.

"The lifeboat will have a lot of fun trying to catch us. We're already two miles from the *Izumrudny*." He took another swallow of beer and smiled.

I'd been kidnapped.

Chapter Seven
"Hello, I am Your American Suitcase"

WHEN YOU ARE stinking drunk, there is nothing more breathtakingly beautiful than riding an open lifeboat in heavy seas by moonlight at two in the morning. The waves curl lovingly upwards to plant salty, wet kisses on your brow; the foam froths by as if you were riding on a wedding cake. Moonshine fills the sky, pouring though the edges of silver clouds, forming halos everywhere you look. You anticipate the swoops and dives of your boat, and roller-coaster-like, you wedge yourself into your seat and shriek for the very glee of it, for the wonder of it. We swooped through another watery glissando, and I gazed dopily through the darkness at the lights of the *Muis Yegorova*, a quarter mile ahead of us.

Matt had been right—the *Izumrudny*'s holds had been topped off with the *Golden Hope*'s last tow, and now I was jobless until the off-loader came, anywhere between two days and a week from now. We'd partied relentlessly aboard the *Alexandrovsk*. Matt's captain, Anatoly Vasilievich, among others, had been eager to test the low reputation of American women: I'd spent several evenings being plied with drink, keeping an elbow cocked.

Anatoly's opinions as to the looseness of American women were not unfounded; many of the female reps in the fleet ended up with Russian paramours. Months at sea with a very male crew tended, willy-nilly, to break down inhibitions. The consequences of an affair varied. Frequently, the goon—the fleet's KGB agent—made an appearance on board and took a cabin next to the unfortunate paramour, the better, apparently, to monitor conversations. Most often, that person simply didn't show up again the next year. Gone—who knew where. The Americans had their own problems: at least one rep that I knew of had venereal warts. The Russian practice of reusing needles had contributed to the spread of AIDS, but from what I'd heard, no one in the fleet had had a case. Yet.

Laura, sensing party activity aboard the *Alexandrovsk* and intuiting that I had become a free agent—or loose cannon—with the topping off of the *Izumrudny*, had invited me over to the *Yegorova* for a few more days of vacation after my interlude on the *Alexandrovsk*. Captain Alex had needed little coercion to send a lifeboat over to pick me up as Matt's birthday party began to spin into entropic disarray. I had nothing but the clothes on my back, but given my present circumstances—profound inebriation—I wasn't particularly concerned.

In one of those time leaps that somehow occur only when you are drunk, our lifeboat was suddenly beside the *Yegorova*, bumping washboard-like in the low chop of her leeward side as the men secured the block and tackle to the rings on the lifeboat's bow and stern.

A familiar face peered over the *Yegorova*'s railing: Laura. "Hey, Barb, long time no *vizhu*. Wanna *peet'* some more?" She tapped her throat meaningfully, the rep Creole adding luster to her speech. I gave her the high sign as the lifeboat was hoisted aboard, and she grabbed me in a tipsy embrace and dragged me off toward the captain's cabin.

"Randy from the *Karenga*'s here," she said. "He doesn't speak Russian for shit, but he's okay. He's been promising me a candlelight dinner to get lit by, and now he's finally paying up." We reached the captain's cabin. Laura whacked the door with her fist and proceeded in without waiting for a reply. The usual Russian custom on board ships is to simply galumph into a cabin. A knock is *not* a question as to whether or not anyone's home, but rather a warning that whoever's knocking is coming in. The feeling is that if you really didn't want somebody to come in you'd lock the door.

A small forest of candles embedded in a pool of wax at the center of the table lit the cabin. The flames flickered as the ship swayed, sending shadows chasing over bottles, hands, and faces. Smoke from the deadly Russian cigarettes choked the crowded room. Even thicker than the smoke was the reeking, musky odor of vodka and sour beer.

"I don't think you've had a chance to meet Leonard yet," said Laura, introducing me. Leonard smiled crookedly and said something incomprehensible in an alcoholic slur, wiping a hand on oily black hair. "And here's Randy. I believe you already know Pavel Alexeyevich."

I did a double take. Pavel Alexeyevich was the *Izumrudny*'s doctor. "What's he doing here?" I asked in startled English.

"Our second mate, Misha, had an abscessed tooth," Laura said in Russian. She pointed across the table to a gaunt young man with a swollen cheek seated beside Leonard. "Our doctor is just *awful*, and besides, he doesn't know anything about pulling teeth. So we got your doctor to pull it."

God, and I thought *our* doctor was bad.

Misha smiled, a drunken, painful smile. "He did a good job, too. Where'd you learn how to pull teeth so well, Pavel Alexeyevich?"

"A friend taught me," said the doctor off-handedly.

"Actually, this party's for Misha," Laura whispered in English. I nodded. Since there were no anesthetics aboard any of the boats, alcohol was the only pain killer around—as Ben had discovered. The usual technique for minor—and major—surgery was to get the patient drunk and hold him down while the doctor performed the operation, then keep him drunk afterwards until the worst of the pain wore off.

"Barbara, you are here at last!" I was enveloped in a hairy embrace by Captain Alex, shit-faced as always. He grabbed a bottle off the table and poured me a shot. "It's tequila. I saved the worm for you."

I downed the shot. The worm hit bottom and found new life; I burped.

"Coffee makes good chaser," Alex said. He poured a cup of hot water from a kettle perched precariously on a ledge, then dumped what looked to be a half cup of instant coffee into the mug, stirring vigorously. "Bottoms up."

I drank. The coffee tasted like acid, and was the equivalent, I knew, of about twelve No-Doze.

Laura was now busy translating for Randy in the corner as the doctor told a joke. Randy caught my gaze and motioned me over.

"Pleased to meet you at last," he said. I recognized his deep baritone from the radio. He was a little thinner than I'd imagined, with startlingly platinum blond hair. We shook hands and he scooted in to make room for me at the table.

"I'm what you might call a token rep," he said, smiling. I couldn't help but smile back. "It would really help if I could speak Russian."

"What are you doing out here if you can't speak Russian?" I asked.

"I think the company liked my resume. I've got a master's in business administration from Harvard; my specialty's marketing. They want me to get a little experience out on the boats before I hit land to do my thing." He tipped his glass in my direction. "This *is* an experience, but I'm not sure it's going to help my marketing."

"Did you ever study Russian?" I asked loudly. The second mate had fetched a guitar, and despite his swollen jaw, now sang handily.

"I took one semester as an undergraduate five years ago. When I got out here to the *Karenga* I introduced myself by saying," Randy's mouth screwed up and an abysmal imitation of Russian followed: "Hello, I'm your American suitcase."

I suppressed a grin. Laura didn't.

"*Chemodan, chelovek*—suitcase, person—geeze, they all sound pretty much the same to me." Randy took another hefty belt from his glass. "You think that's bad? You should see me going through my 'two syllables' and 'sounds like' routines on the bridge. Thank God I'm going back in next week. I'm afraid I'm going to get someone killed."

Fleet scuttlebutt was that he'd already come close. Last week the *Raven's* steering had gone out just as one of their men had gotten his foot caught in the ropes of a codend being passed off to the Russians. The *Raven's* skipper had screamed at Randy to do something, but Randy could not tell the Russians what was going on. In desperation he'd finally told the crew to cut the cable, which they did just as the Americans cut the cable on their side. The crewman had been pulled free, and the twenty-ton codend, free now of any restraints, had sunk like a stone.

Randy poured himself another drink and reached over to splash vodka into my coffee cup. Through the porthole I could see daylight breaking on the horizon. I leaned back in my seat, giddy, my ears buzzing from the caffeine. I was exhausted, but it felt good to relax aboard Captain Alex's loosely run ship, away from the Shevchenko-brand of communism.

"Hey, you guys want to watch TV?" Captain Alex's voice rose momentarily above the din.

"No," we chorused. Laura looked disgusted. "There's nothing like translating reruns of 'The Incredible Hulk' to make you realize the depths American culture has sunk to."

"What about the religious program that comes on at tea time?" I asked.

Laura laughed. "I told everybody that one was a sitcom."

I mulled it over: the latest twist in creative translation.

Alex's voice rose once more above the hubbub. "How about some dancing?"

"Only if you've got some good sex-musik," said the doctor. Sex-musik was the Russian appellation for any type of American music with grunts, pants, and wails.

"Michael Jackson?" the captain asked, pronouncing it the Russian way—Meekhail Djackson.

The doctor gave an approving thumbs up.

We pushed the table back and danced for hours. When Laura and I finally tired, Klavdia, the captain's waitress, took over the floor, and the music went from funk to an elfin-wild folk as the sounds of balalaikas, concertinas, and whistles filled the air. Each time the *Yegorova* thudded into a wave, the record skipped, and Klavdia gave an extra laughing twirl, screaming and stomping like a banshee. As the record shuddered toward a final rousing crescendo, she stepped recklessly onto a chair, and the captain and the doctor, mindful of what was next, grabbed the few undrunk bottles from her path. In seconds she was up on the table, and empty bottles were flying everywhere as she kicked with wild abandon. Then the captain put on more music and the men drew Laura and me back to our feet to dance again.

We danced until the sun clawed its way high into the sky, glaring through the curtains like an unwelcome guest. We danced until we were all nearly too tired to move, until the candles had guttered themselves out in the heaving pools of wax that had grown like mountains on the table. Then the doctor and Klavdia disappeared, Randy and Leonard passed out, and Laura lent me a pair of shorts and a clean shirt.

Fifteen minutes later the survivors, Captain Alex, Laura, and I, were up on the flying bridge, bedecked with reflectors and slathered with tanning lotion, to sunbathe in the chill air of the cloudless maritime sky.

"How do you like working with Shevchenko?" Alex asked. He was lying in the netting that stored the ship's vegetables, lounging as if it were a hammock. His bulging beer belly spilled over a skimpy pair of red shorts; with his sunglasses he looked like a youngish Santa Claus on a Hawaiian vacation. As he talked, he rooted around the vegetables at his side, pulling a cabbage from among the turnips and onions. He peeled a leaf off and took a bite, staring expectantly at me.

"He's different," I admitted, watching as a sea gull hovered above us. "I still can't really figure him out."

"He believes in the system," said Alex. "We all do, to some extent, because with Russians the only alternative to the system is anarchy. You're the first American Shevchenko's ever met, by the way. He's scared of you."

"Of me?"

"Yes." He pulled another leaf off the cabbage and stuck it in his mouth. "His commissar's a stupid man. Those are the most dangerous kind. And the commissar's never met any Americans before, either. They both know you're a spy, and they're afraid you'll contaminate the crew."

So Captain Alex had me figured for a spy, too. At least he didn't seem to care about it.

"Now, my commissar is smart. He stays out of the way, and we all just hate him at a distance." Alex turned his full attention to the head of cabbage, eating the raw leaves with gusto. He offered a piece to me. I shook my head. "But it's all changing. Who knows where we'll end up."

The *Yegorova* began to turn, and the wind shifted, blowing in on the flying bridge from the unprotected railings on the side. I suddenly realized I was cold, and without the constant drip of caffeine into my system to take the edge off the exhaustion, I began to fade. Laura lay on the deck between us, snoozing in the sunshine. She rolled over as the wind hit her, blinking in the brightness.

"Barb, is that you?" she asked.

"I think so," I said.

"Why aren't you sleeping?" she asked. "We're heading into port this afternoon—you need some rest before we go. By the way—they're sending me to Alaska."

Reps in Alaska received up to $100 a day for their services, which sounds pretty good until you realize that you actually got paid about minimum wage, since you were expected to work close to twenty-four hours a day. The word "work" in the Alaskan fleet is not quite correct; what you really do is *stay awake*. Fishing for yellow-fin sole goes on round the clock, with a codend being taken on board every two to three hours, night or day. All of the Soviet trawlers in the yellow-fin fleet are the older variety, and you must stand outside in the freezing cold (if you're lucky) or sleet (if you're not) in order to watch the codend being brought on board. By the time you've gone inside and warmed up from a bout on deck, it's time to go outside again. Sleep consists of tiny catnaps caught here and there between codends, meals, drunken bacchanals, and simply staring at the walls in utter exhaustion. Come to think of it, it sounded a lot like being down here in the hake fleet, but worse.

A rep in Alaska, it seemed, had quit when he was unable to get medication to help control his herpes while out at sea. (There *are* no secrets on boats.) The fleet needed an experienced replacement and fast. Laura wasn't too thrilled at the idea of going, but this was her second season with Marine Resources, so management tapped her for the job. Leonard had decided to send both Laura and me in on the Coos Bay bound *Golden Hope*—Laura to catch a plane, and me to get a few hours shore leave before the off-loader arrived on Thursday and the *Izumrudny* was back in commission.

We left at two that afternoon, with Captain Alex seeing us off, alternately waving from the railing and turning to gulp beer through the open porthole of his cabin. Gary, Laura, and I exchanged a few perfunctory comments as we boarded, then I hit the sack in my clothing to sleep seventeen hours straight.

We arrived in town at 8:00 a.m., with six hours ashore together to do as we pleased before the *Golden Hope* put out to sea again and Laura's plane took off for Portland. Most of the morning we spent buying gifts, getting film developed, eating unaccustomed fresh fruit on the steps of the local supermarket, and having diarrhea.

"Maybe we'd better head back to the *Golden Hope*," I said, as Laura looked down to check her list. "Your plane's due to leave in two hours."

Laura gazed at me as if I were a complete nincompoop. "We haven't hit the most important place of all yet." She folded her list and stuck it back in her pocket, turning to begin walking briskly down the street. "Come on." I lowered my head and trudged after her, arms loaded down with groceries and four fat Sears catalogs.

The bell of the liquor store jingled pleasantly as we stepped inside. Laura marched straight to the counter, pulling a wallet from her pocket.

"May I help you?" asked the clerk.

Laura paused to eye the shelves. "I'll take a case of tequila, a case of whiskey, a case of peach schnapps, and..." she hesitated again, consulting either memory or whim: "...and a couple cases of Bud. Oh yeah, and two cases of Michelob."

"Will that be all?" The clerk looked bored. I remembered that Coos Bay was a fishing town.

"A case of scotch, too."

"No vodka?" I asked in a low voice.

"Alex can't stand American vodka." She opened her wallet and peeled off a stack of crisp one hundred dollar bills. I watched, mouth ajar, as the clerk handed her a couple of ones in change and stepped into the back room.

"Where did you get that kind of money?" I asked.

"Frank, the captain of the *Jackdaw*, gave it to me to get presents for Captain Alex."

"Oh." Fishermen were nothing if not expansive when they wanted to be. I was certain the *Jackdaw* would be getting preferential treatment from

Captain Alex. "How are we going to get this stuff back over to the *Golden Hope*?"

Coos Bay is laid out on both sides of a large estuary at the mouth of the Coos River. The town proper is situated on the southern side of the estuary; the *Golden Hope* was at a small boat dock on the northern side. To get across the estuary Laura and I had borrowed a small boat. Actually, it wasn't a boat, but rather a homemade platform consisting of two layers of railroad ties bolted together to form a heavy, tipsy raft with a motor rigged to one end. The dock owners used the whole ungainly rig to putter from one pier to the next without going around by land. The whole contraption—a wobbly four feet wide by ten feet in length with no railings—was only inches above the waterline. I didn't think it would hold one case of booze safely, much less eight.

Laura winked at me and snapped the wallet shut. "You got a phone?" she asked the clerk as he shuffled back out toward the counter with a pile of boxes on a dolly.

"Outside."

I opened the door as the clerk scuttled past; within a few minutes we were loading cases of booze into a taxi, along with the rest of our purchases.

"Take this to the *Golden Hope* on the north dock," Laura said. She pulled a crisp fifty from her wallet and thrust it in the driver's hand. The driver grinned. "Sure thing."

"Our work is complete," she said, turning to me as the taxi pulled away. "Now. Fast Food."

"Shouldn't we be getting back to the *Golden Hope*?" I asked again.

"Where's your sense of pride?" Laura said, head high. "We haven't hit shore until we've hit McDonalds."

We headed down the block to a set of familiar golden arches, where Laura ordered onion rings, french fries, a milk shake, and three Big Macs. She ate in reverential silence, venturing to speak only as we left to ask the clerk if there was a Kentucky Fried Chicken nearby.

"Jesus Christ, Laura, you're going to founder," I exploded. "We'd better get back to the boat."

"We've got plenty of time," said Laura, but we turned our steps back toward the edge of town, where we'd parked our raft against a stand of cattails below a Dunkin' Donuts poised over the estuary. Our pace had slowed considerably—we'd both been out to sea for close to three months now, and between the lack of fresh food, minimal exercise, dearth of sleep, and relentless partying, we were both flabby and out of shape.

"I don't remember there being mud flats," said Laura as we walked along the edge of the highway, glancing out toward the broad, low waters of the Coos River. A heron perched one-legged atop a lone post standing a hundred feet out in the midst of the muck.

"I thought this was a river," I said, "but it looks like it's close enough to the sea to get a tide here."

"I think you're right," said Laura. "And you know what? I think the tide's going out." We looked at each other and broke into a shambling run.

The water was just lapping away from the sides of our platform as we got to it. Laura got down on her hands and knees on the dirt bank and began pushing. "Come on," she yelled. "I'm going to miss my plane." I stepped cautiously onto the deceptively smooth surface of the mud and instantly sank to my thighs. "Push, damn it," Laura yelled.

We pushed with all our might, then got around behind the contraption into waist deep mud and pulled. The heavy raft didn't budge.

"Any more bright ideas?" I asked.

Laura glanced across the mouth of the estuary to the north shore a half mile away. The receding tide revealed stretches of stinking mud-flats. A quarter-mile long raft of logs passed in the water between us and the north shore. Up river, a barge load of timber was just coming into view. "Swim?" she said hopefully.

"Not on your life," I said.

It took a slimy one hundred dollar bill to convince the taxi driver to take us. Laura missed her plane. I headed back out to sea with the *Golden Hope*.

And I found Ben.

"I don't know what hit me," said Ben, sipping coffee with a sideways grimace as we idled, feet propped on chairs, in the *Golden Hope*'s galley. Both Ben's eyes were purple, with flecks of red, green, and turquoise making for a nearly iridescent display. A cut ran from his mouth along his chin toward his ear. Between his face and his bandaged hand he looked as if he'd been in a car wreck.

"All I said was that I was working out on the Joint Venture," he continued.

"That's enough," I said. "JV people aren't always real popular in this town." Ben had made the mistake of talking to some fishermen in the bathroom of a north shore bar the *Hilo*'s crew had taken him to. He'd been dragged out the back and clubbed silly: local fishermen didn't take too kindly to people working with the foreign competition. The *Hilo*, having little patience for observers, had simply left him behind when they were due to leave and Ben hadn't shown up.

"I should have told them I was an observer," Ben said morosely.

"It wouldn't have helped. They might have beat you up even worse."

Ben nodded and glanced back out the *Golden Hope's* porthole. I could see the fleet growing larger in the distance—nearly a dozen Soviet trawlers, and even more American catcher boats. The fleet had moved closer to the mouth of the Coos River while we'd been in to port—it took only two hours to get back out to join them. According to Leonard, the transport vessel had shown up as soon as Laura and I had left the fleet, and the *Izumrudny* was busy now off-loading her packed holds.

"Barb?" Gary shouted down from the bridge.

"Coming." I slid out from behind the galley table and trotted up the steep and narrow steps to the bridge.

Gary's human deck cranes, Brian and Bob, were former carpenters, and it showed in every inch of the *Golden Hope*. The bridge itself was a cunning mixture of paneling and equipment—the area around the captain's chair in particular seemed a study in space-age technology artfully inter-twined around fine old-fashioned woodwork. Fish finders, Loran (a type of radar), and other navigational equipment were placed below the front windows in a low semi-circle around the chair. Above the windows was a row of six radios. Microphone cables dangled everywhere. The captain's chair itself was plush, luxurious leather, trimmed with seat belts. Gary swiv-eled to greet me as I emerged from below.

"Leonard's calling you on channel nine," he said, holding forth a microphone.

"*Muis Yegorova*, this is the *Golden Hope*," I said.

"Hi, Barb," came Leonard's voice. "Sorry we didn't get much of a chance to talk when we finally saw each other."

"Sometimes the work's just too demanding," I said. "What's up?"

"Bad news for you. I was over on the *Izumrudny* today, poking around while we're all tied up together with the transport vessel. I'm afraid the goon's just taken up residence on your boat. You'd better be careful."

"Thanks for the warning," I said. "*Golden Hope* out." I turned to a questioning Gary and shook my head.

The fleet KGB agent had arrived on the scene.

"Glad to have you back aboard," said Shevchenko, giving me a courteous hand over the side of the lifeboat. Ben, who needed more assistance than I, was left to help himself. "We missed you. That goddamned *Alexandrovsk*—we nearly lost the *Golden Hope*'s codend without you here. I'm going to tie you onto the ship with a little golden chain. No more leaving the ship for you." He sounded, surprisingly enough, as·if he meant it.

Strange as it seemed, I'd missed the *Izumrudny*, too—even Shevchenko. If nothing else, I'd missed the challenge of dealing with him.

A shriek—half terrified, half delighted—sounded behind me, and I turned toward the bow to see a barred metal contraption, rather like an oversized bird cage, passing on an overhead series of cables from the transport vessel onto the *Izumrudny*. The cook and her assistant, plump as dumplings, were stuffed inside.

"That looks like fun," I said, nodding toward the cage as it swooped over the open holds to land on the far side of the ship. Lena screamed again as a final bit of momentum tipped the basket with a crash onto its side. The crane operator climbed down and dragged them out, giggling with excitement.

"That's what you'll use to go between ships, if you go," said Shevchenko.

"Fine with me." It looked like *lots* of fun.

"Yes. Females are only allowed to use the basket when going between ships," said the commissar, coming up to stand beside Shevchenko. A pudgy young man with a broad, baby-smooth face took his place beside him. The man wore a bright yellow polyester shirt and alligator shoes.

"Women must only use the basket?" I asked, my voice suddenly low. I would make it a point not to ride the basket. "How do the men go across?"

"They use the Jacob's ladder," said the commissar. "I'll show you." We trooped over to the *Izumrudny*'s starboard side, which bobbed against the transport vessel. Rubber bumpers, six feet long and four feet in diameter, bounced in the water between the two boats, squealing with rubbery melancholy. A rope ladder looped fifteen feet down the *Izumrudny*'s side to curl back and climb up the side of the transport vessel. As I watched, a man began climbing down the ladder, slowing as he neared the point where the ropes curved back up. The transport vessel rose on the back of a wave, and the crewman was suddenly balancing precariously on all fours as the ladder shifted, pulling out and up beneath him. If the *Izumrudny* had risen any higher, the man's feet would have been up over his head. The wave passed and the *Izumrudny* eased back down; the man grabbed the rungs of the far side of the ladder, climbing ignominiously up to the transport vessel to the tune of raucous catcalls.

"That's why we don't allow women to go over on the Jacob's ladder," said the commissar, with a certain amount of satisfaction.

"I should think you wouldn't allow the men to go over on it," I said. The polyester-clad man looked as if he were hiding a smile. I looked questioningly at Shevchenko.

"This is Vladimir Ivanich," said the captain. "He's the, ah, senior fleet refrigeration engineer."

Vladimir looked a little young to be a senior anything to me. And somehow I couldn't picture a fleet refrigeration engineer wearing alligator shoes. Everyone looked uncomfortable. So this is the goon, I thought.

"I guess I'll go get washed up," I said. I grabbed the paper bags full of purchases I'd made on shore and headed for my cabin.

Irena was busy preparing for dinner in the mess next door, and after taking a spit bath and donning a clean set of clothes, I greeted her with a hug and settled down in a chair near her station, handing over a heavy Sears catalog that I'd wrapped in a newspaper. "A present," I said.

Irena looked surprised and grabbed the package with both hands. She sat in a nearby chair and carefully unwrapped and folded the newspaper.

"Oh, Barbara," she said, her eyes misting as she saw the catalog. "This is so wonderful of you." She flipped the book open to gaze dreamily at the slick pages before her. "Would you," she stopped and swallowed. "Would you autograph this for me?"

"Sure," I said, embarrassed. I took the heavy book back and pulled a pen from my shirt pocket: "To my good friend Irena, from Barbara," I wrote on the cover. Irena smiled and clasped the book to her chest. In celebration, we slipped next door to my cabin to open a screw-top bottle of currant wine that I'd bought on shore. We chugged it as if it were cherry pop, laughing like school children.

We shoved off from the transport vessel around supper time, and with nothing better to do I went up to the bridge to find Shevchenko pacing the deck in a foul mood. We were supposed to have headed out immediately from the transport vessel to pick up a codend from the *Golden Hope*, but Leonard had decided at the last minute to instead give the *Hope*'s tow to the *Alexandrovsk*, whose captain had complained that he needed the fish more than we did. The *Golden Hope* was nearly ready for the transfer, but now the *Alexandrovsk* wasn't answering the radio.

"*Alexandrovsk*, this is the *Golden Hope*," Gary's voice crackled over the receiver. "*Alexandrovsk*, *Golden Hope*." There was no answer. I knew without being told what was going on: the *Alexandrovsk*'s rep was busy partying in the captain's cabin—no one bothered to monitor the radio on the bridge.

"They take my fish, and then they don't even bother to answer the radio," said Shevchenko. He glanced angrily out the windows toward the *Golden Hope*, a couple miles off our port bow. The *Alexandrovsk* drifted aimlessly a mile or so to her side.

"*Alexandrovsk*, *Golden Hope*," came Gary's forlorn voice over the radio: "*Alexandrovsk?*"

Shevchenko smashed a fist down on the window sill. "Helmsman! Fifteen degrees to port!"

"What speed?" Seryozha asked.

"Full speed," snapped Shevchenko.

The *Izumrudny* spun slowly to port, and I went to pour myself a cup of tea, wondering what Shevchenko was up to. Vladimir, I noticed, had crept unseen onto the bridge and was now seated near the fore windows, watching me.

"*Izumrudny*, this is the *Golden Hope*. You there, Barb?"

"Right here, Gary."

"Is that you I see coming up on me from the south?"

"Sure is."

"Maybe you could give me a hand trying to raise the *Alexandrovsk*."

"No problem," I said. I called the *Alexandrovsk* several times, with no answer. Shevchenko's face wore a growing look of happiness.

We circled as we approached the *Golden Hope*, coming around behind the starboard side to sweep past her. Just as if, I noticed, we were picking up a codend.

A staccato blast of Russian emerged suddenly from the static: "*Izumrudny*, *Alexandrovsk*. What are you doing by the *Golden Hope?*"

In three steps Shevchenko was at the radio. "You weren't answering your radio, so Leonard gave the *Golden Hope*'s fish back to us. We just picked up the codend."

The radio's silence was suddenly louder than words.

"Those were our fish," came a new voice at last: deeper, sterner, more authoritative. The *Alexandrovsk*'s captain, I presumed. Shevchenko's former boss.

Shevchenko grinned, glancing behind us at the *Izumrudny*'s empty decks. "It was a beautiful codend, Anatoly Vasilievich. Thirty tons; all good sized hake."

"You bastard," said the *Alexandrovsk*'s captain.

"You should answer your radio occasionally," said Shevchenko pleasantly. Behind me, Seryozha began guffawing.

More silence. Then an accented English came back on the air: one of the mates, most likely, who could speak a little English. "*Golden Hope*, this is *Alexandrovsk*."

"*Golden Hope* back."

"You give *Izumrudny* codend?" said the accented voice. Shevchenko bent over and began laughing.

Gary hesitated, unsure. "No, I haven't given the *Izumrudny* my codend. I'm ready to have it picked up, though."

"You give *Izumrudny* codend?" the voice repeated.

"No, I didn't," said Gary. There was another long pause.

"*Izumrudny, Alexandrovsk*," the radio crackled. It was Matt's voice, sounding as if it came from fifty fathoms. "Hey, you there, Barb?"

I took the mike from Shevchenko. He winked at me, and I winked back. "Right here, Matt. What can I do for you?"

"The crew over here is pretty excited. They tell me you've just picked up the *Golden Hope*'s codend. That was supposed to be our fish."

"There must be some mistake," I said. "We didn't pick up the *Golden Hope*'s codend. In fact, I think Gary's trying to get hold of you right now for you to pick it up."

"That's right," Gary interjected.

There was a disgruntled silence again from the *Alexandrovsk* as I translated my exchange for Shevchenko's benefit.

"*Izumrudny, Alexandrovsk*," came the voice of the *Alexandrovsk*'s captain.

"*Izumrudny* here," said Shevchenko. He reached over to switch the channel, still smiling.

My eyes drifted over to Vladimir. He avoided my gaze and jotted something down on a small pad of paper at his side.

I went downstairs to find Irena crying alone at her station in the officer's mess.

"What do you think the problem could be?" I asked Ben, as we sat popping popcorn in his cabin. The pungent odor wafted through the room, nearly eliminating the stink of the fish-meal plant.

Ben shook the pan on the makeshift burner and looked out the porthole toward the back deck. We'd taken our second tow of the day a half hour before. We weren't expecting another for three hours, so we had time to spare. "I think it's that damn KGB agent, what's his name..."

"Vladimir Ivanich," I supplied.

"Yeah. Vladimir. I think he was probably giving Irena a bad time about being your friend."

"You really think so?" I said doubtfully. "It's not like we plan any anti-communist plots. We never even talk politics."

"Shoot," said Ben, brushing a pinkie against the side of the hot pan as he picked it up to pour the now-done popcorn into a large bowl. He sucked the finger momentarily. "From everything you've told me, the guy sounds like a creep." Vladimir had been up on the bridge again this morning, watching my every move and jotting down occasional notes.

"Barbara, please come to the bridge immediately," came Pasha's voice over the loudspeaker.

I grabbed a quick handful of popcorn. "You may be right. Be back in a second."

At the end of the corridor I could hear Irena busy putting up silverware in the officers' mess. I hesitated, then slipped down the hallway and peeked into the mess. Irena glanced up at me and frowned, putting her finger to her lips. She lowered her finger and pointed toward the commissar's door. I nodded. So Ben was right. I slipped quietly back out the door and continued on to the bridge.

"The *Krakatoa*'s calling you," said Pasha, indicating the radio as he leaned against the steering wheel. Leonard had assigned the *Krakatoa* to us this week. She had her trawl in the water now, working to supply us with our next codend.

"*Krakatoa, Izumrudny*," I said.

"*Krakatoa* back." It was Kenny, the *Krakatoa*'s redneck skipper. "Hey Barb, could you ask this ship here to get off my tail? He's too close for comfort."

I turned to glance out the window at the *Krakatoa*. Not fifty feet to her starboard lay a large vessel with a scarlet Soviet flag flapping in the breeze over her stern. Antennas fairly bristled off the larger Russian boat:

five large parabolic reflectors were mounted in a circle on the bridge super-structure; smaller reflectors, interspersed with horn antennas, ran along her sides. Loop antennas bristled at both bow and stern, and a variety of monopoles stood on whips, spikes, blades, and cones that sprouted like weeds throughout her length.

"What's that boat?" I asked, looking to Pasha.

Pasha looked uncomfortable. "That's a research vessel."

I looked again at the Soviet ship: "What are they researching?"

Pasha answered with a smirk.

"Isn't that the Coast Guard?" I pointed to an American cutter a mile off our port. "Aren't you going to tell the captain?" Normally when an American Coast Guard vessel was observed, both the crew and the captain were notified immediately.

"The Coast Guard." Pasha's smirk grew. "They're not worried about us right now. They're busy following the research vessel."

"What's the research vessel doing?" I asked. The Soviet ship *was* awfully close to the *Krakatoa*.

"Following one of your Trident submarines."

"Oh." I noticed an even larger boat on the horizon. "What's that?"

"An American aircraft carrier," said Pasha.

"And what's *that* doing here?"

"Following our research vessel." Now Pasha looked embarrassed. Vladimir sat watching me, his face expressionless.

"Do you know the research vessel's name?" I asked Pasha.

Pasha's gaze flipped over to Vladimir. "No, I don't."

I thumbed the mike on the fleet channel: "Soviet research vessel, this is the *Izumrudny*." There was no answer. I paused, then switched to channel sixteen, the international hailing frequency. "Soviet research vessel. This is the *Izumrudny*." Again, there was no answer.

"Is there a channel these people are monitoring?" I asked Pasha. Pasha shrugged, raising his shoulders unconvincingly.

"*Izumrudny, Krakatoa*," said Kenny. "Barb, these guys are getting *close*. Could you get them to move away?"

"I'm trying to reach them right now," I said. I turned to Pasha: "Why aren't they answering me? Would you give it a try?"

Pasha seized the mike unwillingly. "Soviet research vessel, *Izumrudny*," he mumbled. "They're not answering." He shoved the mike back into my hand as he glanced nervously toward Vladimir. "Why do you need to talk to the research vessel?"

I pointed toward the *Krakatoa*. "Look." The research vessel was cutting even closer toward the *Krakatoa*.

"Barb, they're getting awfully close," Kenny repeated, his voice growing loud.

I keyed the mike again: "Soviet research vessel, this is the *Izumrudny*." I flipped back to the fleet channel and hailed once again.

"JESUS FUCKING CHRIST, THEY'RE GOING TO RAM ME!" Kenny screamed.

"Get Captain Shevchenko," I yelled. "Get the captain *now*!" For once Pasha didn't argue.

"*Muis Yegorova, Izumrudny*," I said.

"*Yegorova* back," came a Russian voice.

"I need to speak to the fleet commander."

"Just a moment."

I heard a weird rattle, and glanced over to the companionway to see Shevchenko crawling up the stairs. He emerged at the top and climbed to his feet, rocking to and fro in inebriated cadence with the waves. "What do you want, little lady?" he slurred.

"THEY'VE CUT THEIR GODDAMNED ENGINES. I CAN'T GET AROUND THEM," Kenny shouted. I glanced back again at the *Krakatoa*. She had turned hard port. Her trawl cables hung loose as she lost forward momentum. The research vessel looked to be not ten feet off her bow.

"Your damned research vessel is trying to ram the *Krakatoa*..." I yelled.

"*Izumrudny, Muis Yegorova*." It was the fleet commander.

"DO SOMETHING!" Kenny screamed.

Shevchenko looked confused.

"Fleet commander, tell the research vessel to move away from the *Krakatoa*!" I yelled into the mike.

"What research vessel?" said the fleet commander.

"The one right out there!" I kept my eyes glued to the *Krakatoa*. Had they managed to scrape past each other?

"What makes you think there's a problem with the research vessel?" said the fleet commander. "Let me speak to Shevchenko."

"Here," I fumed. I handed the mike toward the captain, who pulled at his tee-shirt in an attempt to summon dignity.

"I'm afraid Barbara's overreacting," said the fleet commander. "She has no concept of navigation. Please explain to her that everything is really quite safe."

"THOSE FUCKING ASSHOLES JUST FOULED MY GEAR!"

I grabbed the receiver from Shevchenko's hand. "Look, you pint-brained pip-squeak. I may not be a navigator, but the captain of the *Krakatoa* is a goddamned captain. When he says he has problems, he means he has problems. *Do* something, lard butt!"

There was momentary silence from the *Yegorova*, then the fleet commander's voice returned: "Soviet research vessel, *Muis Yegorova*, he said meekly. There was still no answer.

"Goddamn it, Barbara," Kenny fumed. "It's going to take me hours to get straightened back out now. Why didn't you fuckin' call them?"

"Barbara, you're always overreacting," said Shevchenko. "You see, nothing happened. By the way, that Sears catalog is great. Do you have another one?"

I shook my head and headed for the stairs.

Vladimir followed.

In the next days a pall fell over the ship. Where before my friends had greeted me with cheerful salutations and wry jokes, they now turned away when they saw me, doggedly resisting all attempts at conversation. Once when I was out on deck I managed to strike up a conversation with Gregori, but he broke off in the midst of a sentence, glancing up toward the bridge and muttering "There's an old Russian saying: A giraffe, because of its build, is very visible." Then he hurried off. I glanced up behind me to see Vladimir watching us from the bridge.

The many pleasant hours I had spent before the radios, listening absently to the conversations of the fishermen, noting who was taking a lot of fish, who wasn't, and observing in general the mood of the fleet, now turned into a sour occupation. I felt a pariah—even happy-go-lucky Kolya would have nothing to do with me, and Seryozha returned my question of "How's tricks?" with a stolid, oblivious stare.

My brief sojourn on shore began to seem a distant, dreamlike interlude of sanity. Bored and lonely, I took to walking down on deck to inspect the nets, a good excuse to see Ben, the only one on board I could visit with comfortably. When that conversation wore thin I took to talking to the incidental catch: rockfish, salmon, giant skates, squid—all poor conversationalists; all indisputably dead. Occasionally the deck crew, also bored, would rig the skates out with cigarettes in their mouths and dress them in ragged shirts. I watched from a distance, and Vladimir watched with me—moving into the cabin next to mine, sitting next to me at meals and on the bridge, eyeing me from above when I went out on deck; even loitering outside the toilets when I went to the bathroom.

After a week and a half, I decided I'd had enough.

"Kolya!"

Kolya turned to face me with a stony look.

I shot him, point blank, in the eye.

"Seryozha, now it's your turn."

Seryozha took one look and ran to cower behind the steering column. Vladimir, seated quietly in his usual observation perch, smiled for the first time in days.

"Don't do it, Barbara," said Seryozha, peeking out from behind the wheel. His cauliflower ears had flushed a bright pink. "I'm too young to die."

I shot him anyway, then turned my water pistol toward Vladimir. "Hold it right there, comrade."

Vladimir was up and out of his seat in a dive toward the door. I stopped to distribute some of the other water pistols I'd bought on shore, then pounded out after him. A cursory glance down the balcony showed Vladimir nowhere in sight. I hesitated, then ran down toward the deck, intent on mayhem.

"Surprise," I yelled, popping into the deck crew's team room. Gregori, Danielich, and three others looked up in astonishment as I drew a watery bead on them. I dodged back out and headed for my cabin to reload.

"Take that, you capitalist spy!" I ducked just in time to miss a healthy squirt as Vladimir appeared suddenly from around a corner. He'd apparently borrowed one of the squirt guns I'd given out on the bridge.

I sprinted for my cabin, and Vladimir ran after me

"Surprise!" Kolya yelled, standing up from the lifeboat as we bounded past. He squirted Vladimir, then leapt lightly from the boat to head toward the back deck. Vladimir turned to follow.

I reloaded, then crept back out of my cabin up the corridors toward the bridge.

Seryozha stood at the helm, drenched from head to toe. He grinned as I came up the companionway.

"How'd you get so wet?" I asked.

He pointed wordlessly toward the back deck, and I went over to the rear windows to get a bird's eye view of Vladimir being shot at by Kolya and Danielich as he bounced over a heap of netting near the starboard scuppers. The erstwhile refrigeration engineer stopped to spray his attackers, then retreated in the face of superior firepower—only to run face-first into a solid wall of foam as three of the deck crew who had been waiting patiently at his back plastered him with buckets of sea water. Vladimir dodged sideways, then galloped over to center deck to bolt up the stairs on the port side, heading forward.

I scurried out the starboard door of the bridge and climbed up the ladder to the flying deck. Gregori was perched on the other side of the platform, a large bucket of sea water by his side. He grinned over at me, then, as Vladimir pounded past below, casually dumped his bucket over the side. Vladimir roared, and Gregori and I both scampered back down the far ladder, screaming with laughter.

Vladimir proved to be a master of deception, lurking everywhere lurkable and generally terrifying the population—except for the deck crew, who were on the alert with endless buckets of sea water. We squirted, doused, drenched, soaked, and ambushed each other for nearly two hours, running breathlessly the length of the ship, hitting anything and everything that moved. No one was sacred—I even spotted Shevchenko bolting for his cabin, squirted stains etching a dark pattern over his chest.

And in the end, after we had all collapsed, soaking and dripping and laughing on the flying bridge, Vladimir reached a hand toward me. I automatically extended mine to shake. Instead, he took my palm in his and brought it up to kiss the back of my hand.

"Thank you," he said.

That night, he left the ship.

Chapter Eight
Deadly Ennui

WE HAVE BEEN WORKING for over four months now: the fishing season is drawing to a close. And one thing is becoming increasingly, painfully clear—a ship can only be out at sea for so long before provisions begin to dwindle. Some provisions are used up more quickly than others. Potatoes, for example, are consumed much more quickly than the lowly cabbage and the bland turnip. Sour cream and tomatoes, available in the first few weeks of the voyage, now appear only when one of the Russian vessels goes into port—a rare occurrence. Beef is infrequently served at best, and now, with nearly five months at sea, we are lucky to see even a piece of gristle-and-bone-chip-laden hamburger. The meals revolve monotonously around cabbage, fish, and bread, and since eating is a high point around which much ship-board life is centered, everyone has become dispirited with the tedium.

Shirts that were laundered and torn and patched and repatched, now disappear, to be replaced by blouses that appear distinctly Slavic—and homemade. Radios and televisions have broken and remain silent because there are no more spare parts. Tea and coffee, once given out generously, are now hoarded—and sugar, that indispensable builder of strong bones, is non-existent.

The crew endures all this with stolid ennui. Most have been to sea for years. They are used to doing without—it is not all that different from life on shore, except for one thing: on shore you can always get alcohol. When the liquor supply on ship disappears, there is no more, and no possibility of getting more any time soon.

People have aged noticeably in the months I have been aboard the *Izumrudny*. Tempers have begun to flare, with irrational acts becoming commonplace. Several nights ago two crewmen awoke Ben by barging into his cabin in a crazed search for alcohol. Ben had no idea what was going on; in desperation he fled down the hall to my cabin, tailed by both intruders. They asked me for vodka with haunted eyes, and when I finally succumbed to their interminable begging and gave them a small bottle I'd been holding since my trip to shore, they grabbed it, the sudden smirk on their faces all but announcing their thoughts: you dumb schmuck. They quickly asked if I had another bottle, and when I answered no, one tucked my bottle under a shirt as they both turned to run back down the hallway—without a thank you or a by your leave. The Soviets have always been proud of the fact that there was very little use of illegal drugs in their country. The truth was they didn't need it—alcohol filled the bill quite nicely.

Simply being together with the same small group of faces day after interminable day for months on end has become an ever-increasing strain. I have begun to discover some very interesting things about myself—chief among them being that I am not the nice, easy-going person I had thought I was. I keep trying to stop my calculated rudeness toward those on board who annoy me, but I have great difficulty restraining myself. One can only listen to the commissar begin so many conversations with "How many religious believers are there in America?" before one begins to feel like gutting and filleting this product of Soviet pedagogy.

The atmosphere in the dining room is often tomb-like, even when full of people. We have all been around each other too long—most of what can be publicly discussed has been discussed. I am the only un-known quantity remaining, so that when the commissar puts a question to me everyone immediately stops eating to stare, waiting expectantly for my answer even if the question is one that has been asked, and answered, a dozen times before. I feel as if I am in a goldfish bowl, and the pressure has begun to tell.

One unhappy afternoon during tea several weeks ago, I got a bit per-turbed, stood up, and announced that I would make a point of missing tea from now on if the commissar continued to ask the same obnoxious ques-tions. The commissar was quiet for a week after that outburst, but now he has rebounded, and I have reached the state of mind where I answer his questions semi-politely, curious as to what idiocy he will come up with next. Today's question was: "Barbara, why have the American fishermen decided not to catch fish today?" "Go ask the captain," I'd said, sipping my watery tea. The chief mate had chimed in with his own opinion: "Pavel Alexandrovich is too thick-headed to understand that fishermen don't just *decide* not to catch fish." The commissar left in a huff, and has not been to tea since.

But now it is the factory director who has begun to annoy me. He eats with his nose in his food, loudly slurping anything slurpable, getting rid of the bone and gristle by bending his face down and disgorging the offensive material with a loud "ptui" on the saucer. The factory director always sits directly across from me, and at times I can hardly bear to attend meals.

Pasha, the second mate, has also unwittingly earned my complete enmity, which is unfortunate, because his stupidity is at heart good-natured. I have cured him of his habit of interrupting me on the radio by walking up and beginning intense conversations with him whenever I catch him on the mike. He irritates me with a constant barrage of witless prattle; one minute stating how peaceful and non-warlike the Soviet Union is, the next talking about how the Americans shouldn't be disagreeing with the Soviets, but rather joining with them against the Chinese. Pasha discusses with unthinking vacuity how honorable it is to die in battle, and how dishonorable it is to be captured; displaying the standard Russian belief that if you are captured by an enemy and do not kill yourself you should be considered a traitor. He, as do most Soviets here, castigates me for American attitudes of prejudice toward blacks, then displays a completely unconscious anti-Semitism that I find shocking.

Through sarcasm and profane force of personality I have bludgeoned Pasha's chauvinism into retreat, but a macho narcissism remains in force. Recently he appeared prancing before me on the bridge, his hair newly washed and styled in a high and silken pompadour. I ignored him until he could stand it no longer: "Barbara," he asked, running his fingers over his curly locks, "how do you like my hair?"

"It makes you look like a woman," I growled. He slinked off the bridge in hurt silence. To be truthful, I am amazed that both Pasha and the commissar can still be polite and nice to me, considering how rude I am to them. It speaks well for them—certainly better than of myself.

Unfortunately, a part of my problem out here on the boats is simply being female. Pasha is not the only one who thinks it perfectly acceptable to interrupt my work constantly with trivia, or to tell me not to worry my pretty little head about something. In fact, nearly everyone seems to assume that, no matter what I am doing, I should drop it immediately in order to hear whatever they happen to feel like talking about at the moment. It irritates me because of the underlying assumption that what I happen to be doing is of no importance. All of the women on board are treated this way. The doctor is particularly guilty of this habit—hiking up to begin showing tricks and telling jokes at the least opportune moments, as for example, when I am lying prone doing pushups on the flying bridge.

My exercising is the subject of innumerable comments: chief among them being the question as to whether I know karate. Russians hold a fascination with the Asian martial arts that borders on mystical fanaticism, chiefly because the study of the discipline is illegal in the Soviet Union. Karate is the province of espionage and the underworld, and unfortunately, the Russians here seem to think that if a woman exercises she is automatically some sort of superspy in training.

I have begun to think in Russian, but I've found that this, too, creates problems. I am not as bright in Russian as I am in English: if I don't know the word for a concept in Russian, then, when I'm speaking and thinking in Russian, it's more difficult to think of that concept. I have labeled this phenomenon the Conceptual Russian Dumbshit Syndrome.

Shevchenko himself is really beginning to grate, what with his private and not so private suspicions, and his intense, secretive nature. He is becoming increasingly unhelpful, particularly since the last of the alcohol disappeared. When Kent on the *Barroom* asked for a little help in fixing a trawl last week, the *Izumrudny's* lifeboats proved to be suddenly out of commission. A few hours later, when Kent asked us to search ahead for fish, we couldn't, as the *Izumrudny's* engines were having problems. Shortly thereafter, however, another Soviet trawler called to ask if we wanted to exchange films. Suddenly our engines were started, the lifeboats lowered, and off went the deck crew.

Just yesterday Shevchenko took it into his head that he had to run south to "check out" a spot for fish. When we arrived at the spot, it turned out that by happy coincidence the *Yegorova* was there waiting for us, with magazines and letters for the crew. Shevchenko seems incapable of being honest about what he is doing.

Indeed, the only way I can find out whether we have problems on board is through careful observation of the ship's tempo. We've slowed or stopped and they've called for the chief engineer? I'd better ask; we've probably got engine problems that may put a stop to our next codend transfer. The fish aren't in the bunkers? Better go take a look; there may be bunker feeding problems. A call for the chief electromechanic? Problems in the factory.

And why do I have to do this? Because the captain, awash in his paranoia about Americans and secure in the fact that knowledge means power, won't tell me anything. In fact, the one time I can be sure something is wrong is when the captain assures me something is all right. That's when I get sneaky and ask others whether that "something" is fixed yet. They always say no and then tell me what's wrong. Nine times out of ten the matter is really not of any importance. I keep it up because that tenth time comes fairly often, and then it does matter.

I have become physically worn out. Several nights ago I just couldn't keep my eyes open, so I went downstairs to take a brief nap in my cabin. The chief mate broke in an hour later to tell me I was needed on the bridge. I found out that the rep on the *Aragonit* had been calling me for an hour, so I bawled the watch out for not getting me up. That's when I found out the watch had phoned me twice, announced over the loudspeakers for me three times, peeked into the cabin four times, and scoured the ship looking for me. They were convinced I'd fallen overboard when the chief had made one final check of my bunk and found me. I'd apparently forgotten to lock the door to my cabin (the captain had asked me to do so whenever I slept), so they'd assumed I wasn't there when they'd knocked and peeked inside. No one had thought to peer *behind* the door to look at the bunk until the chief mate had done so. They couldn't believe I would sleep through all the pounding and fuss.

I am phoned frequently at night—sometimes by a blathering Pasha, sometimes by an unknown person who says nothing. I have tired of this, and have taken to answering my phone in a variety of fanciful modes, none of which are particularly polite, but which provide me a great opportunity for venting steam.

Even seemingly innocent objects have left their mark on me. The stainfully pervasive Russian paint has taught me new lessons in the art of personal adornment. Russian paint is a special substance that normally takes about two weeks to dry. And just when you decide it is dry—that's when it really gets you, because it's just the outer skin that's dry, and if you bump that skin very hard, or in the case of a handrail, grasp it, it immediately explodes, leaving you with dirtied hands, pants, face, shoes, and/or shirts, all of which, at some time or other, I've managed to soil on some innocent looking piece of ship.

The ship itself is falling apart. Several nights ago there was a big meeting in the officers' mess next to my cabin. Ranting and raving went on for hours as I listened, staring sleeplessly at the ceiling. The upshot of the meeting was that the *Izumrudny* would return to Nakhodka within the week: engine and steering problems had been getting worse, and the winches weren't working right, either.

But of course, Shevchenko overrode the crew's decision: we didn't leave. Instead, we tied up to the offloader and unloaded everything in the holds. It's funny how Shevchenko can pull these tricks and get away with them. The *Alexandrovsk*, our sister ship, also had problems and the crew there voted against staying; as a result they headed home to Nakhodka. But Shevchenko was in the running for top captain, tonnage-wise, in all the fleets. If the *Izumrudny* left early there would be no way he could achieve this honor.

The fish factory has presented the most significant problems. It is falling apart, spewing ammonia until even in the best of times it is impossible to work. Last week we stopped production for two days while repairing the gas lines. As soon as we started up production after the repairs, the lines began spewing ammonia again. I'd gone down myself to see what was going on, but I could stand no more than a couple of minutes before I had to leave, my eyes as red and tearing as if I'd just peeled a bucketful of onions. We sent for the fleet refrigeration engineer, the real one, but to no avail: he came over, got soused in the chief mate's cabin, and told me as he was leaving: "You guys can just learn to live with it." It is no wonder everyone wants to go home so badly. In general, the whole ship, as well as the crew, is just plain beat.

In the face of such overwhelming exhaustion, there was only one thing to do: organize a party.

"Yee ha!" hooted Kenny, the skipper of the *Krakatoa*. He grabbed the towel Irena held and wiped his face, then began peeling off his survival suit, revealing damp jeans and a plaid lumberjack's jacket. We'd picked up the *Krakatoa*'s crew, as well as Arnie, the young replacement skipper on the *Yoda*, in our lifeboat, but Kenny had wanted to see what it was like coming over like a codend, so we'd obligingly dropped the cable into the water and dragged him aboard.

"I am very pleased to meet you," said Shevchenko, extending a hand. "Would you care to come up to the officers' mess?"

"Be glad to," said Kenny. The other Americans stood uncertainly about me, staring at the deck and the trawl gear. "Do you think he'd like to smoke a joint?" Kenny whispered, indicating Shevchenko with his thumb.

I gazed back at Kenny, horrified. "No." Kenny had no idea that Shevchenko was the communist equivalent of a John Bircher. I hurried to catch up with Shevchenko and the commissar. The other Americans followed; the *Krakatoa* crewmen each carried a case of what looked to be vodka. Arnie struggled along with a couple cases of beer. We dropped several of the bottles of vodka off on the bridge for the mates and continued down to the mess.

Preparations for the party had been going on in the officers' mess all evening long. I wasn't exactly sure what kind of spread they were laying out: the doors were kept locked, no doubt to keep out errant liquor pilferers. Not that there was anything much to pilfer.

The commissar unlocked the door before us, ushering everyone into the mess: "Could you tell the Americans that we are very pleased to have them aboard our ship, and extend to them the friendly hand of communism?" I turned to Kenny, standing beside me just inside the entrance to the cabin. He interrupted before I could speak: "Like, wow, man, get a load of this shit." He pointed.

Just inside the door was a large table covered with leaflets about communism and life in the Soviet Union—all in English. Over the table had been hung a large banner with the words "Take what you would like, please" neatly lettered in both English and Russian. I turned to glare at the commissar, but he moved away and sat, carefully avoiding my gaze. "Have a seat, everyone," he said, as Irena entered the room, followed by Danielich, the factory manager, his assistant, and Ben.

The table bore a poor man's version of the feasts I had been used to. Where plates of potatoes and tomatoes had previously decorated the scene, now plate after plate of simple coleslaw lined the center of the table. Two bottles of vodka stood on the table, one on each end. I was surprised to see Shevchenko had any left.

Introductions were made all around, then Shevchenko got down to business. "A toast," he said, "to the overworked and underpaid fishermen of America."

I frowned at Shevchenko and then translated.

"Fuckin' A we're underpaid," Kenny responded. Arnie and the others nodded.

"It's different for us," said the commissar, "and so much better. We are paid very high wages to do the work we do, and we are always assured of our pay. We never have to worry about being unemployed, or about our retirement." I translated reluctantly, trying to find a way to ease the conversation onto a more neutral subject. Kenny and Arnold listened with half an ear, eyeing Irena as she came over to pour some tea.

"Get a load of the broad," said Kenny. "Best looking butt I've seen on a trawler."

"What's he saying?" asked the commissar, politely.

"He's very glad that the fleet has been getting along so well," I said lamely.

Kenny took a sip of the tea and nearly choked. "Hey," he said, holding the tarry glass up with a look of respect, "this stuff's better than cocaine."

"Please tell our American guests..." said the commissar.

"Speaking of..." said Kenny, overriding the commissar.

The commissar raised his voice with irritation: "...that we Russians do not want war, that we are a very simple people."

"...cocaine, do you think the skipper here would like to try some?"

"I don't think so, Kenny," I said. I rolled my eyes at Ben while the captain poured another round.

"Do Kenny and the others know that our Soviet constitution prohibits war?" asked the commissar. "Please tell them that."

Irena bent beside Arnie to reach across the table for an empty bottle. "I'd like to fuck your butt," said Arnie. Irena turned to smile uncomprehendingly.

"Gentlemen, please," I said.

We settled down to a sullen round of drinking.

Arnie leaned over and whispered something to Kenny, who said: "Ask the captain if the doctor has any drugs he'd like to do."

"I don't think he does," I said.

"Last year the doctor on the *Muis Yegorova* whipped us up a cocktail and we were all high for four fuckin' days straight."

I tried to change the subject: "Is there anything we could be doing to make the fishing go a little easier for you?"

"Yeah. Could you ask the captain to get his mates to zigzag right in front of us? They're always too far off to the side or behind us or something, and it doesn't help at all."

I turned to the captain: "Kenny wants to know if you could get our mates to zigzag in front of us instead of to the side." I felt an inner glow of vindication. I'd been trying to tell Shevchenko this for months.

Shevchenko stared at me. "Those are not our mates, Barbara, those are *my* mates."

"All right, then," I said. "Tell *your* mates to do the job right."

"It is not your place to tell me how *my* mates should be doing their work," Shevchenko said.

"I wouldn't have to if you were on the bridge supervising them when you should be," I said. We glared menacingly at each other. Even Arnie and Ken looked surprised and a little intimidated. The cabin had suddenly become very quiet.

"Here's to friendship," said the commissar, raising his glass.

The ship lurched sickeningly beneath us.

The engines died.

The room went pitch black.

Shevchenko's chair grated backwards: he bolted out the door.

"This is what you call an emergency? Yes. An emergency shutdown," the commissar said with drunken assurance.

Arnie and Ken headed for the door. I followed with Ken's crew in the second wave, fumbling toward the bridge as the lights flickered and power resumed.

"Hello, Barrrbarrra," said Kolya, rolling the r's out to an immensely long trill as I came up the stairs. He was leaning against Seryozha, who was propped against the front window. They were both drunk. How can this be? I wondered. We'd left the bottles of vodka on the bridge less than half an hour before.

"Pretty," said Kolya, pointing aft. "It went boom boom."

I headed out the side door to join the rest of the Americans at the railing.

The *Yoda* lay just off our stern, her blunt bow now looking even blunter. A suspicious dent creased her side.

Arnie looked stricken. "My boat," he said. "Elmer will kill me."

"You should have parked it further away," said Kenny, obviously more experienced in Soviet partying techniques. Kolya had managed, while in his cups, to back up the *Izumrudny* a half mile into the *Yoda*.

"I told Mike to take her half a mile to the *Izumrudny*'s stern. I never thought she'd be bothered there."

Kenny looked smug. "I left Nick aboard the *Krakatoa* with strict orders to take her five miles away from us, and not come an inch closer until we called. Live and learn, Arnie."

"I guess this is it for me for this evening," said Arnie.

"Me too," said Ken.

"I think they'd like to go on back to their ships, now," I said to the captain.

"Wait," said the commissar. He darted inside, to emerge a few moments later with some brochures in his hand. "This is for Arnie and Ken and the others to keep," he said, thrusting them toward the Americans. I looked down and groaned inwardly. The brochures were English translations of the Soviet constitution. Ken and Arnie accepted the leaflets and wadded them into their pockets. In a few minutes they were gone.

"You didn't have to hand them copies of your constitution," I said to Shevchenko as we walked back inside. Pasha had replaced Kolya at the helm; he, too, had shaved his head. "It would be the equivalent of me coming on board with a bunch of Russian versions of the Bible and handing them out to the crew."

"Have you ever read the Bible?" Shevchenko asked.

"Of course," I said.

"No you haven't," he said. "You've read a translation of the Bible."

"Well, yes, the same as you have," I said.

"Oh no. I've read the authentic version of the Bible, in Old Church Slavonic." Old Church Slavonic is a sort of proto-Russian, rather like the Old English of Beowulf. To a modern Russian it is scarcely comprehensible.

I laughed. "Do you think Jesus spoke in Old Church Slavonic?"

Shevchenko looked uncomfortable. "Well, it was a language very much like it."

I unexpectedly found myself inside Shevchenko's cabin, joined by the other five Russians who had been in the officers' mess. Irena shuffled in with one of the heavy cases of vodka. The captain took a bottle out, sniffing it as Irena set out glasses.

"Here's to the ultimate victory of communism," said the commissar, raising his glass. I didn't raise mine.

"And to peace," Irena chimed in. I raised my glass and we all swallowed.

"This American vodka is nasty," said the factory director.

"It's nowhere near as good as our vodka," said the commissar. I had to admit the Soviet Stolichnaya went down a lot smoother.

"Did you know that we Russians used to own Alaska?" said Shevchenko.

"Yes, and you had posts all the way to California," I said.

"They tell you that in your history books?" said the commissar. I nodded. "We were fools to give it up." He took a fatalistic swallow of vodka and continued: "Fortunately, we're not imperialistic, like you are."

I let the bulk of the Soviet empire stand and said nothing.

"I don't understand how people can want to live under your system," said Fyodor, the assistant factory director. "Here, we never have to worry about unemployment."

"Or about getting sick," said Gleb. "We are taken care of by the state. We don't worry about not having money to pay for a doctor, like in your country."

"In our country we have certain freedoms," I said. "One of these freedoms is the freedom to take responsibility for your own actions."

"I wouldn't want your kind of freedom," said Shevchenko. "I wouldn't want the freedom to go walking in a park and get shot, or to be robbed by a bunch of hooligans on drugs, or to be sued every time I sneezed by the same lawyers who are unable to protect you against common criminals."

Shevchenko had a point. Everybody likes to complain about lawyers, but, like the weather, nobody ever does anything about them. Except in the Soviet Union. Sometimes I wondered if the Russians had simply taken Shakespeare's dictum to heart: "The first thing we do, let's kill all the lawyers." The United States had about 700,000 lawyers. The Soviet Union had 20,000. Consequently, the Soviet approach to law was much less complicated than the American; more along the lines of: "He's guilty—shoot him."

"And the terrible things your own people say about their country," Shevchenko continued. "No self respecting person should ever say things like that about where they live. Not if they have any respect for their history and their culture and their race. Not if they have any patriotism."

"You can't teach patriotism," I said glibly.

Shevchenko gave me a disparaging look. "Of course you can. We do it all the time."

"Why don't you ask some questions about the Soviet Union?" asked the commissar.

I stared at the four hostile faces surrounding me: Gleb, Fyodor, the commissar, and the captain. Danielich and Irena sat quietly off in the corner. It was four against one, tough odds when you're speaking a second language and you're drunk.

"How old are kids when they first start school in the Soviet Union?" I asked, trying to pick a non-controversial topic.

"Did you want the war in Vietnam?" asked the commissar, brushing aside my question.

I turned to stare at him. "That," I said, "is a very stupid question." The others laughed and the commissar flushed.

"You ask why I don't have any questions," I said. "Well, here's one for you. Did you want the war in Afghanistan?"

"That's different," said Fyodor, "the government there asked us to come in."

"Do you really believe that?" I asked. The room froze into a brittle silence.

"I think it's getting late," said the captain.

"I think I'd like to get some sleep now," said the commissar. We all stood. I caught a glimpse of Shevchenko as I walked out the door, alone now, and suddenly haggard with weariness. He was pulling another bottle from the box.

The phone rang once again that night, around three o'clock. I answered sleepily.

"We're going to visit the United States—we'll be putting in at Portland, Oregon, in two days," said the captain. There was a long pause. "Come to my cabin. I want to make love to you."

I stared at the phone, then slowly put it back in its cradle.

Chapter Nine
The Soviets Meet America

I STARED AT THE poster thumbtacked onto the hallway wall with undisguised interest. Its caption read: "Rules of Conduct while within the United States."

The first rule read: "Keep your passport safe at every moment while ashore. Remember, the CIA will be tailing *you* in an attempt to steal this important piece of documentation."

The second rule read: "If you buy ice cream in a store—eat it while you are still in the store. Walking the streets dripping ice cream reflects poorly on Soviet Socialist Mankind."

I skipped down toward the bottom of the list, suppressing laughter. There were thirty-seven rules, each beautifully lettered in italic Cyrillic; each sillier than the next.

Most of the Soviet trawlers in the fleet had already managed to sneak into port at least once this season to replenish supplies. For the crews, it was a welcome relief from the tedium of the never-ending shipboard routine, as well as an opportunity to spend hard earned "*valyuta*"—foreign currency—on items difficult to obtain in the Soviet Union (which meant nearly everything).

The *Izumrudny*'s crew had received news of their impending shore leave with a mixture of exhilarated avarice and naked fear: the fear fostered largely by frenzied rallies which the captain and the commissar began holding twice daily in the crew's mess. As Irena had told me privately, neither Shevchenko nor the commissar had been to the United States before, and they had no idea what to expect. They were terrified that someone would decide to defect, something they had little physical control over once the crew hit shore. The meetings, Irena said, were full of diatribes against America and Americans, emphasizing the dangers of the American way of life: drugs, ghettos, homeless—and dangerous—street people. These were calculated efforts to put the damper on excitement about the materialistic West, and as such, they were successful. Now some of my former friends shunned me in embarrassed silence, and I missed their companionship. As for Shevchenko himself, he was by turns petty, bitter, and mean in his dealings with me. I wasn't sure if it was our political differences, the rejection from the other night, the stress of the impending visit to America, the lack of alcohol, or a combination of any or all of the above. With Shevchenko, in fact, I was never sure of anything.

I turned away from the poster and caught a glimpse of the commissar from the corner of my eye. He was standing quietly at the end of the hall, watching me covertly. I ignored him and headed up to the bridge, where I grabbed a mug of weak but steaming tea, and stepped outside to join Kolya at the railing. We were steaming up the Columbia River now, and had been ever since we'd met the coastal pilot at five in the morning. Even in the hottest days of summer, the cool, moist air of the Pacific Northwest kept the trees and grasses on the banks before us as green as emeralds.

"What are you going to do when you get to Portland?" I asked, eyeing the rippling greenish-brown waters below us—so different from the gray swells of the Pacific.

"I'm not sure yet," said Kolya. "I'm not sure what any of us will be doing—we don't know yet how we're going to be able to get away from the ship to visit the city." The Portland docks were several miles from the city proper—too far for the Russians to walk in the limited time they had available.

"Can't you get a bus?" I asked.

Shevchenko slid in beside us. "We're working on that," he said.

"If you'd like I could call Portland on the ship-to-shore radio-telephone to see about chartering a bus for you."

Shevchenko watched as a small tug passed us, heading down river with a barge of logs. "I'm sure you could." He hesitated, his mouth curving into a caustic smile. "It might even be cheaper for us if you did, since the CIA would pay for the charges."

I turned on my heel in disgust. This was the third time today Shevchenko had annoyed me; only this morning I'd offered to see if I could rent a video for the crew when we hit town. The captain had demurred, stating the video would probably be "*s podtextom*"—with subversive overtones. Next, he had stood listening intently beside me while I'd called my family over the radio, trying with all his suspicious Slavic might to figure out what I was saying. When that effort had failed, he'd asked point blank what kind of "relatives" these people really were.

I'd worked with Shevchenko now for over four months—trying hard to keep the *Izumrudny* supplied with fish and to ensure no accidents happened. It hurt to see that count for nothing in the midst of Shevchenko's errant certainty that I was a spy.

"Wait," said Shevchenko as I walked down the corridor. He stepped away from the railing as I stopped and turned. I wondered if he had it in him to apologize.

"I want the film," he said in a low voice.

"What film?" I asked.

"You know what film."

"Huh?" The only meaning I knew for "*plyonka*"—the thing Shevchenko asked for—was film, as in photographic film. I didn't have any photographic film that Shevchenko would be interested in. I wondered if "*plyonka*" had some obscure meaning nobody'd ever bothered to tell me about.

"You know exactly what film I want."

"I don't know what you're talking about."

"Yes you do. I want the film of the pictures you just took of the 'Rules of Conduct'."

"Pictures? Of the 'Rules of Conduct'? You've got to be kidding. I didn't take any pictures of your 'Rules of Conduct'."

"Yes you did." Shevchenko's bloodshot eyes narrowed; he shot a hand up to push back his grizzled hair.

"No I didn't."

"Did too."

"Did not."

"I have pictures," said Shevchenko triumphantly, "of you taking pictures."

Pictures of non-existent pictures. Now that was a neat trick. "Oh yeah? Let me see them."

"They're not developed yet."

"It figures," I said. Shevchenko stared belligerently at me, and I stared angrily back. Kolya had disappeared onto the bridge.

The commissar, I thought. It's the commissar. He was the one who'd seen me looking at the poster, and for some reason he had imagined I was taking pictures. He'd reported his suspicions to the captain—hence the intense interrogation. Where on earth had the commissar gotten the idea I was taking pictures? I hadn't even had anything in my hands when I'd been looking at the list.

The *Izumrudny* had been out to sea for nearly five months, now. She had come inland to a port well within the borders of the United States, the object of Shevchenko's obsessive mistrust. And there'd been scarcely any alcohol on board for weeks. I stared at Shevchenko's wide, accusatory eyes and shivered.

It took us eleven hours to make our way up the Columbia; the *Izumrudny* docked at the seamy piers of Portland around four in the afternoon. Shevchenko swallowed his pride enough to invite me back into his cabin to translate for the ship's chandler—the American agent who supplied comestibles and other necessities to the ship.

The operative words here are "other necessities." I'd thought I was good at creative translation; compared to the captain, I was a rookie. "Five hundred pounds of potatoes," which Shevchenko carefully inscribed in the *Izumrudny*'s log books, translated, with some explanation, into five hundred cases of beer. One hundred and thirty pounds of sour cream became one hundred and thirty cases of vodka. Rum became radishes; tequila became tea. A variety of foods were also ordered: tomatoes, cabbage, turnips, potatoes, sour cream, cooking oil, fresh fruit, and eggs. These less important items were to be delivered the next day. The "other necessities" were to be delivered that evening.

With the departure of the ship's chandler, my work was finished for the day. I left to go look up old pals in Portland's Siamese twin city— Vancouver, Washington. When I returned to the ship late that evening, a friendly—and dead drunk—Shevchenko greeted me. We partied until dawn, when, in an abrupt and drunken about-face, he turned the entire crew over to my care.

"We'll meet at the bus here at six o'clock," I repeated vehemently through the bus's loudspeaker system.

"No we won't," said the chief mate. "Nobody wants to spend all day here. We want to see downtown Portland."

"But there aren't as many stores there, and it's more expensive. The captain recommended we stay here at the shopping center." I knew what was on the chief's mind—there were far more bars in Portland's downtown area than in the shopping mall.

"We all want to see downtown," said the chief stubbornly.

"All right," I said. "If you're so sure everyone wants to see downtown, we'll do things democratically and put it to a vote. We are now in a democratic country, after all," I said with pointed sarcasm. "Whatever the majority wants to do, we'll do."

The chief mate grabbed the mike from my hand and turned to the crew. Seventy-six flushed and excited faces stared up at us. "Crew! We're going to stay here in Jantzen Beach Shopping Center for three hours. Then we're going to pack up and," the chief raised his voice to a shout and lifted a clenched fist, "head for the best part of town and spend the rest of the day there! Now who's for it?!!"

There were a few desultory "me's."

"Great!" exclaimed the chief: Soviet democracy in action. "We'll meet back at the bus in three hours. Now let's go!" The herd began to pour off the bus toward the great double doors of Sears.

"They look so *real*," breathed Katya, gazing in astonishment at the mannequins in a clothing display before us. We women had ducked temporarily into Nordstroms, that venerable Northwest clothing store with a flair for marketing and a taste for the offbeat.

"I can't believe my eyes," said Irena. She bent down and squinted up at the mannequins—a darkly handsome man and a sophisticated looking woman—standing motionless before us. The woman was seated in a curved wicker chair; the man was bent over as if he were about to kiss her.

"It's amazing," said Katya, circling the display to get a better view. "They have fingernails—and there's hair on the back of the man's hands. Their skin is perfect, just like a real person's—and those eyes!" She stopped and stepped closer to crane her head down to within a few inches of the woman's face.

The mannequin burst into laughter.

"It's alive!" Katya shrieked, jumping back to stand behind me. "Heaven help us!"

I began laughing, too. "Those are living models, Katya. They're real people. It's okay."

Katya crossed herself and gave a shaky smile. Irena broke into a grin beside me. "What will you Westerners come up with next?"

"Barbara, come over here," Danielich shouted from the perfume counter. Some fifty of the crewmen were clustered around the perfume-testing station, squirting each other with fragrances in search of gifts for their loved ones. The clerks were wild-eyed.

"What does this mean?" asked one of the men, thrusting a bottle under my nose and pointing toward the label. He reeked with a musky odor.

"*Strast',*" I said. Passion.

The men turned as one and began grabbing bottles of Passion from the shelves. Within seconds the supply was exhausted and the Russians had congealed around a cash register, babbling happily away at the sales clerk.

"I don't understand," said the clerk, leaning nervously away from the counter. "Wha—what do you think they want?" she said to the woman stocking shelves beside her. I waded through the crowd and leaned over the counter, "Don't worry, they're Russians. They like your perfume."

Danielich, nearest the cash register, thrust a twenty dollar bill in the clerk's general direction. She took it and dutifully counted out change while Danielich rolled his eyes at me. "She's pretty," he said, winking. "Why don't you ask her to go out drinking with me?" He tapped his throat meaningfully. "Come to think of it, where's a bar?"

Fifty pairs of eyes swiveled to note my response: "It's too early for a bar to be open." There was a collective sigh.

"How about watches, Barbara? Where's the best place to get watches?" came a voice from the back of the crowd.

"K-Mart—where's K-Mart?" came another voice. Everybody knew about K-Mart.

With the perfume purchased, we walked as a group toward the other side of the mall, where K-Mart lay. The Russians darted into stores like children: everything was new and exciting—there was so much to see that nothing could hold their interest long. There were runs on cassette decks and "sex-musik" tapes, sunglasses, and of course, blue-jeans. K-Mart proved to be a good source of calculators, digital alarm clocks, and cameras. They gazed in awe at video machines, and I noticed a number of the men slipping furtively into the "blue" section of a video store to stare longingly at the covers on the cassettes. One man bought an oak toilet seat in a housewares shop, which he carried with pride, constantly taking it out of the bag to show the others.

All too soon it was time to head back to where the bus was parked toward the rear of the mall. I was amazed to find everyone there—but there was a reason for the punctuality. The commissar had organized the seemingly inchoate shore party into groups of three people each. The ship's rowdier types, as well as the politically suspect, were each provided with two steady partners. Unfortunately, there weren't quite enough Rock of Gibraltar types to go around, so the commissar did everything he could to keep the entire group together at all times.

The bus jerked into motion, and within a few minutes we were rumbling down the back streets of Portland, heading for the downtown area. I leaned back in my seat and catnapped.

"Look everyone," said the commissar. I opened my eyes to see the ship's political officer bending down from a stance at the head of the bus to point authoritatively out toward the train station. "There is a bum."

I glanced out the window to where an undeniably pathetic looking man huddled in sleep beside a boxcar, a filthy backpack at his side. The crew gawked from the windows of the bus, those with cameras snapping pictures.

Nobody, I mused, had bothered to take any pictures inside the shopping center. Now I knew how the Russians felt when they complained that Americans saw only the bad in the Soviet Union, never noticing the good.

"See how filthy the streets are," the commissar continued. "And how the garbage lies everywhere?" I glanced at the Styrofoam cups and random newspapers blowing in the wind along the edge of the road. Someone had dumped a bucketful of oil in the dusty weeds growing out of a crack between the street and a chipped cement-block fence. I'd driven through back streets like this thousands of times in my life, but somehow they'd never looked this bad before.

"And look at that warehouse there," the commissar continued, pointing to a corroded building with smashed and boarded-up windows staring out on an abandoned street. "This is typical capitalistic decay. There are millions of people begging for jobs in this country, yet you can see that there is no work made available for them, even when it is needed." I hunkered down into my seat, wishing we would get to the better part of town. The commissar prattled on, and the crewmen listened, absently juggling their purchases on their laps.

"Where's a bar?" whispered a crewman seated in front of me as we pulled up to our destination: a bus stop near the old Fox Theater.

"Is there a liquor store near here?" asked his companion.

The *Izumrudny*'s crew descended on the bars of downtown Portland like a hoard of ravaging locusts, sweeping into taverns in groups of twenty-five or more; scaring the cocktail waitresses with their number, unwashed disorder, and incomprehensible speech. They would down between five to ten shots, then flee in search of more drink elsewhere. They augmented their shy English with hand signals and fists full of money, pinching waitresses and purloining coasters; downing zombies, hurricanes, planter's punches, and Manhattans: in fact, anything they could see other people ordering. I hustled from bar to bar on the strip, explaining the situation to the waitresses, translating here and there, glancing at my watch. Six o'clock, the time the bus was supposed to meet us, could not come soon enough.

The commissar, with all his self-righteousness, disappeared, to reappear drunk several hours later in a tiny bar at the far end of the street, passionately proclaiming the divine attributes of communism to a bleary-eyed non-Russian speaker propped up against the counter.

Around four o'clock, someone discovered a liquor store several blocks up the street, and drunken mobs of Russians tore out of the bars to congregate in the store and loot the shelves of hard liquor. The clerk told me he had never seen anything like it. I simply nodded.

Around 5:30, possessed of some sort of drunken homing instinct, Russians began to accumulate around the bus stop where we were to be picked up. Most were still mobile; all were loaded with clinking bags of bottles. I routed the commissar from his perch; we both then combed the bars seeking the remnants of the crew.

Six o'clock found seventy-six smashed Soviets hanging around the corner near the Fox Theater, waiting for the bus. The commissar and I circled the crowd like dogs, nipping at the heels of the strays.

By 6:15 the bus hadn't arrived.

At 6:30 the bus still hadn't arrived.

By 6:45 I'd called the bus company (no answer), the ship's chandler (ditto), and the police ("Wait and see if the bus comes.").

By 7:00 the crew had descended once more into the bars. Gregori had blackened the eye of a barkeeper.

By 7:15 a fight had broken out between the owner of the toilet seat and three of his shipmates. The toilet seat was broken over its owner's head.

By 7:30 the crew's mood was turning ugly. Half the crew was at odds with the other half, and the other half of the crew was at odds with the Americans. The commissar had passed out completely, the chief mate was incoherent, and Kolya and Pasha were too busy arguing to be of any help.

At 7:45 I threw up my hands and called the police again. This time three barkeepers backed my call.

By 8:00, no one had shown, and I was getting desperate.

By 8:30 the Russians were dropping like drunken flies, with only Irena, Katya, and me left at least partially sober.

At 9:00, a bus showed.

By 10:00, we were back at the *Izumrudny*.

"Barbara!" said Shevchenko, showing me in. The party was in full swing, with cigarette smoke thick enough to climb onto and raucous laughter abounding. Irena giggled shyly in a corner. Other Russians from the *Tigil*, which had also steamed upriver with us, glanced curiously at me. From the cushions behind the table, the commissar smiled innocuously toward me, tipping a glass in my direction as the captain continued: "How I missed you—my favorite translator. I am going to put a little golden chain around your neck so that you can never leave my vessel again." He chucked me under the chin, smiling wolfishly.

Was it that he had decided Americans were not so dangerous after all, or was Shevchenko just drunk? The latter, I decided, eyeing him and smiling back.

Three bottles of vodka stood amidst the potatoes and loaded ashtrays. Shevchenko seized one and doused a tumbler. "This is for you." He refilled his own glass and cleared his throat. The hum of conversation in the room instantly fell silent.

He raised his glass.

I raised mine, forestalling him. "To the Joint Venture," I said quickly.

The cabin remained quiet. I noticed Irena looking to Shevchenko, waiting to follow his lead.

Shevchenko looked down at his glass. The recent flush of alcohol seemed to have cleared his bloodshot eyes—his whole demeanor was more relaxed than I had seen in weeks. He didn't answer, instead staring into his glass, looking deep inside, as if it were a crystal ball.

I took a breath and held it. The commissar opened his mouth and then closed it. The cabin remained silent.

A knock sounded from the bridge, and Seryozha poked his head through the door: "Captain..."

Shevchenko whirled, straightening, pulling himself up so that he seemed, suddenly, two feet taller. "In a moment," he said peremptorily. He turned to face us, weighing his thoughts carefully, lifting his glass.

"To the Joint Venture," he said, at last. The group, myself included, obediently raised our glasses.

Shevchenko smiled.

Interlude

I prefer always to remember Shevchenko thus: glass raised, eyes bright, a wolfish smile slicking his lips. In my mind's eye his wild frizz of hair has become blurred, his eyes shadowed—his slight frame has taken on an uncanny translucence. And yet, despite the entropy of memory, somehow I see his essence now more clearly than I ever saw it when I stood before him. He has assumed something clearer in my memory as the years have passed. Something has smoldered, embers glowing. And now, only now, has it caught fire.

The painter Robert Pope writes that time must elapse between an original experience and its re-creation: "During this gestation period, the creative faculties act as a filter where personal opaque and chaotic data is made public, transparent and ordered. This is a process of mythologizing. Myth and dream are similar: the difference is that dreams have private, personal meaning while myths have public meanings."

What is myth? Is it a story rife with adventure? Is it a feel for a place and a time where mores were different—more free, perhaps, wilder? Is it a flavor of the past, made golden by the distance of time?

Myth is all those things, and more. We think of the old West, for example, and somehow we know about the stink of the outhouses and mounds of dead buffaloes and the cries of those who lost their minds at the harshness of it all. We know all these things, and yet we mythologize it—we yearn for it. We realize there was something special about those times, something about the freedom of an imagined infinity of resources, all there for the taking. We knew that men and women then were in some sense on the brink—pitted against something elemental, both in themselves and in their surroundings.

As it was with the old West, so it was with the Joint Venture. It has become a myth, in my mind. Something pinned against the brink of legend.

The demise of the Soviet Union was, for most Westerners, an overwhelming shock—a sudden and historic schism predicted by few. Even trained Sovietologists were taken by surprise. The evidence of the death of the Soviet system lay all about me on the trawlers as I worked, yet even I did not realize the meaning or importance of the notes I scrawled as I lay hungover and seasick on my bunk. Even I did not realize what I was chronicling: the end of an era.

"Once you've eaten all the fish, you know how many there used to be," says Ransom Myers, a population biologist. Fish stocks worldwide are in crisis: the fate of the cod, fished to near oblivion off the Grand Banks, is now offered forth as the fate of the lowly pollack, and the hake. For all its complexity, the time of the Venture was a simpler time, because, like the West of yore, we could believe that our resources were without end.

No. I knew not what I was witnessing as I sat laughing that evening, watching as Shevchenko raised his glass to his lips. Shevchenko with his photograph of Stalin on the wall. Shevchenko with his "Yob tvoyu mat'." Shevchenko with his truculent ambition that joined him more than he would ever have acknowledged with his capitalist arch-enemies.

Shevchenko and Fisher, and Talbot and Jack, and all the rest of them were indeed something special: a paradigm for our times.

They were the last of the buffalo hunters.

But our story is not done. A few weeks after our sojourn in Portland, the 1982 fishing season ended. I returned to the University of Washington to spend the winter studying electrical engineering, and to begin reflecting on my experiences, like new wine placed in an oak barrel to age.

In early spring, I received another phone call from Marine Resources. The 1983 fishing season was soon to begin. Would I come to Alaska to work on the yellow-fin sole fleet?

As I hung up the phone, the sardonic Shevchenko shifted in my mind. Making room.

Chapter Ten
Interlude on the Pribilofs

"WHAT DAY IS THIS?" a raspy voice inquired. I turned to my left, surprised. It was Yuri, captain of the *Chasovoi*, mobile at last.

There was a gritty burp as the loudspeakers over the back gantry came to life, and sounds from the old rock band Queen poured out over the deck, lending a surreal muzak to the scene.

There is a curious feeling in the air, a mixture of tension and that "what the hell" feeling we get late at night, when the commissar sleeps. I need this time like a drug: the *Chasovoi* is truly nowhere as political as the *Izumrudny*, yet the ship's political officer still casts a shadow wherever he goes.

Yuri burped beside me in the darkness. If I'd thought Shevchenko was bad, downing vodka by the case, it was as nothing compared to Yuri. I'd seen Yuri sober exactly once, when he'd gone for a medical consultation to the *Severodonetsk*, a gigantic surimi trawler with far better medical capabilities than the *Chasovoi*. He'd returned looking considerably chastened, and had remained bone dry for three days. Then we'd gone to visit an American, Sven of the *Oslo*, for some drinking: "The Doctor says my liver won't be getting well for a long time," Yuri had explained, "meanwhile, I might as well enjoy myself."

I have been aboard the *Chasovoi* for two months now, long enough for even the ship's dogs, vicious at first in the face of the unfamiliar American smells of Woolite and Ivory Soap, to become accustomed to my presence. The *Chasovoi*, isolated from the prying eyes of the Coast Guard in the far reaches of the Bering Sea, had three canines: Kachagar, Aleut, and Rosella. Aleut had gamboled aboard during a day's layover in Dutch Harbor—the crew hadn't the heart to shoo her away. She'd immediately grown fat, then showed why efforts to put her on a diet failed—she had eight puppies, all of which, with the exception of Rosella, were distributed among the other five trawlers of the small Soviet yellow-fin sole fleet.

Kachagar, an old Husky-type dog with crystal blue eyes, had greeted my appearance on board by pinning me when I came out of the ship's head, barking and lunging at my throat. With the aid of the fatty gristle from my "meat" rations, he has grown to tolerate my presence, although we both keep a wary eye on each other. Kachagar has spent seven years at sea: long enough to know where the real danger on board the ship lies—in humans. He makes friends carefully, and no one messes with him. Rosella, a fluffy, bright-eyed puppy, was too friendly. She is gone now, thrown overboard in a storm by a drunken factory worker.

The cold is one thing I can never get used to here in the far north. In the wee hours of the morning my defenses are always down, so the raw wind and the sporadic shafts of driving sleet and snow rip effortlessly through my clothing to chill me to the core. I envy the deck crew their work; at least it keeps them moving, and thus a little warmer.

Flexing my fingers in my pockets, I stamped my feet on the grilled floor of the stanchion, easing slowly into the beat of the music. I gasped as a freezing blast of wind gusted through the fur of my overcoat.

"Good tune, eh, Barbara?" Nikita, the second mate, slid into place on my right. I nodded. Nikita bopped appreciatively as captain Yuri stared into the darkness. My walkie-talkie crackled to life: "*Chasovoi*, this is the *Oslo*. You there, Barb?"

"Right here, Sven. Cable's going out now."

I've worked with Sven quite a bit—we've gotten to know each other about as well as his reticent Scandinavian nature will allow. I met him once; despite his reassuringly stolid behavior on the radio, I discovered that he too has found comfort in a hair of the dog. "Barb," he'd asked in all seriousness as we'd sat alone in the privacy of the *Oslo's* bridge. "Do you think a quart of whiskey a day is too much?" Sven and Captain Yuri are fast friends.

Sven spent his teething years on whalers off the coasts of Africa and Antarctica, then moved to the United States to go through four ships and five wives in rapid succession. He's found a home of sorts for himself in the Bering—free to live and work the eccentric lifestyle he desires. I understand his laconic happiness completely. Underneath the exhaustion, buried behind the pain and the boredom and the drinking, I am beginning to love the people I work with and the things I do.

Although I am loathe to admit it, I am having the best time I have ever had in my life.

Captain Yuri has been on his latest bender for six days, loading up on the pure spirits of alcohol the chief mechanic orders for cleaning tools. Yesterday I had to see Yuri twice to get fuel receipts signed. The first time he had at least been able to sit up at his desk, although his only words were: "Barbara, you are looking at a drunk Russian captain." The second time had been at 2:30 yesterday morning. I'd been a little tipsy myself, having had a couple stiff belts with the trawl crew. Fortified by Dutch courage, I'd simply pounded into the captain's cabin when it came time to have the receipts signed. Yuri had been lying out cold on his bunk: I'd stuck a pen in his hand, shaken him awake, and told him to sign.

"How many more times do I have to sign this stupid thing?" he'd complained after a few moments.

"Just once more, Yuri Antonich," I'd said. "But this time you've got to move your hand."

When he is drunk, Yuri reminds me of an infant going through the terrible twos. Everything is "no, no, no." He throws a mean pout and dispenses snits like Popsicles. And if you think it's tough trying to talk a sober Russian captain into doing something he doesn't feel like doing—try talking a *drunk* Russian captain into doing it. It is impossible. "Just have one drink here with me," he'll say beguilingly, "and I'll do whatever you want." I fell for that ploy once, and had a two-day hangover to prove it. We have spent the past week fishing two hundred miles south of the rest of the fleet because Yuri, in his cups, refused to go north in what he insisted was a futile search for fish. Louise, the lead rep, had pleaded with Yuri to go, then had made me plead with him, and finally had had the fleet commander give him a direct order to rejoin the fleet—all to no avail. Yuri simply stopped speaking to me and refused to come near the radio, making sure the *Chasovoi* headed south all the while. The upshot was that the rest of the fleet didn't catch a thing all week, while the *Chasovoi* and her two American catcher boats, the *Oslo* and the *Mary Jane*, raked in several hundred tons of fish.

Despite his fishing intuition, however, it is still amazing to me that Yuri is actually **The Captain.** During our visit to the *Oslo*, for example, Yuri became too drunk to stand—so he refused to even try. The chief mate, well aware that we had fish to pick up from the *Mary Jane*, simply poured another tumbler full of Jack Daniels and popped it into Yuri's eager hand. Forty seconds later Yuri, anesthetized, toppled nose first into his spaghetti, from whence he was plucked, trussed like a hog, and hauled forty feet up the *Chasovoi*'s side to be deposited nicely out of everyone's way in his bunk.

For all Yuri's problems, however, I've grown to like the little son-of-a-bitch enormously. The crew adores him. Indeed, it would be hard for anyone to dislike a Soviet captain who keeps a four-foot-tall stuffed pink bunny rabbit tied over the barometer on the wall of his cabin.

"It's all yours, Barb," Sven's voice crackled over the walkie-talkie. I glanced toward Yuri as I translated, then followed his bloodshot eyes past the stern ramp and the tattered Soviet flag snapping above it, toward the American boat accelerating away from the now taut cable.

The *Oslo* shone like an angel in the blackness, wings of foam leaping from her bow as she cavorted in the waves, feather-light without the twenty-ton weight of the codend. Beyond her I could see the running lights of the *Mary Jane*, holding position as she waited.

"Yo, Barb. 'Radio Free' *Mary Jane* here." It was Tim Henson on the walkie-talkie; he was, as usual, barely audible in the overwhelming swell of music from his heavily muscled stereo system. Tim loved music; loud music—he had four separate hundred-watt speakers crowded onto the *Mary Jane*'s bridge, four more speakers in the galley, and a number of loudspeakers on deck. Tim enjoyed cranking up the volume on his system after a successful tow, so that at times we on board the *Chasovoi* could hear the strains of the Grateful Dead or Led Zeppelin reverberating off the *Mary Jane* from a mile or more away.

"When are you mother-fuckers going to be done?" Tim asked. Yuri cocked an ear toward the familiar voice on the radio, holding his worn Soviet army jacket closed with one hand while the other hoisted a rumpled pair of pajama bottoms. His huge slippers and slight build made him look like a kid at Christmas, hiking around in his old man's shoes.

"Just a few more minutes," I said, "it won't take long to get an estimate for Sven." Nikita was fast at the winches—the *Oslo*'s codend was already sliding into place on deck. Tim lowered the background music and I could suddenly hear the sounds of impatiently drumming fingers. I was due to transfer over to the *Mary Jane* as soon as I finished with the *Oslo*'s fish, and Tim was anxious to get me aboard. Today would be a welcome day of relief from the tedious routine of fishing: I would be heading for the Pribilofs.

"What's that?" Yuri croaked suddenly. He pointed toward a lump of netting wadded beside the still jiggling codend.

Nikita leaned over the railing on the other side of me: "I saw it, too."

I stared at the netting, seeing nothing.

"Deck hands. Get your gaffs!" yelled Nikita with the sudden quivering attentiveness of a pointer.

"There it is!" yelled Yuri. He grabbed at the mike for the ship's intercom and switched it on. "Attention. Attention all crew. Bring Kachagar to the back deck immediately." He dropped the mike to shove past me and down the companionway toward the deck.

"There it goes," shrieked one of the deck crew, slashing at the meshes with a gaff. A flurry of activity ensued, and then something cat-sized scuttled from the webbing.

It was a rat.

Kachagar burst from the door to the crew's quarters, tail raised in an alert arch as he sensed the crew's excitement. "Get it!" yelled the captain. Kachagar put his nose to the deck and ran forward, trying to track by smell what everyone else could clearly see.

"Kachagar—here!" Yuri cried. He grabbed Kachagar and pulled him by the scruff of the neck toward the rat, his slippers flapping like clown shoes on the hard wood of the deck. The rat darted aft, then, blocked by a man with a boat hook, scrambled toward the far side of the deck, Kachagar and the captain hot on his trail.

"Here he is! Get him, Kach!" The rat, cornered between the captain and Kachagar on one side, and three advancing crewmen on the other, slipped deftly around the captain and headed forward toward the open area beneath the stanchion. I craned my neck, leaning out over the railings in a vain attempt to peer beneath me as Kachagar and the captain lunged after their quarry. The rest of the deck crew followed in a ragged mass, waving boat hooks, gaffs, and sledgehammers.

"Got you, you..." came the captain's voice.

"Damn it!"

"Get it, Kach...."

There was an indecipherable welter of curses, and then: "There it goes!"

The team boiled back out from beneath the stanchion, Kachagar in the lead with the captain right behind him.

"Where *is* everybody?" I jumped at Tim's voice in the walkie-talkie and looked to starboard to see the *Mary Jane* pulling toward the *Chasovoi*.

"Just a sec," I said into the mike. I cupped my hands: "Hey, you guys—the *Mary Jane*'s here."

The fore section of the deck crew hesitated, then split off to head for the bulwarks and drop the heavy rubber bumpers that would prevent the American and Soviet vessels from slamming into one another in the swell. A few moments later the *Mary Jane* was fast to the *Chasovoi*'s side.

"I've got to grab my bags, Tim," I said into the radio, still watching the deck. The captain was now clambering over the full codend we had just brought aboard; Kachagar was scurrying around the front, hackles raised.

"No problem," said Tim. "I'll just head on up with a couple of my boys and give you a hand."

"Not so fast," I said. The last time Tim's crew came aboard they had loped around pounding on doors, light-fingering trinkets, propositioning women, and in general creating such a ruckus that they'd finally been kicked off the ship.

"Come on now, Barb. You're not going to let a few bygone high spirits ruin a wonderful working relationship, are you?"

"Yes."

I knew why Tim wanted his crew over to visit: barter. The *Chasovoi*, along with most of the other Soviet and American vessels here in the Bering, is barter crazy. I myself have joined the fun; I presently have two new rabbit fur hats, for which I will give the second radio operator my little cassette recorder when the voyage ends; and a nutria fur hat, for which I am trading two pairs of size 36 jeans which I have asked Tim to get next time he is in port. Likewise, the officers' stewardess has ordered two pairs of sunglasses, two tee-shirts (red or blue, not white), five sex-musik cassettes, and two boxes of Oreo cookies; all in exchange for one fur coat, one new gray rabbit fur hat, and a sweater.

This is just part of the story. The third mate has a nutria hat which he wishes to exchange for two pairs of size 34 jeans. The cleaning woman wants to trade a bottle of vodka for a bottle of anything American (anything alcoholic, that is), and the second mate wants to exchange jeans for a coat and hat both. The chief mate, undercutting the rest, is willing to trade a nutria hat for one pair of jeans.

Bennie of the *Mary Jane*, on the American team, seems to hold the record in trade for an evening—nine hats and two coats in one quick foray through the lower decks of the *Tigil* whilst the captains and the representative sat upstairs getting drunk. One needs no translator where such matters are taking place. The year before, Bennie told me, he had been aboard the

Mary Jane when a man clambered down from the *Archangelsk* with a thirty-one-inch walrus tusk under his coat. Snokkered past caring, the guy had exchanged the tusk for five bottles of vodka; not a bad deal for the Americans, considering the tusk was worth around $5,000. The man had then clambered back aboard the *Archangelsk* and disappeared. About fifteen minutes later Bennie spotted the erstwhile tusk owner being held by a couple of crewmen while the Soviet officer in charge clubbed him unconscious.

"Why don't you just trade through the portholes like everybody else?" I asked Tim irritably.

Tim keyed his mike, but for a few moments I heard only the overwhelming sounds of the stereo. "I—umm. It's too big."

"Oh." God knew what they were trading.

"Come on, Barb," he wheedled. "I'm taking you to the Pribilofs, after all."

What the hell. "Okay, but keep the guys under control this time, will you please?"

"Absolutely. See ya in a minute." Static filled the air. I glanced down toward the now-silent deck. It looked like the ragtag bunch of rat killers had headed up toward the bow.

I went for my things. Theoretically, I would be away from the *Chasovoi* for only the day, but I knew better than to go on that assumption. I also had two weeks of laundry I wanted to do in the *Mary Jane*'s small washer.

I'd been hoping that I'd have a chance to visit the Pribilofs ever since I heard I was heading for Alaska. The Pribilofs are the fabled breeding grounds of the northern fur seal, as well as a stopping point for nearly two hundred different species of birds. Located smack in the middle of the Bering Sea, with the nearest land roughly four hundred miles away, the Pribilofs consist of five islands. There are two larger islands—St. Paul and St George—and three smaller ones: rocks, really, too small or close to sea level to be inhabited by humans. The islands lie in an area that has been described as the "cradle of storms." There are usually only thirty or so clear days a year, and the wind blows an average of seventeen miles an hour, with gale force winds common. There are no trees except for an extremely dwarfed willow. The highest temperature ever recorded was sixty-four degrees; the Pribilofs do not have enough growing days for crops.

But the islands are perfect breeding grounds and nesting areas. Humidity is high, a condition necessary for fur seals to stay cool. And the numerous cliffs provide ample nesting space: the Pribilof bird cliffs are, in fact, some of the largest sea bird nesting colonies in the northern hemisphere.

Under normal circumstances, some birds can be seen only in the Pribilofs: the red-faced cormorant, for example, or the red-legged kittiwake.

The Russians opened recorded history in the area with a genocidal bang, destroying native villages all along the Aleutian chain, abducting women, and kidnapping children to ensure their fathers would hunt through the winter.

As ruthless as they were with the Aleuts, the Russians dealt even more harshly with the natural resources that had attracted them to the area. They hunted the sea cow to extinction by 1768. The near extinction of the sea otter came close to sinking the entire Russian fur hunting enterprise in the area—until the enterprising Chinese discovered a method for stripping the guard hairs off the pelt of the northern fur seal. This method of processing left only the fine, dense (over 300,000 hairs per inch) undercoat. The undercoat formed a rich fur perfect for coats, cloaks, capes, and linings.

With the rising value of the fur seal pelt, the race was on to find the seals' breeding grounds, where the animals went ashore and could be killed easily. In 1786, fleet master Gerassim Pribilof, cruising north of Unalaska, heard the unmistakable sounds of roaring, barking, and bleating through a dense summer fog. He landed to discover St. George, the smaller of the two inhabitable islands, and an abundance of seals, sea otters, sea lions, walrus, birds, and foxes. He had found the fur-bearing mother lode.

The Aleuts, far better hunters than the Russians, were quickly brought to the area and forced to capture seals. By the early 1800s there were several permanent Aleut communities on the islands. Inhospitable as the place was, it became the Aleuts' home.

The Pribilof Aleuts are a special people, heir to a unique mixture of Aleut and Slavic traditions and culture. They have withstood decimation through disease, forced repatriation during World War II, and a condescending American attitude that has seen fit to describe the Aleuts as a "people still in a state of semi-civilization." In 1946 the governmental food schedule for the Pribilof Aleuts provided for 1,700 calories a day. German prisoners of war had been given 1,900 caloric units daily during World War II.

But with the growth of native rights, a governmental reevaluation of the living conditions and human problems of the Bering Sea native communities, and a modicum of tourist trade, life for the Pribilof Aleuts has changed remarkably. The Aleuts can speak their native language in public now without fear of retribution. There is a school on the island, a power plant, running water—as well as tooth decay, hypertension, alcoholism, heart disease, an increase in cancer, and a suspicion of mercury poisoning from some of the seafood.

Through it all the Aleuts have remained open, friendly, and vulnerable. "I took my grandchildren to Seattle once," a man from St. Paul remarked, "and they said hello to everyone on the street. They didn't understand why no one answered."

I was more than ready to get away from the shipboard routine and visit these unusual islands. Floating beside the *Chasovoi*, my chariot—the *Mary Jane*—awaited.

"What in the hell are they doing?" Tim asked. Below us on the fore deck the captain, winded, leaned against a railing as a group of crewmen beat at a tangle of ropes with their makeshift array of weapons. Kachagar barked excitedly nearby.

"Trying to catch a rat," I said. "Shall we go now?" It had only taken me a few minutes to get my things together, and I was anxious to get going before Tim and Yuri decided to have another go at cementing Soviet-American relations.

"Can't leave without saying hi to the good captain," said Tim. My heart sank. "Yuri, *ezdruzvui!*" Tim shouted in a passable imitation of hello.

Yuri glanced up, his face splitting in an ear-to-ear grin. "Tim! Welcome! One minute." He pushed off from the railing and shuffled toward the hatch leading to the bridge.

Tim and Yuri were, on the face of it, as unlikely a pair of friends as you could find anywhere. Where Yuri, for all his drinking, was the well-respected captain of a large Soviet factory trawler, Tim looked like nothing so much as a juvenile delinquent, and his small ship like a trash barrel. Tim tied back his long, greasy hair to reveal a delicate gold earring. His combination of hawk nose and receding chin gave him, as he put it, "a stupid look on my face."

But looks were deceiving. The *Mary Jane*, for all her small size and party atmosphere, always kept a respectable amount of fish coming aboard. She also had the fewest repair problems of any of the American boats. The rapport Yuri and Tim developed was in large part responsible for the *Mary Jane*'s—and the *Chasovoi*'s—success. Yuri made sure the *Chasovoi*'s watch officers did everything they could to assist Tim by searching for fish ahead of the American vessel and helping repair any mechanical problems quickly. As a result, Tim and Yuri had some of the best catch records in the fleet.

"My good friend!" said Tim as Yuri arrived on the bridge. He reached forward to give Yuri the Slavic bear hug traditionally given to a soul mate met through repeated bouts with a bottle.

Yuri leaped back. "No, no. Very sick." He clutched his side protectively. "Oh. Sorry."

"Is okay." Yuri shrugged and waved a deprecatory hand, keeping his elbow close to his side. Behind the captain, I suddenly got a glimpse of the commissar chugging up the bridge's companionway.

"Uh oh," I muttered. Tim swiveled, and in a flash had stepped back around and behind me.

Where the commissar on the *Izumrudny* had been a dapper, fanatically thin little man, the *Chasovoi's* commissar is a teddy-bear. He is the kind of guy you imagine playing Santa Claus at Christmas, or being your kid's cub scout leader. A perfect Friar Tuck—until you look into his eyes.

Or, more properly, don't.

The commissar's eyes have never met mine—never once, in the two months I have been aboard. He nodded politely in my direction when we first met, eyes drifting. After that he ignored me completely, eyes floating over and around me as we sat together in the mess, or passed one another in the hallways, until as the weeks passed I began to feel as if I had some sort of communicable disease.

Last week, however, the commissar recognized my presence for the first time. Kachagar had found his way into my cabin and lay at my feet as I sat entering the day's catch into my log. The commissar walked past, then stopped and returned to poke his head in the open door. "Kachagar," he asked solicitously, "what's the matter, turned traitor?"

The deck crew refers to the commissar, among other, less polite terms, as "the Snake." Several evenings ago, after we all had polished off some vodka the *Oslo* had sent over on the back of a codend, the senior trawlmaster re-filled one of the bottles with water and left it sitting on his table. "The commissar will get a nice surprise," he said laconically, "when he confiscates this."

This commissar, like all the others I had met, was a zealot. And he was approaching me now. Behind me I could hear Tim, rustling about as he centered himself behind my back. Captain Yuri, beside me, seemed to wilt.

Suddenly the commissar's nose was against mine. The skin beneath his left eye jerked spasmodically; I watched, fascinated. Behind me, Tim shuffled back. Yuri, to my left, swallowed, then began to cough, his breath suddenly coming in short, choking gasps. He bent over, whooping, and I leaned over with him, pounding him on the back in a futile attempt to help him catch his breath. The commissar stepped deliberately around me, coming face to face with Tim.

"Okay," the commissar said. He leaned forward, his baby-talk English at odds with his ferocious baritone: "You go bye-bye."

I had thought I was tired down south, but it is as nothing to how I feel here on the Bering Sea. The round-the-clock fishing has made my nights run into days run into endless marathons of sleeplessness and work. Occasional glances into a mirror show a ghost-eyed woman with aged, sallow skin. Not me, certainly.

Often I return to my cabin too tired to move, too cold to sleep, too weary to think. I simply stare silently, listening through the cabin's paper-thin walls to the screams of Anatoli Pavlovich, the chief radio operator, who lives next door. He is far gone into alcoholism, and frequently has the D.T.'s. Between the screams and his drunken, creepy advances, I am beginning to hate him. Actually, the never-ending fatigue occasionally finds me hating everything. Even my sink is beginning to drive me nuts; in heavy seas it sloshes and gurgles like a continuously flushing toilet. I have fiddled with the plumbing, cleaned the crap out of the stinking pipes, readjusted valves, and played with the spigots. In the end I have found the only way to sleep in peace is to unscrew the pipes under the sink. With vague dimness of somnolence I frequently forget to reconnect the pipes before running the water. Now the floor has moisture bubbles under the seedy linoleum.

This interlude on the Pribilofs is just the break I need.

"Tell Lucy to get his ass down here," roared Tim from "Studio *Mary Jane*," a.k.a. the *Mary Jane*'s bridge. I glanced up from the galley sink, surprised at hearing anything at all over the painfully loud stereo. It was five o'clock in the morning; I was busy cracking crab.

The mood aboard the *Mary Jane* was celebratory. This was the first non-fishing day in weeks, and we were preparing to live it in style. Last night, still aboard the *Chasovoi*, I'd fulfilled the letter of American law by helping throw overboard the halibut and king crab the Russians had brought aboard in the last codend. Of course, Tim had made sure the *Mary Jane* was alongside the *Chasovoi*, directly below me when I'd thrown. Now, in the topsy turvy world of round-the-clock fishing, we were busy preparing a 6:00 a.m. dinner of the freshest king crab and halibut I'd ever seen.

There was a slight bobble to the galley floor beneath me. Lucy, the *Svetlaya's* rep, was boarding. Tim had carefully invited only Lucy and me on this trip to shore. Last year he had invited one of the observers, who had feasted merrily on the illegal crab and halibut, got swacked, had a hell of a good time, and turned them in to the authorities as soon as he left.

Engines revved and the *Mary Jane* bounced against the *Svetlaya's* side, then rebounded to head out and away from the Soviet ship, setting a choppy course for St. Paul, the largest of the Pribilof Islands.

"Barb!" Lucy said. His six-foot-three, heavily muscled frame nearly filled the doorway.

"Lucy!" I jumped up to give him a hug, my hands leaving shreds of crab meat on his jacket.

"Please," Lucy said, disentangling himself and grinning. "I do have a real name, you know."

Lucy's real name was Dave Fletcher. Unfortunately, there were four Daves in the fleet—in fact, every rep on the yellow-fin except Louise and me was named Dave. Dave Fletcher had had the misfortune of being the last Dave to arrive. "Hi," he'd said to Tim upon boarding the *Mary Jane* for his trip out to join the fleet. "My name's Dave."

Tim, according to fleet scuttlebutt, had given him a single disparaging look: "No it's not. Your name's Lucy. We've already got too many Daves."

The *Mary Jane* began to thud rhythmically against the swell and I felt a momentary pang of nausea. One unfortunate aspect of seasickness is that, although you seem to eventually adjust to the motion of the sea— once you've gone through enough misery—actually you've only adjusted to the motion of your own boat. The pitch and yaw of a 270-foot Soviet trawler is entirely different from that of the smaller, wilder-riding American vessels. Being accustomed to the one did not necessitate being accustomed to the other. What it *did* mean was that I occasionally suffered *mal de mer* when visiting American catcher boats. It also meant that a swaggering tough American, having laughed at the Soviets' "smooth" ride aboard their far larger vessels, would arrive for a visit only to seek refuge in the ship's head as the weather worsened.

"God, it's good to take a break," said Dave/Lucy. He took his coat off and threw a bag of what looked to be laundry toward a corner. "Working with Gunnar will be the death of me."

"I know, I know," I commiserated. Gunnar, the pistol packing hotshot of last season, had already distinguished himself this year with an extraordinarily foul mouth and vile temper. I was glad I'd never had to work with him.

"Last night," Dave continued, "Gunnar had the gall to tell me he's never been treated so shabbily by a rep in all the sixteen years he's been working the Joint Venture."

I laughed with Dave. The Joint Venture had only been in operation for five years.

"That's not so bad," I said. "I made the mistake of asking Fat Frank what the 'A' on the *Valkyrie*'s bow stood for."

"You didn't," said Dave. Fat Frank, also known as "the Drag Buddha," was not a particularly friendly individual. He was also a trifle touchy about the large "A" he'd painted on the prow of the *Valkyrie*, which was surrounded by a thick black circle that made the logo look like an avant garde symbol for asshole. Fat Frank's "A" was the laughing stock of the fleet—behind Frank's back, of course. But still, he suspected.

"What'd Frank say?"

"He said: 'It stands for Amundson.' End of conversation. He hasn't spoken to me since."

"I'll bet." We both laughed again and Dave helped himself to a bottle of vodka Tim had left tucked into one of the side bars, offering me a shot only after he'd taken his first swallow. I declined, determined to enjoy a respite from alcohol.

I was tiring of the overwhelming sea of liquor aboard the Soviet vessels; tiring of the pitiful deterioration of both the officers and crew that seemed to occur even as I watched. But even if I had little further stomach for booze aboard the Soviet boats, I knew better than to simply refuse to drink; those few reps that did so were ostracized by both officers and crew, making what could be a very unpleasant environment even worse. Recently I'd found myself developing a surprising number of sly techniques for maintaining my liver—and my sanity. The direct route was best—dumping the stuff under the table when no one was looking. But there were often times when this technique proved ineffective, because someone *was* looking. An alternative was to drink a shot in one gulp, then put a thick piece of bread in my mouth—the kind the Russians frequently used as chasers. The bread sopped the booze up quite nicely. Then I threw it away. Sometimes I asked for a glass of water or juice to use as a chaser. I would drink the chaser three quarters of the way down immediately, then use it as a repository to disgorge vodka into. With everyone drunk, they never noticed that the chaser glass was going from empty to full rather than the other way around.

But here on the *Mary Jane*, away from the Russians, I felt I could get away with no alcohol. I could indulge instead in my one true vice—coffee. I reached for the pot and poured another cup: my fourth in the past few hours. My head buzzed in a glory of caffeinated frenzy.

Our early morning supper was delicious; the seafood was garnished with mashed potatoes, corn on the cob, Jell-O, and pumpkin pie—everything American in the world, it seemed, save Dave's vodka. Dave was filled to bursting with fleet gossip: the *Otradny's* National Marine Fisheries observer had fallen in love with one of the deck crew workers. He'd been arrested. She'd gone home to her husband. A letter from Laura was waiting for me on the fleet flagship—it had been slit open. The fleet's "Safety Inspector" was actually a KGB agent. The fleet commander's medication (for his liver, natch) was lost in transit and a new batch had to be flown out from Montreal. Nick of the *Vargas* had been surprised and attacked by a bear as he'd sat steaming clams in the hot springs just outside Port Moller....

Listening intently, swept up in Dave's increasingly drunken patter, I was surprised to catch a sudden glimpse of a hillside through the porthole behind him. The verdant green of the slopes swirling out of the fog was shocking after months of nothing but gray skies and waters.

It was, I knew, St. Paul island. Dave and Tim rambled on, adrift in boozy conversation. I excused myself to slip outside to the back deck.

The approaching shoreline held a rocky beach and low-slung grassy hillsides. In the distance, I could hear a deep rumbling chuckle that gradually resolved itself into a multitude of roars, snorts, bellows, and farts—fur seals engaged in a cacophony of life. I rested my hand on the railing and stared as mist curled indecisively about me: now light and thin, now thick and heavy as a curtain. The *Mary Jane's* deck was low to the waterline. I could reach over the railing and touch the water more easily than I could touch my toes.

Suddenly a thick black fin, tall and hooked as an oversized beak, jutted out of the water not five feet away. A killer whale. I gasped and snatched my hand back. The fin rode slickly, inexorably by, as if to say "This is my world. Be warned. Be wary." A putrid exhalation filled the air, and with a wave of an enormous flipper, the fin was gone, leaving a lapping wake that gradually subsided in the still waters.

Through the haze I glimpsed another boat, perhaps twice the size of the *Mary Jane*, anchored a few hundred yards off a small promontory of the rocky shore. The ship was, I knew through rumor, a Greenpeace boat fresh back from a trip off the Soviet coast to harass the Russians for illegal whaling. The fog closed back in and the ship disappeared.

Gradually I became aware of being watched. I scanned the thickening mist, my eyes moving back and forth in the gray, but there was nothing. I held my hand up before my face, catching the prickle of vapor, then glanced down.

A pair of soulful puppy eyes met mine, whiskers all a quiver under a perky nose that looked as if it should be bouncing a striped beach ball. It was a fur seal. Another seal poked its head up beside the first, and then another, until I was surrounded by playful watchers, squelching and barking and frolicking in the water as if it were a vast playground. A tufted puffin skidded into view, its orange crest gleaming with a moist sheen. Beside it, a cormorant bobbed to the surface, rising from a dive to unknown depths. Overhead flew a small flock of stocky seabirds of a type I'd never seen before.

The world was alive with movement and sound, all the more noticeable when the only water life I'd seen for the past month had been the dying catch we brought up in the nets. Here in the midst of the cradle of storms, wrapped in a shroud of foggy cottonwool, we had come upon an eye of vibrancy. The mist parted once again to reveal the beckoning grasses of the shore.

This was the Pribilofs.

We had arrived.

Two dark-eyed children regarded us solemnly as Tim, Dave, Bennie, and I rounded the final corner of the red clay road leading toward town. The taller of the two looked to be about five years old, the shorter around three. They stood beside a three-wheeled, all-terrain vehicle parked in the middle of a large rusty-colored mud puddle. I smiled, and beside me the others did the same.

"Hi," said Dave. We stopped walking. I couldn't help but notice how cute the kids were, dressed in identical parkas, obviously brothers.

The *Mary Jane* had set anchor about a half mile off shore. We had landed in our inflated lifeboats—zodiacs, as they were called—just north of Tonki Point, a few miles away from the single settlement on the island. We'd been greeted by a single fur seal, an old bull forlornly holding down the beach; Bennie and Tim had immediately grabbed their cameras and ventured in for "photo ops" until the animal had taken a gash out of Bennie's boot. Then we'd headed inland to hit the single dirt road running the eastern length of the island. There we'd found the children splashing gleefully through the mud.

The kids eyed us with interest, then exchanged a knowing glance. The younger child thrust his little face forward belligerently: "You're fucking Greenpeace."

Tim hunkered down. "I'm not fucking Greenpeace." He pointed toward the child: "You are."

"No I'm not. I'm a fucking Aleut." The child stared up at us with huge, innocent looking brown eyes, then turned to point toward a weather-beaten sign rising out of the sedge behind him.

"Welcome to St. Paul," said the sign. "Population 537. Largest Aleut Community. Home of the largest northern fur seal herd in the world."

"We just came in from working with the Russians," I said.

"We're fishermen," said Bennie.

The kids continued to eye us warily. The Pribilof Aleuts are not particularly fond of Greenpeace, which had done all it could to stop seal harvests—one of the few sources of income on the islands. The Aleuts felt they controlled the harvest of their seals very well, for the most part killing only the extra males that were of little importance anyway, reproductively speaking. The general Aleut opinion was that Greenpeace got upset about fur seal killings because seals happened to be cuter than cows.

Worse, though, was that several national conservation organizations had lobbied to have the Aleuts removed from the Pribilofs altogether. As the president of one such group suggested: "It would be a small thing for our government which annually moves thousands of families to build highways, to move the 120 Pribilof families in a body to the mainland." It seems more than a little insensitive to recommend the Pribilof Aleuts leave a land they settled forty years before the American Civil War.

Or so, at least, the Aleuts think.

"Is there any place around here where we can rent a car?" asked Bennie. We had only a few hours to see as much as we could of the island; Bennie's idea of sightseeing was to see how fast he could get away from wherever he was. Strictly speaking, Bennie was a hunted man—he owed, including fines, over $400,000 in back taxes. The motto among crewmen was frequently "Pleasure before Business." By the time the IRS had finally caught up with the immense amount of money Bennie had made in the last few years' work with the Joint Venture, he was in big trouble.

"First place after the road forks," said the older boy. "You can rent motorcycles there."

Bennie's eyes lit up. "Thanks."

We walked on while the boys climbed onto their ATV and splashed out of the puddle past us, the five-year-old throttling the engine like an expert.

The knolls and banks of St. Paul were low and gentle: they sported unimaginative names like Slope Hill, Low Hill, Ridge Hill, and Cone Hill. Their lush green reminded me incongruously of Ireland. The lack of brush and trees lent the place the well-trimmed atmosphere of a park, while distant mists softened the spill of the slopes into the sea. We walked briskly, our pace quickened by the chill of the damp air, and gradually the little town of St. Paul, with its lines of small white houses overshadowed by a large Russian Orthodox church, materialized out of the fog. "This must be the place," said Bennie as we passed a road branching off toward the rookeries southwest of town. A medium sized ranch-style home stood just off the street, a large cement block garage at its side.

We rented four Honda 125s (Bennie, disappointed, had clearly expected something far larger). The garage mechanic also doubled as the pastor of the First Church of Christ; he suggested, for reasons he was reluctant to discuss, that we avoid town.

We straddled our mounts and headed north, tooling along the bright red clay roads to North and Northeast Points, racing each other and stopping to climb out toward the cliffs, where tens of thousands of murres, fulmars, kittiwakes, and other seabirds packed the ledges. In the distance, we could see the seal rookeries, where seething masses of blubbery flesh— the harems— pressed upon each other.

We spent a fruitless couple hours searching for the reindeer herd the mechanic told us roved on the north end of the island. Then, tiring, we ignored the mechanic's warnings and headed for town.

Somewhere a door opened and a voice yelled something indiscernible. The door slammed shut and the back of my neck prickled. I gunned the motor of my bike and kept going.

The town's streets were curiously deserted, the scrubby white houses looking like uprooted farm outbuildings. In the distance I could hear a wild ululation, as if of hundreds of car horns sounding. I slowed, and the other three behind me did the same.

It *was* the sound of car horns. We edged to the side of the road and throttled to a stop as a pickup rounded the corner heading our way, honking with a long, steady rhythm. The bed of the pickup was loaded with grinning Aleut children, their faces painted a wicked red. Some of the kids appeared to be holding buckets of a repulsive looking substance; others held wads of the same stuff in their hands. We dismounted and stood as a second pickup rounded the corner, and then another.

"What's going on?" Dave asked of no one in particular. "Looks like some kind of parade."

"Wonder why the kids are painted all red," I said.

"What have they got in their hands?" Tim asked, as the first pickup began to pass us. And then: "Shit."

A large chunk of blubbery, bloody goo hit Tim dead square in the center of his jacket. There was laughter from the pickup, followed by a bloody barrage. Dave was hit twice, Bennie once, and Tim caught another one directly over his heart. A smaller missile hit me in the leg, and I reached down to grab it before dancing back out of range of the screaming children. The back of the pickups all seemed to be overflowing with kids, and still more vehicles rounded the corner every minute.

"What the hell's going on?" Tim bellowed as the others dodged back with me.

"Excuse me, sir," came a quiet voice. We turned to see a small older man standing with a woman well back from the road, his hands shoved into his pockets. "Today's the last day of the seal harvest. It's a festival we like to celebrate."

"What's with the kids?" asked Tim, brushing ineffectually at his bloody jacket.

"It's a custom for the children to throw seal blubber and whatever other scraps they find at anyone within reach."

I opened my hand. A curiously human-looking seal eyeball stared up at me. Quaint custom, I thought.

"And most of the kids think you're from Greenpeace."

"We're not," said Dave.

"I know. The Greenpeace boat left this afternoon, but not everybody's gotten the word yet." The man turned and spoke to the woman—his wife?—in what I assumed to be Aleut. It sounded like a muted dog fight.

"You must be working with the Soviet trawlers," said the man.

"Yes, how did you know?" I asked.

He waved an arm. "Let me show you around."

He led us off toward the town's main street, blithely introducing us to all and sundry as we passed. A large dump truck full of skinned and bloody seal carcasses roared by, followed by more pickups. Most people, I noticed, stood well back from the road, out of the children's lobbing range.

The cafe ($4.95 for one small hamburger with no french fries) was run by St. Paul's Russian Orthodox priest, an Aleut who had grown up on St. George and had taught himself Slavonic and the ritual of the church. In fact, according to our informant, about half the residents of St. Paul spoke Slavonic, the old Russian language of the liturgy.

I bought ten Granny Smith apples and some popcorn in the town's one grocery store, along with a passel of postcards. With everything being flown or shipped in from the mainland, the prices were exorbitant—one-and-a-half times those of the already-healthy prices of Anchorage. The store's curio section had little to offer—a few damaged seal pelts, slides, film, and jewelry made of fossil walrus ivory. I was surprised to learn that all the green pelts were shipped for processing to a little company in South Carolina—the Fouke Company—which has since 1915 held an exclusive contract with the United States government to process Pribilof fur seal pelts using a highly classified tanning and dyeing method.

Once it became clear just who we were, or rather, who we weren't, we were overwhelmed with friendliness. It was with regret that we declined an invitation to the evening's ceremony, a blowout to commemorate the end of sealing. The *Chasovoi* would be close to finishing her off-load by the time we returned. We needed to get back to work.

Five o'clock found us heading back to the beach, an ugly storm brewing overhead.

A few hours later, I nearly died.

Chapter Eleven
Farewell

I DANGLED BY ONE arm over the twenty-seven degree water, trying desperately to lift my feet above the bumper as it slammed heavily into the side of the *Chasovoi*. The Jacob's ladder had flipped around backwards so that I was trapped between it and the *Chasovoi's* side. Facing the *Mary Jane*, I was aware only of the rough gnarl of the rope in my right hand and the empty groping nothingness in my left.

This time there was no tumbler's belt to catch me if I fell.

Water washed at my legs and I prayed it was blown from the top of a wave. If my legs were in the swell itself this would be the last thing they ever felt before the locomotive weight of the *Mary Jane* crashed against the bumper, which was backed with the thousand ton weight of the *Chasovoi*.

The salty taste of the spray on my mouth mixed with the sour bile of fear. "Don't think don't think don't think just *do* it; grab that rope and *don't* look down."

My left hand connected with a knot on the edge of the ladder and my fingers tightened with prehensile instinct.

Deep breath.

Feet still dangling. Can't lower them to catch in the rungs.

"Use your arms—climb! CLIMB!"

I was suddenly thirty feet up, at the top of the ladder, with husky arms helping me over the bulwark. "*Vsyo khorosho?* Everything okay?"

"Sure," I said. "Just fine." I looked at the pale faces of the deck crew surrounding me, the streaks of rain on their cheeks and chins sparkling in the fluorescence of the deck's ghastly yellow-white lighting. The deck crew looked worse than I felt—except that I was shaking now, breathless and trembling.

The tumbler's belt was a nuisance that had been used occasionally when I first boarded the *Chasovoi*. It had been used less often as my climbs between boats became more routine, as trip after trip with no untoward occurrences made the hop from the American boat, to the bobbing rubber bumper between boats, and finally to the Jacob's ladder dangling off the side of the Soviet vessel seem as normal to me as walking from my cabin around the corner and up the stairs to the bridge. You forget that miscalculations multiply as the weather worsens. You forget that one miscalculation can kill.

I stood, still shaking, and glanced over the *Chasovoi*'s gunwales. A wave splashed over the *Mary Jane*'s deck, and the American boat whomped against the bumper separating the two ships. Tim's bloodless face stared back up at mine—he'd been preparing to follow me up the *Chasovoi*'s side when I'd nearly fallen.

"It's too rough," Tim shouted over the growl of the swells. "I'll wait." I nodded and thrust a thumb up. Tim was demonstrating the common sense I should have used. At the very least I should have asked for a belt. But I'd been anxious to board the *Chasovoi* for yet another reason.

Louise had told me something else in our radio conversation.

The fishing season had ended. One more week, and we would all be going home.

I flipped my tattered journal open, fingering the rough stubs where I'd sliced out swaths of pages, stuffing them into envelopes and passing them in waterproof bags to the Americans to be mailed home on their next trip to shore. This had been my form of protection for those I wrote about. Behind me the sink gurgled again. Irritably, I shut the journal.

We'd spent our last week by Port Moller, scraping up a final few hundred tons of yellow-fin to round out the quota. This morning we'd taken our last codend. Now we were preparing to go our separate ways.

I wrapped the remnants of the journal carefully with a fiber-back scrubber the cleaning woman had given me, then placed the bundle at the bottom of my knapsack. Katya had woven the scrubber of mending twine begged off the Americans; weaving back scrubbers, along with *"avoski,"* netted bags, was a common shipboard hobby for men and women alike. It whiled away the boring off-duty hours with the emotionally soothing feel of creation. I had three *avoski* already packed—presents from various deck and factory crew workers. I used the *avoski* to pad a hand-carved wooden spoon and a multitude of postcards the captain had given me, as well as a pristine Russian edition of *The Three Musketeers* from Gala, the captain's stewardess. Three Soviet flags, presents from the second mate, filled the lower portion of my duffel. They cushioned a bottle of Armenian cognac from the chief engineer. I also had a sack full of *znatchki*, the little decorative enamels of animals, people, and commemorative events the Russians so like to collect. Everyone, it seemed, had one they wanted to give me.

I had plenty of room for these treasures. Having traded half the goods I owned for a wealth of hats, coats, and Red Army belt buckles, I'd given away the other half. My precious dictionaries, much thumbed, I had wrapped and given to the third mate, who had wasted untold hours of my time getting me to translate illegal English karate manuals he'd managed to obtain. My calculator had gone to the factory manager; my camera, to Yuri. The only pants I now owned were canvass dungarees; the blue jeans were long gone.

The *Chasovoi* was enveloped in a muted frenzy of excitement. Spontaneous parties had broken out like riots throughout the ship—I'd been dragged to three in the past day and a half, and had disengaged myself with difficulty. I needed to get packed; with the evening I would be heading with Yuri and the crew of the *Mary Jane* to the *Turkul* for the fleet farewell party. And once I left the *Chasovoi*, I would not return.

The farewell party was being held aboard the *Turkul* for an important reason—the *Turkul*'s captain, unlike the other captains in the fleet, could not leave his ship.

I'd met the *Turkul*'s captain, Igor, several weeks ago. He was a remarkable man who I at first unthinkingly took for a cook: he wore a shapeless, once-white tunic from which it would have been possible to sample a complete selection of any of the previous week's meals. He combed his hair straight back from his receding forehead down to his shoulders, although it didn't need to be combed, since even a typhoon's winds would have had difficulty moving a single strand in the thick sludge of grease that had accumulated over his scalp.

And Igor was fat. Fabulously fat. Breathtakingly fat. The kind of fat where you just stand back and whisper in fascinated horror to whoever's standing next to you: "Wow."

Igor's fat was unique in that it had no firmness. It hung as if ready to seep away from him, with folds and crevices and pendulous immensities everywhere. Igor jiggled as he walked; a human lard receptacle coated with the colorful remains of his feed. Like the ship's cooks, Igor was far too fat to make the trip from his boat to another without the cumbersome assistance of a multitude of cranes. So the season's blowout would be held aboard Igor's boat.

I cinched my duffel shut and took a last look around my cabin. The bunk was, for once, made up. I'd left the porthole open; the cabin needed fresh air, and the cleaning woman would close it soon enough. The bookshelves hung empty over my former desk, the shelves' edges curbed with a side railing to keep books and trinkets from sliding as the *Chasovoi* rolled.

So much time at sea, both here and on the *Izumrudny*...

Would I miss it? Would I miss the seasickness and the lack of sleep, the stink and the squalor, the treacherous ladders and the inky, icy waters? Would I miss the Rambo-strong tea and the endlessly monotonous meals balanced at the thin edge of spoilage? Could I not miss the wispy, wee-hour sunrises, when the catcher boats tossed on the far horizon, prancing through the glistening foam in search of the morning's fish? Or my friends in the deck crew, tipsily walloping each other with fish? Or the songs, or the laughter; the friendships, or the convoluted, paranoid camaraderie?

My sink gave another aspirated gurgle and I glanced at it in irritation. How many hours of sleep had I lost to that endless gargle? I reached in disgust for my bags. The damn sink wouldn't even let me have a good-bye reverie in peace.

Wait a minute. Shampoo. I'd forgotten my shampoo. I dropped my duffel and crossed to open and grope behind the cabinet doors underneath the sink. Nothing. I bent down and peered inside the cabinet, craning my neck until I finally saw the green bottle wedged somehow at the very back of the cabinet. I reached forward and my hand brushed against a rubbery something that had rolled behind a piece of piping. I withdrew the something—a rubber stopper for the sink. I reached back in for the shampoo, then stood and stuck the stopper in the sink.

The toilet sound disappeared.

"How do I look?" asked Yuri, giving the tie one last wiggle to settle it into place. He wore a trim sports coat and slacks, and would have looked altogether quite respectable if it weren't for his plastic sandals.

"Good," I said. In truth, I thought he looked adorable. There was something about Yuri—his small frame, his kid's laugh, his effervescence, that often made me want to hug him. Except when he was in one of his recalcitrant moods, when slugging him was dreadfully tempting. As it was,

Yuri's cheeks were flushed and his eyes glistening, souvenirs of the drinks we'd had with Tim aboard the *Chasovoi* before heading for the *Turkul*. Yuri, I suspected, had also been privately partying on the side.

Yuri, Tim, and I were among the first of the twenty-five or so guests expected aboard the *Turkul*. We'd quickly been led to the officers' mess, where the long table groaned under its weight of caviar and Soviet crab, apples, oranges, cookies, smoked fish, pots of tea and the steeped fruit drink called *kompot*, fried potatoes, fresh tomatoes, and bowls of garlic: the standard party accouterments. A small American flag, mated with a Soviet flag, rose from a stand in the middle of the table. The table itself stood under a formidable reproduction of Karl Marx, looking as if he'd just suffered a bout of indigestion.

"Good evening." A slender woman with long dark hair entered the room. It was Louise, the lead representative. Yuri clicked his heels together and bowed. Tim, already busy stealing pieces of smoked fish from the table, turned to grin a greeting. Technically, Louise was my boss, although I rarely saw her. Louise had the same problems I did in working with the fishermen, except that, given the obstreperous nature of all the individuals involved, her problems were mine multiplied by ten. She, along with the Soviet fleet commander and the senior American captain—the "troika"—had to keep all fifteen Soviet and American skippers working together and happy.

Louise—poised, calm, deeply intelligent, thoroughly pleasant—has a will of iron. The fishermen, crude and rude though they may be, treat her with the utmost respect, and she deserves it. The only person I'd ever met who hadn't liked Louise was Laura, who thought Louise's occasional wearing of dresses and high heels a little out of place on the trawl deck. Laura may have been right, but everybody had their own eccentricities, and as such, I thought trying to look nice on occasion pretty minor.

Actually, I've found all the reps on the yellow-fin fleet to be remarkable people: witty, diligent, likable, and sociable. And each of the fishermen seems to be an exceptional character in his own right, with a strong personality rarely found in the outside world. It would have given me an acute inferiority complex if it weren't for the fact that I was so constantly busy, and so often too tired to care.

"Yuri Antonich," said Louise, extending her hand toward my captain. Yuri looked poised to flee. "So you've decided to rejoin the fleet."

"Why, er, yes," said Yuri. He glanced guiltily at me. Tim, with no knowledge of Russian beyond hello, looked lost.

"It would be very helpful if you would come to the radio when the fleet commander or I call you."

"Yes. Of course," said Yuri. He looked to me with baleful eyes. Tim excused himself and wandered off toward the vodka. Yuri eyed him wistfully, held in place by Louise's stare. I folded my arms and smiled.

"So glad you could come." We turned to find the *Turkul's* captain planted like a chunk of suet before us. Beside him stood a medium-sized, craggy-faced man with a heavy cast on his right foot. Louise and I smiled, and out of the corner of my eye I glimpsed Yuri scampering off toward the booze.

"Glad to see you again, Igor," said Louise. "Vladimir, what's happened to your foot?"

"My second mate here managed to break a leg falling down the stairs," said Igor. He balanced his massive frame precariously on one foot and with the other reached over to kick Vladimir's cast. Vladimir winced, gritted his teeth, and gave a thin smile: "It's not so bad."

"Barb!" An effusive Dave Fletcher suddenly enveloped me in a bear hug. Beyond him I could make out the *Svetlaya's* captain and two mates.

"Loocy!" Dave was hugged in turn by me and a grinning Yuri, who simultaneously slopped a generous dollop of vodka down Dave's front. Backed by a fresh infusion of Dutch courage, Yuri now seemed prepped to handle Louise.

"Please," said Dave, "it's my last night. Can't you just call me Dave?"

I caught sight of the *Turkul's* Dave, followed by the *Otradny's* Dave, heading in through the growing crowd. Dave of the *Obrucheva* stood in the far corner, by Karl Marx.

"All you Americans are named alike," said Yuri. He should talk. I'd taken a gander at the *Chasovoi's* roster once; it contained eleven Nicholais, ten Vladimirs, eight Sergeis, eight Alexanders, and five Victors, all in a crew of about ninety. Contrary to my expectations, there were only two Ivans. No wonder Russians often address each other by both their first and middle names.

Igor caught sight of the *Svetlaya's* captain and began to ooze in his direction. The fleet commander, a stocky man with that all-too-familiar Slavic combination of bloodshot eyes and jaundiced pallor, appeared at Louise's side and fixed Yuri with a probing stare: "So when are you going to start answering your radio, Yuri?" he asked.

Yuri took another gulp at his glass. "Soon." Apparently his courage wasn't quite Dutch enough. "Excuse me." He fled toward the bathroom.

Lucy handed me a shot of brandy and I took a slug, scanning the crowd. Gunnar and Tim were busy arguing in a corner. When the party ended, I would be heading straight from the *Turkul* to Tim's boat—the *Mary Jane*—for a ride to Kodiak, the first leg of my journey home.

I wandered toward the table to grab an apple and eavesdrop as two of the captains lectured one of the Daves.

"You really shouldn't have missed it," said the *Svetlaya*'s captain, Boris. "It would have told you the truth about Zionism and the Jewish religion."

"And there was an even better documentary yesterday," said the *Otradny*'s captain, "about the American and Soviet naval forces. It shows just how easy it would be for a missile to be accidentally launched by one of your people."

"That's true," said Boris. "Accidental launches occur all the time on American submarines; they just don't tell you about them."

"And the reason you Americans have all those accidental launches," the *Otradny*'s captain concluded, "is because you rely too much on computers, which can break down, instead of reliable human beings."

I took another swallow of my brandy as the *Turkul*'s captain paunched his way to the head of the table and called the assembly to take their seats.

We drank and toasted and ate and drank, as if the only thing that mattered on this earth was our revelry, and our companionship, and our happiness. As if the knowledge that the season had drawn to a close, like the ending of life itself, made the moments of the here and now more precious, more bitter, more sweet. We could not get enough of each other's company, regaling each other with remembrances of seasons past. With comments and anecdotes of this season. With hopes and dreams for the seasons to come.

We ate and we drank, but above all, we talked, while the hours glimmered past like quicksilver and the warmth of companionship filled the room like glowing coals.

"What?" I asked. I could have sworn the *Turkul*'s third mate, just down from the bridge, had asked if we wanted to go see the volcano erupting. But there weren't any volcanoes erupting in the Bering. None that I knew of, anyway. I wondered again at my knowledge of Russian.

"What'd he say?" Tim asked, nudging me drunkenly.

"Um," I said, looking back at the third mate. The other reps were at the far end of the room arguing about the best method for catching geoducks. Tim, Gunnar, Sven, Bennie, Yuri, and I stood near the doorway spiritedly discussing involving web manufacturers.

"There's a volcano erupting," the third mate repeated. "Doesn't anyone want to see it?"

I shook my head. The Americans looked at me expectantly.

"There's a volcano erupting," I translated hesitantly, then stopped.

The Americans boiled out of their seats as if they'd been set afire, calling toward Louise and the Daves.

"Volcano!"

"It must be Pavlof Volcano."

"No. Shishaldin."

"Let's go!"

I followed the stumbling horde up the companionway to the bridge, where we looked shorewards, toward the black of the low-lying hills.

And saw the volcano.

Everyone talks about the volcanoes of Hawaii and the monthly eruption of Kilauea. Everyone talks about St. Helens. Even Redoubt Volcano, they talk about—mostly because it's close to Anchorage, and people, and life. But no one ever talks about the volcanoes in the Aleutians. No one pays much attention to the far reaches of mankind, where few live, and perhaps even fewer care.

I squinted shorewards, dimly aware of Yuri easing in beside me at the railing. The tip of the volcano's cone burned brightly, eerily, in the distance. It was like watching a devil's cauldron, looking at the glowing fingers of flames rolling down from the volcano. It was like being on the edge of the earth, watching the world being born.

"Barbara," Yuri asked, taking his place beside me in the darkness, "will you come back to work with me next year?"

I stared out at the waters before me, black and gleaming and full of lapping calm on the moonlit night. The stars shown fiercely cold above us, and the running lights of catcher boats and processors gleamed—from what I now recognized to be a safe distance away.

I had been looking for a break: to do something different for a while.

I hadn't known what I was looking for.

But I'd found it.

"Yes, Yuri," I said. "I would like to work with you very much."

We boarded the *Mary Jane* from the *Turkul*, then headed for the *Chasovoi*, where we dropped Yuri off and watched him climb the rope ladder toward the bridge, as loosely nimble as a drunken monkey. He flipped over the top railings and rose moments later to wave, shouting, but I could hear nothing over the growing roar of the *Mary Jane*'s revving engines.

"Til next season," yelled Tim beside me. We peered upwards, our eyes tearing in the cold, but Yuri had already disappeared in the deep twilight of the coming dawn. The *Mary Jane* thudded into the chop, then veered to port, heading south. It would be a long journey down around False Pass and back up the Shelikof Straits toward Kodiak. Toward home. Tim reached up to shield his eyes as we gazed sternwards, back toward the *Chasovoi*.

There was an instant of silence, the silence that comes just before a roll of thunder. Then, suddenly the *Chasovoi*'s foghorn began to blow.

Loudly, the foghorn blew, until I put my hands to my ears to block the sound. Then more loudly, until I could nearly see the pulses slapping through the dense air. Tim and I stood, wind and wet and cold forgotten, as the Soviet ship swung heavily in the darkness, her lights shining like Christmas bulbs, burning bright, clear, and beautiful in the crisp Arctic air.

Loud and long roared the horn. Low and awesomely deep and, at last, fading. Until slowly, ever so slowly, the many lights of the *Chasovoi* resolved into one. Then, as the cold numbed our ears and our hands and the tips of our noses, into none.

Yuri had no need to speak English to say what the horn said, and we, no need of Russian.

I can hear the sound of that horn even still.

Afterword
A Brief History of the Venture

Through a good part of the seventies and eighties a little-known industry flourished in the Pacific Northwest. It was called Joint Venture fishing, and it united Americans and Russians in one of the most improbable of entrepreneurial casting choices. Who would have thought that obscure legislation could result in a new industry? Who would have thought that two world powers, poised at the brink of nuclear war, could jointly create an enterprise that was at once lucrative, closely knit, and border-line cuckoo?

Ever since the 1950s, American coastal fishermen had sought to extend the recognized marine boundaries of the United States from 3 miles to 200 miles from shore. As matters stood, the Japanese and Russians, among others, were disappearing over the horizon with enormous quantities of round and flat fish from off the coasts of Alaska and the Pacific Northwest. Since there was little market for these fish in the United States, there would seem to be no problem. But what American fishermen wanted, and were increasingly determined to implement through enactment of a 200-mile limit, was a chance to eliminate the large and efficient foreign competition so as to be able to harvest this vast resource themselves.

Hake (also known as whiting) and pollack are tasty and nutritious sources of protein. But there is a problem in working with these fish—they must be caught and immediately processed in large quantities to be profitable. This requires huge outlays of capital to build the tremendously expensive factory trawlers capable of catching, processing, and flash-freezing the fish at sea. Many foreign countries, more attuned to the wealth of comestibles available from the sea, had subsidized the construction of these multi-million dollar factory trawlers. The Japanese and Russians in particular had fleets of immense trawlers with which they roved the world raking in millions of tons of fish.

The Americans, on the other hand, had only small, privately owned vessels with very limited "at sea" fish processing capabilities; that is, no large ships that could process, pack, freeze, and store great quantities of fish. Not only was there little American dockside market for the less expensive round and flat fish that foreigners caught with such gusto—there was no way for Americans to even catch and process these fish economically.

Tucked away as depreciated assets on their logbooks, the Soviets had a supply of old, yet still serviceable factory trawlers. The Americans had no such vessels, but needed them if they were to begin catching the fish they so hankered after. It took three men: Jim Talbot, Wally Pereyra, and a hard-headed, party-hearty fisherman by the name of Barry Fisher, to combine the Soviet supply with the American need and simultaneously ram a market into existence to create a new industry—the Soviet-American Joint Venture. Within the rich waters of the 200-mile limit, Americans would catch the round and flat fish previously caught by foreigners, then pass them off at sea for the Soviets to process. The product would be marketed worldwide. It was all perfectly legal; all very profitable.

Joint ventures were not a new concept—they had worked, and worked well, in a few of the third world nations that had the foresight to institute a 200-mile limit in the past. Frequently, a third-world nation with newly claimed maritime boundaries would find that if they supplied a "right to fish," as well as labor, foreigners would supply the necessary capital goods for a fishery. But occasionally, poor countries would team their tiny vessels with huge factory trawlers and shore-side plants built by larger, richer maritime nations to end up with a product—and a profit—for both countries.

In the early seventies, Jim Talbot eyed the renewed efforts toward legislation for a 200-mile limit with more than a cursory interest. He was the principal owner of Bellingham Cold Storage, one of the biggest and most diversified cold storage plants on the west coast. A brilliant—some would say pie-in-the-sky—idea man and advocate for peace, he knew of the successes other nations had had with joint ventures. On a wish and a dream, he'd fired off a letter to the Soviet Ministry of Fisheries proposing a joint Soviet-American fishing venture that would earn hard U.S. dollars— a valuable commodity to the Russians, whose artificially valued ruble was unacceptable in the international marketplace.

Half a year went by with no answer, and Talbot had all but given up on the idea when he received a sudden and enthusiastic phone call from the Soviet Ministry of Fisheries inviting him to Moscow, at Soviet expense, to discuss the possibility of doing business together. Within a few months, the foundations were laid for Marine Resources Company (MRC), a partnership between Bellingham Cold Storage and Sovrybflot, a commercial corporation of the Soviet Ministry of Fisheries. Talbot was a smart man—smart enough to hire a young fisheries scientist, Dr. Wally Pereyra, to head up the budding firm. MRC would charter older factory trawlers from the Soviets, with a guaranteed minimum tonnage to be supplied by American fishermen each day. The processed product would then be sold for dollars worldwide, and the profits split between the Russian and American owners.

The little company faced tremendous obstacles. The Japanese held strong control of the fishing industry off the coast of the United States, most particularly in Alaska. They were partners in some fish processing firms, owners of others. As the providers of both market and capital, the Japanese could—and did—dictate everything from costs to price to quotas. Such products as salmon, crab, halibut, herring, and herring roe—which required comparatively low (although certainly not inexpensive) boat and gear expenses—were bought from American fishermen at fluctuating prices. But the lucrative round and bottom fish industry was reserved nearly exclusively for the Japanese. Americans had never really moved into the money; the Japanese weren't about to let them start. The Japanese hoped to persuade the United States not to enact a 200-mile limit, thus putting a halt to both the Joint Venture and MRC.

But the Japanese lobbying failed. The legislation creating the 200-mile limit—the Fisheries Conservation and Management Act—passed in 1976 and was amended in 1978 with the so called "processor preference" amendments. Fish quotas were to be allocated on a prioritized basis, with first priority going to American fisherman and processing plants, second priority to Joint Venture fishermen, and third to foreign interests. These amendments, along with the original legislation, were calculated to deliver an effective one-two punch against the Japanese, allowing the Americans to pull themselves into the capital-intensive world of deep-water trawling by means of joint ventures, all at the expense of sovereign foreigners—the Japanese, primarily. If a joint venture succeeded, the Japanese knew, there would be a multitude of factory trawlers available to Americans—and the Japanese themselves would be left out in the cold.

The state department also opposed the idea of joint ventures. Foreigners had always fished the waters within the 200-mile limit, and the state department had no desire to offend the burgeoning quasi-democracy of South Korea, or any number of other small but strategic countries, by restricting them access to waters they'd grown accustomed to fishing. Shoreside processors also opposed the joint venture proposals because these facilities had no way to compete with foreign processing vessels which were not subject to U.S. wage requirements, anti-pollution laws, and Occupational Safety and Health Administration regulations. Perhaps even more important than the evasion of various legal and regulatory requirements by foreigners, however, was that shoreside processors didn't want boats escaping from the "company store," i.e., from their control.

And, in the last, and perhaps worst, years of the cold war, communism was still a dirty word to many fishermen. Having any foreign fisherman taking fish from "our" waters was bad enough, but working with Russians was, to many fishermen's minds, condoning their politics while passing a portion of the profits to them. A fair number of fishermen did everything they could to stop legislation that would allow joint ventures. Long after these efforts failed, many a barroom brawl erupted when the Joint Venture fishermen—the JV boys—hit town.

Not the least of MRC's problems was that it proved nearly impossible to attract the fishing barons—the elite boat owners who could be counted on to catch great quantities of fish in their larger vessels. Most of these men were busy making $1.50 a pound fishing king crab in Alaska. The offer of six to ten cents a pound fishing for whiting off the coast of Oregon seemed ludicrous.

Undiscouraged, Talbot managed to talk a group of six fishermen with mid-sized multipurpose fishing vessels into joining him on a Coast Guard cutter to look at a Soviet processing vessel at work off the coast of Oregon. At the last moment, Talbot was stymied again—the state department issued orders refusing to allow him access to the cutter, or any other form of government transportation.

Undeterred, Talbot contacted a friend of a friend—a middle-aged fisherman with a bent for the unusual who would be glad to give the group a ride to the Soviet vessel on his small trawler. His name was Barry Fisher.

While the six fishermen Jim took out to the Soviet processor showed at most a desultory interest in the Joint Venture, Fisher and the Soviet fleet commander clicked in an instant camaraderie born of a zest for living and love of the sea. And Fisher was no stranger to overcoming problems creatively: when, in a typical mode of harassment, the state department refused to allow Talbot and his tiny group permission to reenter the United States from the Soviet vessel, Fisher threatened to defect. Permission to come ashore flashed back from Washington in minutes.

An eighth-grade dropout who'd started fishing as a "catchee" long-lining in dories from the decks of schooners off the coast of New England at the age of twelve, Fisher was used to doing things his own way. He'd entered the Merchant Marines at fifteen, seeing duty in the hazardous convoys to Murmansk during World War II and witnessing death, destruction, and hardship that etched an indelible creed of caring into his character. He earned a chest full of medals in two combat tours to Korea. The lack of formal education hadn't stopped him from picking up undergraduate and graduate degrees from Harvard. In the early seventies, Fisher moved to Oregon to alternate teaching with his first love, fishing. Ever his own man, the lure of the sea had won out, and at the age of forty-five he'd given up a tenured university position to return to fishing full time.

Where the big boys, as well as the six who had accompanied Talbot to the Soviet trawler, scoffed at Talbot's ideas, Fisher saw opportunity. The whole scheme, crazy as it sounded, made sense to him. Normally, a boat is able to spend a maximum of about 25 percent of its time fishing; the rest is spent either going out to sea, coming back, or sitting at the docks waiting to unload. Fisher saw immediately what the others had missed: with a processor following him around to pick up his catch, he could spend better than 80 percent of his time fishing. And fifty to ninety tons caught eight days out of ten at a dime a pound would actually earn much more than thirty to forty tons caught three days out of ten at a quarter a pound.

Fisher believed in Talbot's dream, but he was not a fishing baron; his trawler, the *Excalibur*, was too small to work with the Joint Venture. A superb fisherman, Fisher had long been hounded by financiers eager to put him aboard a larger boat. With the opportunities he alone among the fishermen foresaw in the Joint Venture, Fisher finally decided to take the financiers up on their offer, and in 1977 he commissioned a stern trawler specifically for the Soviet-American Joint Venture.

The *Lady of Good Voyage* was not the first pure stern-ramp trawler built on the west coast—that honor went to Fisher's *Excalibur*—but it was the first sizable one, eighty-six feet long and twenty-six feet in the beam. With the double gantry gear of the traditional European and Asian stern trawler, it was a radical departure from the long-standing configuration of the old drag boats of the west coast. In fact, though mid-water trawling was standard for such maritime nations as Japan, South Korea, Poland, Norway, and the Soviet Union, it was something Americans had never done before. To Fisher, the Joint Venture was a sure thing: the logical and rational plan to follow after a careful analysis of both the finances involved and Fisher's own capabilities. To almost everyone else, the Joint Venture appeared a hare-brained, cockamamie scheme that should never have worked. Fisher was betting the company on an untried, indeed, as yet unbuilt boat, which would require fishing skills no American possessed. He'd be working with a bunch of Communists to boot.

After his first twelve days of fishing with the Soviets, Fisher himself began to have doubts. He spent four nights going without sleep altogether, making every mistake in the book. The gear on *The Lady of Good Hope* was different, far larger than that of the *Excalibur*, and the mid-water trawling he practiced in the pursuit of hake used completely different techniques than the bottom trawling he was used to. As Fisher himself has put it: "I'm not a very bright guy, but I know some things. The first one is if I catch fish, I eat. If I catch a lot of fish I eat goddamned good. And if I don't catch any fish, it's my own goddamned fault." Fisher drove himself, and on day twelve, everything fell into place.

The remaining ten days of the season Fisher caught an average of eighty tons a day. What with the initial down time, everyone still lost money, but the concept was at last proven—the Joint Venture could work. And in those last two days of the fishery, something else happened.

The Soviet fleet commander, Oleg Portenkov, and Captain Nicholai Trushin invited Fisher and his first mate to the Soviet vessel, the *18th Congress*. They asked Fisher to bring every chart he had of the waters from Alaska all the way to California. Fisher brought the charts, and for two days the Soviets pored over them, outlining everything they had learned about the habits of rockfish in twenty years of fishing off the American coasts.

Rockfish were one of the few types of round fish which Americans could catch in commercially viable quantities, and for which a market existed. The wily rockfish tended, however, as its name suggests, to hole up in rock piles that could tear the heart and soul out of the bottom trawls then used by the tiny Oregon fleet. The Soviets provided hard data—exactly how the rockfish schools congregated on grounds Fisher and the others could not work before with bottom trawls, but could now fish by sailing the mid-water trawls over the bad rock piles. The Soviets passed on everything they could—the composition of their catches, where the fish were at given times of year, what the effect of the moon and the tide were. It was a great gift that Portenkov and Trushin gave to Fisher—it is the kind of rare gift one fisherman gives to another in lieu of words that can never be spoken aloud: I trust you. I need you. You are my deepest friend.

Fisher formed an alliance with the Soviets that passed far beyond the petty ties of politics and showed the depths of the bond of the human spirit. In 1983, when the Soviet fleet commander Yevgevny Yermakov fell from a Jacob's ladder stretched between the *Excalibur II* and a Russian processor vessel, he was knocked unconscious—sinking instantly in Bering Sea waters so cold that death is measured in seconds. Fisher's son kicked his boots off and dove, saving Yermakov's life. The next day Yermakov sent Fisher's son the only gifts he could get hold of—a bottle of Armenian Cognac, two fur hats, and three children's coloring books. "Now," said the Russian, "you know what the life of a Soviet Fleet Commander is worth."

And when the newscasts that were played daily on the Soviet ship's intercom rattled in vitriolic response to Ronald Reagan's "Evil Empire" rhetoric, threatening to tear the venture apart in an overflow of jingoistic propaganda, Fisher advised the fleet commander to do one thing, and one thing only: "Turn down the news," he said, "and turn up the music."

The Soviet-American Joint Venture is over, its very success bringing about its demise. U.S. corporations became aware of the profits available in mid-water trawling, and even before the demise of the Soviet Union they began commissioning American-made factory trawlers that continued to fish—and overfish—what once was thought to be a limitless resource. From 1978 until 1990 in the Pacific Northwest and the Bering Sea the Soviet-American Joint Venture caught some 3,000,000 tons of fish, employing up to 3,000 people. It was *perestroika* and *glasnost* long before Gorbachev used the words.

But out of the demise of the Joint Venture have arisen entire new industries—all fueled by the knowledge U.S. fishermen developed while working together with the Russians. In Alaska, a purely American factory trawl fleet arose to handle harvests of pollock, yellow-fin sole, cod, and Atka mackerel that had been previously harvested in Joint Venture operations. Shoreside processing facilities have been built in Dutch Harbor, Akutan, and Kodiak. In 1990, Barry Fisher threw a check for $10,000 on the table, proposing to the Oregon Economic Development Department (OEDD) that they initiate a study on the feasibility of shoreside processing plants. OEDD responded by contributing an additional $122,000. The resulting study was instrumental in the successful construction and operation of five shoreside plants: two in Astoria, one in Charleston, and the remainder in Newport. In 1994 alone, 74,000 tons of whiting were processed—an amount of fish worth $40 million dollars wholesale.

Marine Resources has become an employee-owned company and has helped develop and market products from the fisheries of the Russian far east.

All too often the interaction of two very different societies can be summed up in one word: war. How rare it is when two antithetical societies find a way to cooperate in a mutually beneficial fashion. Of course, Americans and Russians both were blind then to the death throes of a totalitarian giant—throes that would rock the balance of power in the world. They were also blind to the meaning of catching so many fish that nets exploded; of catching so many fish that they rotted on deck before they could be processed; of catching so many fish that a man could walk on their backs over water, as if he were God.

But through it all—through all those brief years of the Joint Venture when we thought the fish were endless; when a tiny corner of a dying empire gazed unbeknownst upon its future—there unfolded a quirky, underdog story, a unique episode that deserves its place in our history, and, because of its very human successes and failures, in our hearts.

Acknowledgments

I WOULD LIKE TO extend my warmest thanks to the following people, whose advice, friendship, and instruction have allowed this book to be born:

Barry Fisher, who provided invaluable information on the early years of the fishery and spent many patient hours shepherding me toward the spare lines of truth. Any remaining inaccuracies are, of course, my own.

Jim Talbot, President, Talbot Investment Company; Anthony Allison, Co-General Manager, Marine Resources; Rod Moore, Executive Director, West Coast Seafood Processors Association.

Vladimir Gross and Nora Holdsworth, who made learning Russian a pleasure.

Gwen Stipek, alias "Sonya," for showing me the romance inherent in the sea, and the faults of my being in too big a hurry in life.

Roberta Skaggs, for her help in the early stages of the manuscript.

Keith Petersen, without whose guidance and encouragement this manuscript would never have been published. Also at WSU Press: Beth DeWeese, Tom Sanders, Mary Read, Nancy Grunewald, Jean Taylor, Wes Patterson, Doug Garcia, Jenni Lynn, and Arline Lyons.

Irene Martin, for her careful and insightful comments.

Alfred Grim, for his encouragement; Pamela and Rodney Grim, who understand.

Marjorie, Daniel, and Jane Oakley, for their help and encouragement through the years of writing.

Roslyn and Rachel and Philip Oakley: the lights of my life.

And, most of all, to the people of the Soviet-American Joint Venture.

About the Author

BARBARA OAKLEY STARTED OUT as a linguist—and buck private—in the Army Security Agency and worked her way up to regular army captain. A *summa cum laude* graduate of Michigan's Oakland University with a masters in electrical and computer engineering, Barbara met her husband, Philip, while working at the South Pole Station in Antartica ("I had to go to the ends of the earth to meet that man," she says). The Oakleys live in Michigan with their two daughters, Roslyn and Rachel.